The Winner-Take-All Society

Robert H. Frank is the author of *The Sunday Times* best-seller *The Economic Naturalist* and *The Return of The Economic Naturalist*. He is the Henrietta Louis Johnson Professor of Management and Professor of Economics at Cornell University's Johnson Graduate School of Management and is a regular economics columnist in *The New York Times*.

Philip J. Cook is the ITT/Terry Sanford Professor of Public Policy at Duke University, and author of *Paying the Tab* (Princeton University Press, 2007) and, with Charles Clotfelter, *Selling Hope: State Lotteries in America* (Harvard University Press, 1989).

D1150951

The
Winner-Take-All
Society

* * *

Why the Few at the Top Get So
Much More Than the Rest of Us

Robert H. Frank and Philip J. Cook

Published in 2010 by Virgin Books, an imprint of Ebury Publishing
A Random House Group Company

2 4 6 8 10 9 7 5 3 1

Published in arrangement with the original Publisher, Free Press,
an imprint of Simon & Schuster, Inc. NY

www.virginbooks.com
www.rbooks.co.uk

Addresses for companies within The Random House Group Limited can be
found at: www.randomhouse.co.uk/offices.htm

The Random House Group Limited Reg. No. 954009

A CIP catalogue record for this book is available from the British Library

ISBN 9780753522264

The Random House Group Limited supports The Forest Stewardship Council
[FSC], the leading international forest certification organisation. All our titles
that are printed on Greenpeace approved FSC certified paper carry the
FSC logo. Our paper procurement policy can be found at:
www.rbooks.co.uk/environment

Mixed Sources
Product group from well-managed
forests and other controlled sources
www.fsc.org Cert no. TT-COC-2139
© 1996 Forest Stewardship Council

Typeset by SX Composing DTP, Rayleigh, Essex
Printed and bound in Great Britain by
CPI Bookmarque, Croydon CR0 4TD

For Mom
—R. H. F.

For Judy
—P. J. C.

Contents

Preface to the New Edition

Income and wealth inequality have been growing rapidly. The trend began in the United States during the 1970s. More recently, it has spread to the United Kingdom, Continental Europe, Asia and elsewhere.

Is this a problem? Many insist not. They argue that large differences in reward stimulate more rapid growth in GDP, which eventually trickles down to middle- and low-income families. Others, however, have begun to focus on the social and economic costs of rising inequality. Of course, a completely egalitarian society would be neither feasible nor desirable. But beyond some point, the costs of inequality clearly outweigh the benefits. In our view, we are well past that point.

If anything is to be done about rising inequality, the most important first step is to understand the forces that have been causing it. Much of what passes for expert commentary on this issue is off the mark. Popular accounts often attribute growing inequality to a breakdown in competitive forces. We're told that industrial behemoths conspire to drive out their rivals, thereby to extort ever higher payments from captive customers; that executives pack their boards with cronies, who agree to pay them exorbitant salaries and bonuses; that hedge fund managers rake in billions through illegal trades based on inside information.

To be sure, such abuses occur. But they're no worse now than they've always been. As Adam Smith wrote in *The Wealth of Nations*, "People of the same trade seldom meet together, even for merriment and diversion, but the conversation ends in a conspiracy against the public, or in some contrivance to raise prices."

If market manipulation is nothing new, why has inequality been rising? Some attribute it to growth in the "skill premium," the higher wage that employers must offer in order to attract the increasing number of highly skilled workers they need. Yes, the earnings differential between college graduates and others is now wider than it was thirty years ago. Yet if we look only at the distribution of earnings among college graduates, we see the same pattern as for society as a whole. For most college graduates, wage increases have been either small or nonexistent in recent decades. The premium for college graduates exists because a relatively small number of the most successful graduates have enjoyed spectacular earnings growth during the same period.

Others argue that globalization has boosted inequality by forcing down the wages of the least skilled workers. Here, too, there is a measure of truth in the claim. Unions, for example, have lost some of their bargaining power as firms have become better able to move their operations to low-wage countries. Outsourcing via the Internet has put similar downward pressure on wages in many non-unionized occupations.

But these global pressures do not account for what's happening in the professions. The growing inequality at the top is even more dramatic than at the bottom, as the most highly compensated corporate managers, lawyers and physicians have pulled away from the pack. In short, growth in inequality does not appear to have resulted from growing market imperfections or just from increased outsourcing to lower-paid workers in developing countries. What, then, has been driving it?

When this book was first published in the United States in 1995, we argued that growing inequality was a consequence of the fact that fundamental changes in technology and market institutions were providing growing leverage or amplification for the talents of the ablest individuals. In the entertainment industries the top performers go after a share of a huge global audience thanks to modern communications technology; there are not many "winners" in this game, but small differences in talent or sheer luck can produce jackpot rewards.

High stakes competitions do not necessarily involve mass audiences, but may involve access to wealth concentrations, as in the provision of services in finance and law, or the control of valuable assets, as in corporate management. The trends we have identified create ever greater leverage for those with the greatest ability, actual or perceived. The associated trends in compensation have been further accelerated by the breakdown of norms and institutions that had the effect of limiting top earnings. This is not a story of artificial limits on competition—rather just the opposite. Markets are actually far more competitive than they used to be.

Reasons for this change differ from case to case. But an important contributing factor in almost all cases has been the information revolution. In the 1950s, telephone connections across the Atlantic were so scarce that some firms hired clerks in the United States to spend their entire workday reading texts over the phone to clerks in European branches, just to keep lines open. In those days, international corporate operations were constrained by the costs of coordination and control. In many product areas, a firm could succeed by being the best producer in a fairly narrow locale.

But the scale and scope of individual markets have grown enormously in the intervening years. If one seller's offering is better than all others, buyers from around the world now quickly get word of that fact. Lower shipping costs, coupled with falling trade barriers, have made it easier than ever to serve buyers everywhere. The upshot is that if an economic opportunity arises anywhere in the networked world, ambitious entrepreneurs are able to discover and exploit it.

Capital markets have also become far more competitive. If a firm was mismanaged in the past, it was usually difficult for small share-holders to do anything about it. Now, large institutional investors hold much more power, and they are often quick to take control of companies whose executives fail to deliver. Ross Johnson, the former CEO of RJR Nabisco, squandered that company's resources in a variety of conspicuous ways. For example, he maintained a large fleet of company jets that flew him and his fellow executives to golf tournaments and other junkets around the country. But Johnson didn't last as long as he would have in earlier days. After a celebrated bidding war, the leveraged buyout firm KKR acquired control of the firm and sent Johnson packing. KKR paid twice what the share price had been under Johnson's leadership, yet still managed to make money on the deal.

The forces driving recent trends in CEO pay shed additional light on the causes of rising inequality. In large companies, even small differences in managerial talent have always made an enormous difference. Consider a company with $10 billion in annual earnings that has narrowed its CEO search to two finalists. If there is reason to believe that one had slightly better judgment than the other, amounting to a 3 percent swing in earnings, then that translates into an additional $300 million. Even if the better performer is paid $100 million, she's still a bargain.

This sort of leverage has long been a feature of corporate management positions. But clearly something has changed. CEOs of the largest American corporations, who were paid 42 times as much as the average worker as recently as 1980, are now paid more than 400 times as much. Similar trends exist in some other developed countries.

Critics complain that the explosive growth of CEO pay proves that executive labor markets are not really competitive—that CEOs appoint cronies to their boards who approve unjustifiably large pay packages. But CEOs have always appointed people they know to their boards, so that can't explain recent trends.

One reason for rapidly growing CEO pay is that companies themselves have become bigger. As the New York University economists Xavier Gabaix and Augustin Landier argue in a 2006 paper, executive pay in a competitive market should vary in direct proportion to the market capitalization of the company. They found that CEO compensation at large companies grew sixfold between 1980 and 2003, the same as the market-cap growth of these businesses.

Still, growth in the size of corporations does not fully account for the changes in how CEOs are rewarded over the postwar period. Take the case of Crawford Greenewalt, a Du Pont son-in-law and CEO of E.I. Du Pont de Nemours in 1959, whose $300,000 annual compensation was (after adjusting for inflation) about one-quarter of that paid Charles O. Holliday Jr, the CEO in 2008, although back in the 1950s, Dupont was still a top performing company and during Holliday's tenure it brought just 2 percent return to its shareholders.

Increased competition for top talent is part of the explanation.

More intense competition has been fueled by a significant increase in executive mobility. In the not-so-distant past, about the only way to become a CEO was to have spent one's entire career with the company. With only a handful of plausible internal candidates, pay was essentially a matter of negotiation between the board and an individual who had no attractive prospects outside of the company. Increasingly, however, hiring committees believe that a talented executive from one industry can also deliver top performance in another.

A celebrated case in point was Louis V. Gerstner, Jr. Having produced record earnings at RJR Nabisco, he was hired by I.B.M., where he led the computer giant, then struggling, to a dramatic turnaround in the 1990s. This new spot market for talent has affected executive salaries in much the same way that free agency affected the salaries of professional athletes in recent decades.

Greater competition also creates positive feedback effects that amplify the growth of salaries at the top. Such effects appear to help explain growing inequality among dentists, for example. The dentists whose earnings have grown the most dramatically are often specialists in cosmetic dentistry, the demand for whose services has been fueled by higher top salaries in other occupations. And the highest paid dentists in turn often demand the services of the most highly paid specialists in other fields.

Beliefs matter. The erroneous belief that inequality has grown because markets have become less competitive has spawned policy remedies aimed at making markets more competitive. For example, a belief that insufficient competition in the university system was fueling rapid tuition growth led the antitrust division of the United States Justice Department to file suit against a group of elite American universities for colluding on decisions about financial aid to applicants. The suit succeeded. These universities are no longer permitted to coordinate their decisions about how much aid to offer specific students.

But if inequality has in fact grown because markets have become more competitive, not less, such remedies will prove counterproductive. Universities were coordinating their financial aid decisions to avoid a costly bidding war for the students with the most stellar credentials.

Their aim was to protect scarce financial aid dollars for the neediest families. Because the government's intervention prevented them from achieving this aim, there will be greater inequality in the next generation of graduates.

Here, too, we see the footprints of positive feedback loops. In chapter 8, for example, we argue that the bidding war for students with the best grades and standardized test scores had become more intense partly because the employers who offer the top starting salaries have been concentrating their recruiting efforts at the nation's leading universities. That change, in turn, reflects the increasing concentration of the best students at the leading universities. These universities, for their part, must continue to attract the top students, lest they forfeit the crucial rankings points that are based in part on the grades and test scores of those students. In short, growing salaries at the top kindle greater demands for elite educational credentials, which kindle fiercer competition among universities for scarce slots atop the academic pecking order. If universities are allowed to use financial aid offers to bid for top students, some will do so, and others will feel great pressure to follow suit. In the end, fewer financial aid dollars will be left for needy families, causing children from these families to graduate with growing debt burdens. It's another example of the "Matthew Effect", coined by sociologist Robert K. Merton and taking its name from a line in the biblical Gospel of Matthew – "For to all those who have, more will be given, and they will have an abundance; but from those who have nothing, even what they have will be taken away," in which success breeds success.

Events of the past fifteen years provide little reason to question our original conclusion that growing leverage in the "winners" positions, combined with growing competition to fill those positions, has been the most important cause of rising inequality at the top of the income distribution. On the contrary, markets have grown more competitive and the most productive players have gained additional leverage since the original publication of our book. Growth in earnings inequality has continued as predicted, with brief interruptions during the two downturns that have occurred.

According to Adam Smith's celebrated invisible hand theory, competitive forces harness the greed of individuals to produce the greatest good for all. Seeking only to increase their profits by winning business from their rivals, producers introduce cost-saving innovations and improved product designs. These efforts succeed in the short run. But over time, other producers copy them, and additional competition drives prices back into line with the new, lower, production costs. The ultimate beneficiaries of all this churning, according to the theory, are consumers, who enjoy better products at lower prices.

To be sure, by extending the reach of the planet's most able performers, the same information revolution that heightened competition in recent decades has created enormous benefits for consumers. But unlike the most ardent of his latter-day disciples, Adam Smith never asserted that more competition *always* leads to better outcomes. His remarkable insight was that it does so under some circumstances. We and others have argued that those circumstances do not reliably include the competition for rank in markets organized like tournaments.

In addition to causing almost unprecedented growth in income and wealth inequality, heightened competitive forces have generated substantial waste. In chapter 6, for example, we argue that most of the millions of people who compete for a limited number of superstar positions in winner-take-all markets actually contribute very little to national output. And in chapter 7, we note that contestants for these positions jockey for position in a host of costly, but mutually offsetting, ways. National income would be higher if there were fewer contestants in these arenas, and if more of the most talented youths went into scientific or medical research rather than finance.

A far more important source of waste spawned by rising inequality involves the escalation of what families must spend to achieve basic economic goals. Consider, for example, the desire of most parents to send their children to good schools. The problem is that a "good" school is a relative concept. It is one that compares favorably with other schools in the same local environment. In some countries, school budgets are financed primarily by local property taxes, which means that the best schools are those in the neighborhoods with the most expensive houses. In other countries, school budgets are nearly the same in all districts, but even in those countries, the best schools tend to be located in the most expensive communities. (In part, this is because school quality depends on student quality, and the children of more successful parents tend to be better students.)

The implication is that for a family at the median income level to send its children to a school of at least average quality, it must live in a district that has such schools—which by and large means spending as much on housing as other families with similar incomes. That's a problem, because rising inequality has spawned an expenditure cascade that (prior to the market crash of 2007) caused the median house price to rise much more rapidly than the median family's income.

The first step in this cascade occurred when the wealthiest families began spending more on housing, a step they took simply because they had much more money. The middle class didn't seem to mind. On the contrary, they gazed eagerly at magazine photos and news footage depicting the lavish new mansions. But the bigger houses of the rich shifted the frame of reference of those just below the rich, who traveled in many of the same social circles. (Perhaps the near rich felt they, too, needed to hold their daughters' wedding receptions at home rather than in hotels or clubs.) So the near rich built bigger. And that shifted the frame of reference for those just below them, and so on, all the way down the income ladder. In 1974, the median new house built in the US had 1,600 square feet of living space. By 2007, it had grown to over 2,400 square feet, despite the fact that the median real wage had not grown at all during the intervening years, and the average household had fewer people.

The problem is that even when all families spend more on housing, half of all children must still attend schools that are below average quality. From the median earner's perspective, the extra bidding for housing thus served only to raise the price of the median house. As in the familiar stadium metaphor, all stood to get a better view, yet no one saw any better than if all had remained comfortably seated.

Similar expenditure cascades have occurred across multiple domains. Because the rich are spending more on clothing, so is everyone else. If the median earner doesn't spend significantly more than before on an interview suit, he'll face reduced odds of getting the job. If he doesn't match the increased spending of others on gifts, he'll risk being seen as someone who failed to grasp the importance of a close friend's wedding or birthday. And so on. Much of this extra spending is purely wasteful, since only relative consumption matters beyond a certain point. When the rich build bigger mansions, they succeed only in raising the bar that defines how big a mansion people in their circle feel they need.

There is little reason to celebrate waste. Yet waste presents opportunity. As we explain in chapter 11, simple changes in tax policy could divert many of the resources currently wasted in positional arms races to much more productive uses.

In chapter 10, we argue that the spread of winner-take-all markets has had a variety of adverse effects on the offerings of media and entertainment producers. Dramatic growth in the economic rewards for publishing best-selling book titles and producing blockbuster films has set publishers and producers scurrying after pots of gold. The result, we argue, has been a growing bias in favor of sequels to hit movies and a growing preference for books by celebrity authors.

Chris Anderson challenged our argument in a 2004 *Wired Magazine* article called "The Long Tail" and a 2006 book by the same name. The information revolution, he argued, has breathed new life into publishers' lowest-selling titles. Titles with only occasional sales are uneconomical for conventional bricks and mortar retail stories to carry, but not so for online distribution giants like Amazon, Netflix, and Apple's iTunes. These firms can hold enormous inventories even of titles that sell only once every few years. The result, Anderson argued, was that future cultural offerings would become more vibrant and diverse, rather than less so.

We were encouraged by Anderson's optimistic view. But recent research suggests that that the winner-take-all trend remains alive and well in culture and entertainment. For example, the top-selling 200 digital music tracks on Amazon had a market share of 18.7 percent in 2008, up from only 14.5 percent in 2004. (We are writing this just as the winner-take-all celebrity dynamic has launched Susan Boyle's first album as the most successful release ever, building on the sensation generated by her performance on *Britain's Got Talent*.) In publishing and movie rentals as well, the share of total sales accounted for by the top-selling titles has continued to rise. To be sure, it is easier than ever to purchase an obscure book or rent a little-known film. But that doesn't mean that producing obscure books and films has become economically attractive. It will be interesting to watch how things continue to develop in these industries. But for now, we see little reason to abandon our concerns about where things are heading.

What is clear, in any case, is that the economic forces that have been causing the spread and intensification of winner-take-all markets have by no means run their course. In non-recessionary times, we should expect continued growth in the intensity of competition on the buyers' side for the best talent, and on the sellers' side for the top positions. The result will be continued growth in income and wealth inequality, and increasing waste.

In late 2008, highly leveraged investment portfolios based on derivative securities helped precipitate the deepest financial crisis since the Great Depression. To combat the crisis, the central banks of the U.S. and the U.K. have pursued policies of aggressive monetary expansion. By all evidence, these policies have made the downturn both shorter and less severe than many had feared it would be. But an unintended side effect has been to create large windfall trading profits for the same financial institutions that assembled and marketed the risky securities that provoked the crisis.

Many outside the financial industry are understandably outraged by the prospect of another round of huge bonus payments at these firms. And although we are generally skeptical of government attempts to micromanage the pay practices of private institutions, the case for intervention in the financial industry merits a sympathetic hearing.

Financial industry executives complain that if they are not permitted to pay large bonuses, they will not be able to attract the talent they need to operate successfully. Nonsense. Productive traders often leave one financial firm for another that offers higher pay, yes, but if there were an across-the-board cap on bonuses, most would stay right where they are. Does anyone really think that the designers and marketers of risky derivative securities face similarly lucrative employment opportunities outside the financial industry?

Even if a bonus cap led some traders to migrate out of the financial industry in the long run, that might not be such a bad thing. As we argue in chapter 6, winner-take-all markets tend to attract talent far out of proportion to their contribution to national output. The financial industry is a quintessential winner-take-all market. The incentives that have lured many of our best and brightest young people to become financial engineers have made our economies both weaker and less stable.

The financial industry needs to channel capital from lenders to those who can invest it most productively. This task requires competent people with sound judgment. But it is not rocket science. If smaller paychecks in the financial industry led some of the geniuses of Wall Street and the Square Mile to pursue other lines of work, so much the better.

As this case shows, there are practical policy solutions for the problems spawned by rising inequality. But we are unlikely to identify those solutions without first having understood the economic forces that have been causing the distribution of rewards to become more unequal, and average earnings to remain static for so long. Former President George W. Bush famously opined that his goal was to "make the pie higher." Well and good, but it is also important that the available pie be shared more equitably. A better understanding of the forces that have given us the winner-take-all society can help us achieve both a bigger pie and a bigger slice for those who don't end up in the winner's circle.

Robert H. Frank and Philip J. Cook
November, 2009

Acknowledgments

Our work on the project began formally in 1988, but our collaboration really dates from conversations as classmates and office mates in Berkeley's economics Ph.D. program more than twenty-five years ago. During the ensuing years, we worked separately on the economics of status competition and of participation in lotteries. These two areas at first seemed to have little in common, but as the 1980s progressed it became apparent that the competition for society's top positions was becoming more and more like participation in a lottery. And with this realization came the decision to merge our research programs and begin work on *The Winner-Take-All Society*.

As our project unfolded, we have benefited from advice from many quarters. Our greatest cumulative debt is to those who suffered through progress reports on our work. For their countless useful suggestions and insights, we thank the participants in faculty seminars at Berkeley, Binghamton, British Columbia, Carleton, Center for Advanced Study in the Behavioral Sciences, Chicago, Claremont Graduate School, Columbia, Cornell, Cornell Law School, Dalhousie, Duke, George Mason, Georgia State, Georgia Tech, Guelph, Harvard, Harvard Business School, Iowa, Lafayette, London School of Economics, Miami of Ohio, MIT, National Bureau of Economic Research, New Mexico, Northwestern, Ohio State, Oregon, Pennsylvania, Russell Sage Foundation, Santa Clara, Southern California, Stanford, Stanford Law School, Toronto Law School, Tufts, Washington, Washington—St. Louis, Wesleyan, Western Ontario, Williams, and Yale Law School.

We are in debt as well to those who read and commented on earlier drafts of all or part of our work. With apologies to those we fail to mention, we especially thank Bruce Ackerman, Anthony Brown, Jim Buchanan, Sudipto Dasgupta, Patrick DeGraba, Andrew Doughety, Victor Fuchs, Alan Garber, Bob Gibbons, Dan Graham, Peter Hall, Jay Hamilton, Bob Inman, Alfred Kahn, Timur Kuran, Edward Lazear, Jim Leitzel, Frank Levy, Glenn Loury, Chuck Manski, Donald McCloskey, Lincoln Moses, Bob Nelson, Dick Nelson, Sam Peltzman, Jim Rebitzer, Jennifer Reinganum, Douglas Rivers, Peter Rogerson, Sherwin Rosen, Dan Rubinfeld, Andrew Rutten, John Siegfried, Lester Telser, Dick Thaler, Ed Tower, Mike Waldman, and Robert Young. For their able research assistance, we thank Ashesh Badani, Pinka Chatterji, Praveen Kulshrestha, Chadwick Meyer, Caglar Ozden, Jonathan Wecker, and Gyeongjoon Yoo. We gratefully acknowledge financial support from the National Science Foundation, the W. E. Upjohn Foundation for Employment Research, and the Center for Advanced Study in the Behavioral Sciences. Finally, we thank Raphael Sagalyn for encouraging us to make our story more broadly accessible and Martin Kessler for his invaluable help in molding our material into its current form.

1

Winner-Take-All Markets

Rabo Karabekian, the protagonist of Kurt Vonnegut's novel *Bluebeard*, is an abstract expressionist painter of modest renown ("a footnote in Art History," as he describes himself). He recognizes that he was "obviously born to draw," just as others are born to tell stories, sing, dance, or be leaders, athletes, and scientists. Speculating on the historical origins of such talents, Rabo muses:

> I think that could go back to the time when people had to live in small groups of relatives—maybe fifty or a hundred people at the most. And evolution or God or whatever arranged things genetically, to keep the little families going, to cheer them up, so that they could all have somebody to tell stories around the campfire at night, and somebody else to paint pictures on the walls of the caves, and somebody else who wasn't afraid of anything and so on.[1]

But Rabo also recognizes that most of these talented people face diminished opportunities in modern societies:

> . . . of course a scheme like that doesn't make sense anymore, because simply moderate giftedness has been made worthless by the printing press and radio and television and satellites and all that. A moderately gifted person who would have been a community treasure a thousand

years ago has to give up, has to go into some other line of work, since modern communications has put him or her into daily competition with nothing but the world's champions . . . The entire planet can get along nicely now with maybe a dozen champion performers in each area of human giftedness.[2]

Now that most of the music we listen to is recorded, the world's best soprano can literally be everywhere at once. And since it costs no more to stamp out compact discs from Kathleen Battle's master recording of Mozart arias than from her understudy's, most of us listen to Battle. Millions of us are each willing to pay a few cents extra to hear her rather than another singer who is only marginally less able; and this enables Battle to write her own ticket.

Rabo Karabekian and Kathleen Battle sell their services in what we call "winner-take-all markets." So do Boris Becker, P.D. James, Carl Sagan, Kazuo Ishiguro, Hakeem Olajuwon, Gabriel García Marquez, Gerard Depardieu, Oksana Baiul, Alan Dershowitz, Alberto Tomba, John Madden, Mel Gibson, Mick Jagger, George Soros, Kip Keino, Jacques Derrida, Sonia Braga, Diane Sawyer, Gary Kasparov, Giorgio Armani, Stephen Hawking, Michael Jordan, Andrew Lloyd Webber, Elle Macpherson, John Cleese, Katerina Witt, Peter Høeg, George Will, Kimiko Date, Arnold Schwarzenegger, and John Grisham. The markets in which these people and others like them work are very different from the ones economists normally study. We call them winner-take-all markets because the value of what gets produced in them often depends on the efforts of only a small number of top performers, who are paid accordingly.

For example, although thousands of people are involved in making a major motion picture, the difference between commercial success and failure usually hinges on the performances of only a handful—the director, the screenwriter, the leading actors and actresses, and perhaps a few others.

Similarly, although thousands of players compete each year in professional tennis, most of the industry's television and endorsement revenues can be attributed to the drawing power of just the top ten players. For example, the Australian Wally Masur, among the top fifty players in the world for many years, in 1993 was a semifinalist at the

U.S. Open. At no time during his career, however, did manufacturers offer tennis shoes or racquets bearing his signature.

Since most of the markets we will be talking about have more than one winner, it would be more accurate to call them "those-near-the-top-get-a-disproportionate-share markets." But this is a mouthful, and hence our simpler, if somewhat less descriptive, label.

The winner-take-all reward structure has long been common in entertainment, sports, and the arts. But, as sociologist William Goode clearly recognized, the phenomenon that gives rise to it is by no means confined to celebrity labor markets. "The failure of the somewhat less popular" is how he referred to this phenomenon: "Grocery stores have only so much shelf space and thus only so much for each type of soap, cornflakes, or maple syrup. . . . obviously the most popular of any class of products or programs will shoulder the less popular off, although in quality these may be close to the most successful in popularity."[3]

The cars that succeed in the marketplace are often only marginally more stylish or better built than those that fail. And even experts sometimes argue about whether the stereo loudspeaker that sweeps the market is really better than the ones buyers rejected.

When only barely perceptible quality margins spell the difference between success and failure, the buying public may have little at stake in the battles that decide which products win. But to the manufacturers the stakes are often enormous—the difference between liquidation and the continuation of multibillion-dollar annual revenues.

These high stakes have created a new class of "unknown celebrities": those pivotal players who spell the difference between corporate success and failure. Because their performance is crucial, and because modern information technology has helped build consensus about who they are, rival organizations must compete furiously to hire and retain them. In the automobile industry, for example, this might mean bidding for an especially talented designer or a highly innovative engineer, or even, in one notorious case, a ruthlessly effective purchasing agent. Little known to the buying public, these individuals often enjoy superstar status in their respective industries.

The markets in which they toil have become an increasingly important feature of modern economic life. They have permeated law, journalism, consulting, medicine, investment banking, corporate management, publishing, design, fashion, and even the hallowed halls of academe. And, although many of the examples we cite are drawn from an American context, the forces that give rise to winner-take-all markets are also at work in other industrial economies —indeed, even in countries in the earliest stages of economic development.

The revolution in electronic communications and data processing, for example, has transformed labor markets not just in the United States, the United Kingdom, France, Germany, and Japan, but also in China, India, Brazil, and Indonesia. The same kinds of trade agreements that have brought workers in Toronto into direct competition with workers in Chicago have also brought workers in Kyoto into direct competition with workers in Munich and Johannesburg. And each year a growing share of people in all these places will read books by the same authors, see films by the same directors, and buy clothing by the same designers.

Winner-take-all markets have already wrought profound changes in economic and social life. And because many of the forces that create these markets are intensifying, even more dramatic changes loom ahead. Some of these changes are for the better. Consumers clearly gain, for example, when modern technology allows the most talented people to serve ever wider audiences. Once the compositor's work is done, a renowned author's manuscript costs no more to reproduce than a hack's. Once the world's hospitals are linked by high-speed data transmission networks, the world's most gifted neurosurgeons can assist in the diagnosis and treatment of patients thousands of miles away— patients whose care would otherwise be left to less talented and less experienced physicians.

But winner-take-all markets also entail many negative consequences, and these will be our primary focus. Winner-take-all markets have increased the disparity between rich and poor. They have lured some of our most talented citizens into socially unproductive, sometimes even destructive, tasks. In an economy that already invests too little for the future, they have fostered wasteful patterns of investment and consumption. They have led indirectly to greater concentration of our most talented college students in a small set of elite institutions. They have made it more difficult for "late bloomers" to find a productive niche in life. And winner-take-all markets have molded our culture and discourse in ways many of us find deeply troubling.

Growing Income Inequality

Despite a flurry of denials from Bush administration officials when burgeoning income inequality first made headlines in the late 1980s, there is now little doubt that the top U.S. earners have pulled sharply away from all others. For example, the incomes of the top 1 percent more than doubled in real terms between 1979 and 1989, a period during which the median income was roughly stable and in which the bottom 20 percent of earners saw their incomes actually fall by 10 percent.[4]

Growing inequality is by no means confined to the United States. In the United Kingdom, for example, the richest 20 percent earned seven times as much as the poorest 20 percent in 1991, compared with only four times as much in 1977.[5] The British gap between males with the highest wage rates and those with the lowest is larger now than at any time since the 1880s, when U.K. statistics on wages were first gathered systematically[6]

As in other times and places, the growing gap between rich and poor has increasingly strained our bonds of community. The top earners are richer now than ever before, yet few among them can feel proud of the social environment we have bequeathed to our children.

Despite a recent spate of books on income inequality, there remains little consensus about why it has grown so sharply. Some commentators mention changes in public policy, citing the Reagan-Thatcher program of tax cuts for the wealthy and program cuts for the poor. Others emphasize the decline of labor unions, the downsizing of corporations, and the growing impact of foreign trade. Still others—notably former Harvard president Derek Bok in his widely discussed book *The Cost of Talent*—mention imperfect competition and cultural factors. Bok sees powerful elites who are insulated from competition and able to set their own terms in a world increasingly unrestrained by inhibitions about greed.

We will argue that the runaway salaries of top performers have not resulted from the policy changes of the Reagan-Bush and Thatcher-

Major administrations, or from the decline of labor unions. Expanding trade, along with cultural forces, may have played a role, but only a supporting one. And if any one thing is certain, it is that growing income inequality has not resulted from any weakening of competitive forces.

On the contrary, global and domestic competition have never been more intense than now. Our claim is that the explosion of top salaries has stemmed largely from the growing prevalence of winner-take-all markets, which, we will argue, is tied closely to the growth of competitive forces. We will describe changes that have made the most productive individuals more valuable, and at the same time have led to more open bidding for their services.

In professional sports, for example, the most productive athletes have become more valuable because of the large influx of television revenue. What is more, owners of sports teams are now forced to compete with one another for the most talented athletes because of "free agency"—athletes' freedom to choose which teams to play for, which resulted from the string of legal decisions that struck down earlier restrictions on mobility. The result has been that much of the new revenue has found its way into the salaries of top players. The San Francisco Giants offered Barry Bonds a $43,750,000 contract in 1992 not because team owner Peter Magowan was stupid but because Bonds's presence helped fill the stands and land a more lucrative TV contract.[7] Bonds was a free agent when he signed with the Giants, and making him a smaller offer would have risked losing his drawing power to a rival bidder.

Growth in productivity of the top performers and the more open bidding for their services have occurred for different reasons in different markets. In broad terms, however, the story in other winner-take-all markets largely resembles the one we have seen *in* professional sports. Disney CEO Michael Eisner was paid more than $200 million in 1993 not because he duped shareholders but because he delivered an unprecedented increase in the company's value at a time when the mobility of chief executives has made them increasingly like the free agents of professional sports. And Danielle Steel gets $12 million apiece for her novels not because conglomerate publishing houses have deep pockets and limited business acumen, but because she sells millions of copies. If Dell/Delacorte had failed to bid accordingly for her manuscripts, Steel could simply have signed with a rival publisher.

The widening gap between the winners and losers is apparently not new. Writing more than a century ago, the British economist Alfred Marshall observed that "the relative fall in the incomes to be earned by moderate ability, however carefully trained, is accentuated by the rise in those that are obtained by many men of extraordinary ability. There never was a time at which moderately good oil paintings sold more cheaply than now, and there never was a time at which first-rate paintings sold so dearly."[8]

What *is* new is that the phenomenon has spread so widely and that so many of the top prizes have become so spectacular. The lure of these prizes, we will argue, has produced several important distortions in modern industrial economies. Perhaps the most important of these involves the influence of market signals on career choices.

The Misallocation of Talent

For any nation to prosper in the face of growing international competition, it must somehow allocate its most talented citizens to its most important jobs. It must steer its best executives to the enterprises that add greatest value, its most creative scientists to the most pressing technical problems, its ablest public servants to the most important cabinet positions. If the economic collapse of the communist countries can be traced to any single factor, it is their dismal performance in these critical assignment tasks. The critics of communism were right all along: The allocation of talent by central bureaucracy is a recipe for economic disaster.

Market economies have done much better by simply letting people decide for themselves which careers to pursue. Although social critics often question the recent wave of multimillion-dollar salaries on ethical grounds, there can be no doubt that these salaries have attracted our best and brightest people. Competition for the top prizes is intense, and those fortunate enough to land them are almost invariably the survivors of a series of increasingly demanding elimination tournaments.

The aspiring major-league baseball player, for example, starts with T-ball, moves on to Little League and then, if he shows enough talent and determination, to Babe Ruth League. Only the best from Babe Ruth League can hope to start for the most competitive high school teams, and only a fraction of those players go on to the minor leagues, where formidable hurdles remain before landing a shot at the majors. Even then, most players who make it onto a major-league roster ultimately fail to land a starting berth, and only a small fraction of starters go on to become stars. As we will see, competition for top positions in other sectors of the economy is no less intense. Almost without exception, the survivors of these competitions are people of enormous talent, energy, and drive.

One of our central claims is that although the competition for top slots in winner-take-all markets does indeed attract our most talented and productive workers, it also generates two forms of waste: first, by attracting too many contestants, and second, by giving rise to unproductive patterns of consumption and investment as contestants vie with one another for top positions.

Consider first the matter of overcrowding. Winner-take-all markets attract too many contestants in part because of a common human frailty with respect to gambling—namely, our tendency to over-estimate our chances of winning. Becoming a contestant in a winner-take-all market entails a decision to pit one's own skills against a largely unknown field of adversaries. An intelligent decision obviously requires a well-informed estimate of the odds of winning. Yet people's assessments of these odds are notoriously inaccurate. Survey evidence consistently shows, for example, that some 80 percent of us think we are better-than-average drivers, and that even more of us think of ourselves as more productive than the average worker.[9] We will describe evidence that many people are similarly overconfident about their odds of prevailing in winner-take-all contests. When people overestimate their chances of winning, the number who forsake productive occupations in traditional markets to compete in winner-take-all markets will be larger than could be justified on traditional cost-benefit grounds.

It is not surprising that there are bad outcomes when people make important decisions on the basis of inaccurate information. What is perhaps less expected is that too many contestants tend to compete in winner-take-all markets even when people have completely accurate assessments of their odds of winning.

The explanation lies in an incentive problem similar to the one that gives rise to excessive environmental pollution. In deciding whether to buy an air-conditioner, for example, people weigh the benefits of their added comfort against the cost of buying and operating it. From the individual buyer's point of view, the relevant operating expense is the cost of the electricity the machine uses. But the machine's operation also imposes an additional cost on others. The more we run the air-conditioner, the more electricity we must generate, and the more we pollute the air in the process. In the absence of regulation, individuals are free to ignore this additional cost, and most of them do so. As a result, when people are driven exclusively by market incentives, we tend to get too little clean air.

By the same token, potential contestants in winner-take-all markets generally ignore an important cost imposed on others by their entry—namely that each additional contestant reduces the odds that someone already in the contest will win. This zero-sum feature leads too many people to compete in winner-take-all markets, and too few to seek productive careers in traditional markets. Thus we will argue that our national income would be higher if some students abandoned their ambitions to become multimillionaire plaintiffs' attorneys in favor of the more modest but more predictable paychecks of electrical engineers.

The winner-take-all payoff structure encourages another form of waste in that it invites—indeed, virtually compels—competitors to take costly steps to enhance their prospects of winning. Book publishing is a lottery of the purest sort, with a handful of best-selling authors receiving more than $10 million per book while armies of equally talented writers earn next to nothing. Under these circumstances, authors naturally jump at any chance to increase their visibility and sales. Witness, for example, this excerpt from Judith Krantz's description of her promotional tour for her best-selling novel *Scruples:*

> Touring for a book—it's the literary equivalent of war. I remember my
> hardcover tour. I'd hit a city—say, Cleveland—at night, unpack, steam

out the clothes that were wrinkled, and, the next morning, get up at six. Because there's always an "A.M. Show," a "Good Morning Show," a "Hello Show" in every city in the country. . . . When you leave that hotel early in the morning, you have to be packed up and all checked out—the publisher has a limo to get you to the studio, and your suitcase is going to be in that limo all day while you make your sixteen different stops. Your arrival at the studio is at seven-thirty or eight, and the author invariably goes on last, but you have to be there an hour ahead of time in order to keep them from going crazy. Then, after I went on, I'd do a whole day of media in Cleveland, finishing up at six o'clock, just in time to catch a plane to Detroit, and the departure gate is *always* at the very end of the airport. You do all that day after day and enough weeks in a row, and you get so that you feel you can hardly function.[10]

That promotional tours like Krantz's are crucial in deciding which fifteen books make it onto the *New York Times* fiction best-seller list cannot be denied. Yet, no matter how much time and effort Krantz and other authors devote to these tours, a simple truth remains: Only fifteen books can make the list each week. Because one author moves up only if another moves down, the rewards of investing in book tours loom much larger for authors as individuals than they do for authors as a whole.

If promotional efforts involve a measure of social waste, they may also help people make marginally better decisions about which books to buy, which films to see, and so on. Many other competitive maneuvers, however, have no such redeeming feature. Consumption of anabolic steroids by professional athletes, for instance, not only does not add to social value, it almost surely diminishes it. National Football League (NFL) fans have little reason to prefer watching games in which each team's linemen average 300 pounds rather than 250. Yet the advantage to any team of having larger players than its opponent can be decisive. And so, in the absence of effective drug testing, widespread ingestion of steroids, with all the attendant health risks, is inevitable.

The incentives for authors to go on book tours and for athletes to consume anabolic steroids are much like the incentives for rival nations to engage in military arms races. Each side suffers an unacceptable loss of position if it buys no arms while its rival does. Yet weaponry is costly, and when both sides buy arms, both do worse than if neither had. We will argue that winner-take-all markets spawn a host of what might be called "positional arms races," which augment the losses stemming from overcrowding.

The Contest for Elite Educational Credentials

Lawyers on Wall Street who specialize in corporate takeovers receive just a small percentage of the total amount of money involved in these transactions. But the amounts involved are often staggeringly large. The RJR-Nabisco buyout, for instance, was consummated at a price of $25 billion. So even when forty lawyers split just one-quarter of 1 percent, we are still talking about a great deal of money for what often amounts to only a few weeks' or months' work.

When such sums are conspicuously reported in the media, bright and ambitious young people naturally ask themselves, "How can I get a job as a Wall Street lawyer?" With so many applicants vying for each entry-level opening, Wall Street firms must be extremely choosy. Even to land an interview at some firms, it is necessary to hold a degree from one of only a handful of prestigious law schools. And how does one gain admission to one of these law schools? The surest route is to have been a leading student at one of a handful of elite undergraduate institutions.

Indeed, the day has already arrived when failure to have an elite undergraduate degree closes certain doors completely, no matter what other stellar credentials a student might possess. Harvard's graduate program in economics, for example, recently rejected an applicant from a small Florida college, despite her straight-A transcript and glowing recommendations from professors who described her as by far the best student they had ever taught. Her problem was that the committee also had a file drawer full of applications from straight-A students with strong letters from schools like Stanford, Princeton, and MIT. On the evidence, the Florida applicant *might* have been as good or better than the others. But committees are forced to play the odds, which tell us clearly that the best students from the best schools are better, on average, than the best students from lesser schools.

The nation's elite educational institutions have become, in effect, the gatekeepers for society's most sought-after jobs. Those who fail to pass through their doors often never have a chance. We will present evidence that realization of this truth has spread widely among our best and brightest high school seniors. Years ago many top students attended state universities close to home, where they often received good educations at reasonable expense to their families. Today these same students are far more likely to apply to, be accepted by, and matriculate at one of a handful of the nation's most prestigious universities, most of which are located in the Northeast. When the rejection letters from these schools are sent out each year in April, recipients increasingly have grounds for feeling downcast. Though many of them are barely seventeen, some of life's most important doors have already closed in their faces.

Of course, there are some obvious advantages to concentrating the best students in a few top schools, just as there are advantages to tracking the best students into separate classrooms in the elementary schools. But tracking also entails costs, and the central question in each case is, How much tracking is best? The debate rages on in the public schools, where the alternatives are usually a limited amount of tracking within each school or no tracking at all. But those are not the choices we face in higher education. There we must choose between tracking at the local or regional level (for example, by putting the best students into honors programs in the state universities) and tracking at the national level (by sending the best students to a small number of elite institutions). The second option is the one we are heading for, yet it is by no means clear that it dominates the first.

In recent years a number of books have lambasted the supposedly cushy working conditions of university professors. *Pro/Scam* author Charles Sykes offers this blustery indictment:

> They are overpaid, grotesquely underworked, and the architects of academia's vast empires of waste. . . . They insist that their obligations to research justify their flight from the college classroom despite the fact that fewer than one in ten ever makes any significant contribution to

their field. Too many—maybe even a vast majority—spend their time belaboring tiny slivers of knowledge, utterly without redeeming social value except as items on their resumes. . . . In tens of thousands of books and hundreds of thousands of journal articles, they have perverted the system of academic publishing into a scheme that serves only to advance academic careers and bloat libraries with masses of unread, unreadable, and worthless pabulum.[11]

Although much of this criticism is overblown (after all, students from around the world increasingly clamor for admission to American universities), it also contains a kernel of truth in several areas. We will argue that the objects of most severe criticism—namely growing salaries and shrinking teaching loads—are best understood as natural consequences of positional arms races in higher education.

Realizing the importance of prestige in attracting top students, schools across the country have attempted to mimic the strategy of elite universities by bidding for the distinguished and visible faculty whose research accomplishments are perhaps the most important emblems of academic distinction. In the process, a superstar phenomenon—albeit a relatively mild one—has emerged in academia: Top researchers' salaries have escalated more rapidly than those of their lesser-ranked rivals, even as the teaching loads of top faculty have shrunk. The quest for academic prestige has also motivated universities to bid aggressively for top administrators, fund-raisers, and others who have demonstrated the capacity to attract and manage resources.

In a world with unlimited resources, these developments might not be cause for concern. But we live in a world in which educational costs have rapidly been outpacing the costs of other goods and services. Undergraduate tuition at the Ivy League schools *(excluding* room, board, and other expenses)—which stood at less than $3,000 per year in 1970—has now reached $20,000, and similar escalation has occurred in tuitions elsewhere. Political pressure has been mounting to control these costs, but unless we understand the forces that give rise to them, we risk costly errors. Excellence in higher education is a critical source of economic advantage, and if costs are to be cut, it must be done in a way that does not compromise this advantage. The winner-take-all perspective suggests a number of practical policy changes that might serve this goal.

Contests for Relative Position in Everyday Life

The winner-take-all markets we have mentioned so far are high-visibility arenas in which people, many with celebrity status, compete for enormous financial rewards. These contests affect the lives of ordinary citizens to the extent that they mold our system of higher education, alter the distribution of income, increase the prices of what we buy, and so on.

But there are also many other arenas in which ordinary citizens are themselves confronted directly with rewards that depend on relative, rather than absolute, performance. The ability to purchase many goods and services, for example, is constrained less by the absolute amount of one's earnings than by how much one earns relative to others. In Los Angeles most people would like to have a home with a commanding view, and yet only a small fraction—say 10 percent—of the home sites there can satisfy that demand. If each family is willing to pay the same fraction of its income for the privilege, the allocation of home sites with views will be settled by relative income alone. If everyone's income were to double, or to fall by half, the winning bidders would be the same—those with incomes in the highest 10 percent.

Because many important rewards in life depend on relative, not absolute, income, people have a strong interest in seeing that their incomes keep pace with community standards. This incentive structure leads to a variety of winner-take-all contests in everyday life.

To land a job, for example, an applicant is well advised to "look good." But what, exactly, does that mean? On reflection, any realistic definition turns out to depend almost completely on context. To look good means simply to look better than most other applicants. One way to do so is to spend more than others on clothing. Since the same incentives clearly apply to all applicants, however, an escalating standoff inevitably ensues. At leading law and business schools, many students don't dare appear for an interview wearing a suit that costs less than six hundred dollars. Yet when all students spend that amount, their attractiveness rankings are no different than if all had spent only three hundred dollars. In either case, only one person in ten can exceed the ninetieth percentile on the attractiveness scale.

As wasteful as escalating expenditures on clothing might seem, the stakes become even higher once cosmetic surgery emerges as a weapon in the competition to look good. Such surgery is expensive, is painful, and entails a small risk of serious side effects. Its use is increasing rapidly and, in some areas of the country, it has already become widespread. In Southern California, for example, morticians now complain that the noncombustible silicone sacks used in chin, breast, and buttocks augmentation have begun to clog their crematoria.

Although surgical enhancement of appearance often clearly serves an individual's goals, its social utility is highly questionable. Indeed, once it becomes the norm, its principal effect is merely to shift the standards that define normal appearance. Many people who would once have been described, nonjudgmentally, as being slightly overweight or having slightly thinning hair now feel increasing pressure to undergo lipo-suction or hair-transplant surgery.

Agreements to Limit Wasteful Competition

It would be surprising if no one had ever noticed that people and firms often find themselves embroiled in wasteful positional arms races, and more surprising still if no steps had ever been taken to curb them. People often are aware, at least implicitly, of these wasteful processes, and have implemented a host of strategies for keeping them under control. Because they function like treaties that limit military weapons, we call these strategies "positional arms control agreements."

The governmental regulations we will identify as positional arms control agreements (whether originally adopted for that purpose or not) come in many forms and apply in many arenas. These include restrictions on the top prizes that individuals may receive—such as income taxes, consumption taxes, and luxury taxes; campaign finance laws; safety regulations, both in the workplace and in product markets; regulations that limit working hours; regulations, or "blue laws," that limit retail business hours; and even laws that prohibit polygamy.

Many such limiting agreements do not involve the force of law. Retail merchant associations, for example, sometimes agree collectively to limit business hours (although enforcement difficulties often lead to a breakdown of these agreements). Private and parochial schools often limit clothing expenditure by imposing uniform requirements or dress codes. Sports leagues impose roster limits, pay caps, drug bans, and revenue-sharing arrangements. And where the antitrust laws permit, industry associations often work out elaborate agreements for sharing the fruits of basic research.

Even informal social norms are sometimes employed to limit wasteful competition. We will offer this interpretation, for example, of social norms that limited the casualties from dueling in eighteenth-century Europe; of contemporary norms in many communities, especially small ones, that frown on conspicuous consumption; and of social norms that discourage cosmetic surgery and other practices regarded as vain.

Some Winner-Take-All Markets Are Worse Than Others

Our claims that winner-take-all markets attract too many resources and generate wasteful spending patterns rest on the standard economic premise that the social value of a product or service is well measured by what the market is willing to pay for it. The top prizes in many winner-take-all markets, however, significantly overstate the social value added by top performers. In these instances the tendency to attract too many resources may be greatly amplified.

The legal profession is a case in point. Without denying that lawyers perform a number of tasks that are indispensable for a well-ordered society, we note that many lawyers appear to receive salaries that far exceed their social value. This is especially the case for lawyers involved in litigation, which usually does less to create new wealth than to redistribute existing wealth.[12] As economist Kenneth Boulding once described the problem:

> [F]or any individual person there is a payoff in having the best lawyer. Under these circumstances, it is not surprising that the law attracts some of the ablest minds of our society and that the payoffs for high ability

are probably as great in the law as in any other profession if not greater. If, however, we could achieve a kind of intellectual disarmament and agree that nobody would be allowed in the legal profession with an IQ above a hundred, the result would be almost exactly similar; people would still try to buy the best lawyers they could, but a valuable intellectual resource would be economized.[13]

We may suspect that when Boulding made this fanciful proposal, almost thirty years ago, he had little inkling of how attractive it might someday seem to a society ravaged by the modern tort system.

Winner-Take-All Markets and Norms of Fairness

Winner-take-all markets have implications not only for efficiency but also for norms of fairness. The economist's theory of wages, which holds that workers are paid in proportion to the value of their productive contributions, was never intended to justify market income distributions on ethical grounds. Nonetheless, many see a certain rough justice when pay is distributed on that basis, for the system rewards not only talent but also the willingness to expend effort. In winner-take-all markets, however, pay distributions will be more spread out—often dramatically so—than the underlying distributions of effort and ability. It is one thing to say that people who work 10 percent harder or have 10 percent more talent should receive 10 percent more pay But it is quite another to say that such small differences should cause pay to differ by 10,000 percent or more. Olympic gold medalists go on to receive millions in endorsements while the runners-up are quickly forgotten—even when the performance gap is almost too small to measure: "The miler who triumphs in the Olympic Games, who places himself momentarily at the top of the pyramid of all milers, leads a thousand next-best competitors by mere seconds. The gap between best and second-best, or even best and tenth-best, is so slight that a gust of wind or a different running shoe might have accounted for the margin of victory."[14] The realization of how winner-take-all markets contribute to income inequality may affect the extent to which society tries to alter market distributions in the name of fairness.

Media and Culture in the Winner-Take-All Society

Social critics have long complained that market imperatives have degraded our culture. What these critics have consistently failed to offer, however, is a reasoned account of *why* this should be so. If the market system is the best mechanism for producing the cars and houses we want, why isn't it also best for books, movies, and television programming?

Still, it is difficult to deny that the critics have a point. The films and books that media conglomerates urge on us will all too rarely speak well of us to future generations. Consider again Judith Krantz, who in the spring of 1994 published her eighth best-seller, a romance entitled *Lovers.* Just what is Krantz urging us to read on these frantic book tours of hers? *The New Yorker's* critic Anthony Lane quoted the following sentence in support of his claim that *Lovers* was one of eight abominable books among the top ten sellers on a recent *New York Times* list: "Did his cousin Billy Winthrop also take a pair of bodyguards with her wherever she went, Ben Winthrop asked himself in mild surprise as he leaned out of his car to give his name to the guard at the gatehouse that stood squarely at the driveway entrance to Billy's estate in Holmby Hills."[15] If passages like these ever find their way onto the reading list of a freshman writing seminar, it will be to illustrate what Lane describes as the difficulty of trying "to cram twice as much information into a single sentence as it was designed to bear."[16]

Of course, defenders of popular culture can cite counterexamples like the novels of John Le Carré, which are consistently best-sellers and yet also consistently draw praise from even the toughest critics. And there, typically, the culture debate bogs down, an apparently un-resolvable quarrel over tastes.

The winner-take-all perspective suggests a possible way of moving beyond this stalemate. We start with the observation that, as social beings, people have a keen interest in reading the same books others read, and in seeing the same movies. Consider a book buyer's choice between two books that, on the available evidence, are of equal quality: Both are on subjects of interest, both have been favorably reviewed, and so on. If one of these books happens to have made the best-seller list and the other hasn't, this tends to tip the balance. After all, we like to discuss books with friends, and a book's presence on the best-seller list means that friends will be more likely to have read it.

As we will see, this success-breeds-success feature is common in many winner-take-all markets, but never more so than in markets for popular culture. Positive-feedback effects in the marketing of books and movies mean that a big launch has become an essential ingredient in the process of becoming a hit. A book that fails to achieve large early sales quickly lands on the remainder tables, and a film that fails to open big is unlikely to survive for long in the theaters.

We will argue that it is the financial imperatives of achieving *quick* market success that have shaped popular culture in the ways that critics find so distasteful. Publishers have learned that the surest way to achieve large early sales is to promote books by authors who have already written several best-sellers. Studios have learned that the surest route to a big opening weekend is to produce a sequel to a recent hit movie. The financial incentives strongly favor sensational, lurid, and formulaic offerings; these incentives could not have been consciously designed to be more hostile to innovative, quirky, or offbeat works, whose charms generally take longer to communicate. The winner-take-all reward structure is especially troubling in light of evidence that, beginning in infancy and continuing throughout life, the things we see and read profoundly alter the kinds of people we become.

The Challenges Posed by Winner-Take-All Markets

Whereas free marketeers maintain that market incentives lead to socially efficient results, our claim is that winner-take-all markets attract too many contestants, result in inefficient patterns of consumption and investment, and often degrade our culture. If these costs are to be avoided, firms and individuals must somehow be restrained from taking advantage of readily available profit opportunities.

This does not mean, however, that detailed, prescriptive government regulation is the cure for all social ills. As conservatives have ably demonstrated, such regulations entail pitfalls all their own, often doing more harm than the problems they were designed to overcome.

The problems we attribute to winner-take-all markets stem largely from participants' failure to take account of the costs they impose on others. In this sense these problems are much like those associated with pollution, and our experience with pollution control offers useful guidance about how best to curb the waste that arises in winner-take-all markets.

The best remedies seldom involve bureaucratic attempts to regulate behavior directly. Rather, alternative policies that require individuals to take into account the full costs of their actions have generally proved simpler, more effective, and less intrusive. Thus, a group of northeastern states eliminated a major source of environmental litter virtually overnight simply by enacting deposit laws for soft-drink containers.

Our search will be for remedies in this mold. Our goal is to discover ways to bring individual and social incentives more closely into line, at the same time preserving freedom of choice to the greatest possible degree. If there are too many attorneys and too few engineers, we are more likely to solve this problem by altering the reward structure than by trying to regulate career choices directly.

But regulation with a light touch is still regulation, and many free marketeers will object to some of the remedies we propose. To these skeptics, we concede that people have every right to seek their fortunes in winner-take-all markets. Yet in an economy permeated by these markets, there can be no general presumption that private market incentives translate self-interested behavior into socially efficient outcomes. Precisely the same logic that justifies community intervention to curb environmental pollution also supports the community's right to restructure the winner-take-all reward system for the common good.

Does Greater Equality Necessarily Reduce Growth?

In virtually every society, we hear of the "agonizing trade-off" between equity and efficiency. Conservative American economists of the supply-side school, in particular, are fond of saying that although they would not mind seeing a more progressive tax system on equity grounds, such a move would produce devastating effects on growth.

The winner-take-all perspective poses a sharp challenge to this argument. The overcrowding problem in winner-take-all markets arises because participation in these markets is misleadingly attractive to individuals. To the extent that many, if not most, of society's highest incomes are the direct result of winner-take-all processes, the effect of higher taxes on these incomes would be to reduce the overcrowding problem.

Moreover, the people most likely to drop out would be those whose odds of making it into the winner's circle were smallest to begin with. Thus the value of what gets produced in winner-take-all markets would not be much reduced if higher taxes were levied on winners' incomes; more important, whatever reductions did occur would tend to be more than offset by increased output in traditional markets. To the extent that most of society's top earners are participants in winner-take-all markets, it follows that a more progressive tax structure would not reduce but actually increase economic efficiency!

As today's young economists look back to the early years of the Great Depression, most are astonished to realize that, less than a lifetime ago, their predecessors thought that the cure for a stagnant economy was to reduce the supply of money. We now know better, of course. For several decades, the Federal Reserve has boosted the money supply at the slightest indication of an economic downturn, and this has helped keep the economy on a remarkably even keel by historical standards.

We may all hope that, one lifetime from now, economists will look back in similar astonishment at the notions that guided late-twentieth-century economic and social policy. The problem of our time is not depression but the multiple evils of rising inequality, budget deficits, and slow growth. Yet the quintessential conservative policy prescription of this era—tax cuts for middle- and upper-income people—is no more likely to cure these problems than monetary contraction was likely to cure the Great Depression. Advocates of tax cuts sometimes concede their negative impact on inequality and budget deficits, but they see these as costs worth bearing in order to stimulate economic growth.

Our claim is that this trickle-down theory simply does not apply in economies pervaded by winner-take-all markets. This is a good thing, too, for it means that the very same policies that promote both fiscal integrity and equality are also likely to spur economic growth. The time-honored trade-off between equity and efficiency is far less agonizing than it appears.

2

How Winner-Take-All Markets Arise

Each spring in northern California, contestants gather for the Calaveras County Jumping Frog Competition. The current record holder is Rosie the Ribbiter, who spanned twenty-one feet, five and three-fourth inches, in three hops in 1986. Rosie competed for little more than honor, but considerably more is at stake when at about the same time each year the world's premier thoroughbreds gather at Churchill Downs for the Kentucky Derby. Jumping frogs, racehorses, milk cows, show dogs, and breeding bulls—all these animals and many more have been contestants in winner-take-all markets.

Besides animals and persons, what other kinds of contestants compete in these markets, and by what processes are the winners chosen? More fundamentally, just what *is* a winner-take-all market? And what forces give rise to these markets in the first place? We must answer these questions before we can tackle larger questions about how winner-take-all markets have transformed society.

Winner-Take-All Markets Defined

Consider this list of winners: best-seller, World Cup champion, Harvard matriculant, Rhodes scholar, first-round draft pick, clerk to a Supreme Court justice, cover girl, prime minister, host state for the first Mercedes plant in the United States, French Open champion. What do they all have in common?

One characteristic they share is that each prevailed in a contest whose payoffs are determined by relative rather than (or in addition to) absolute performance. In tennis, for instance, how much a player earns depends much less on how well she plays in absolute terms than on how well she performs relative to other players. Steffi Graf received more than $1.6 million in tournament winnings in 1992, and her endorsement and exhibition earnings totaled several times that amount. By any reasonable measure, the absolute quality of her play was outstanding, yet she consistently lost to archrival Monica Seles. Seles was forced to withdraw from the tour after having been stabbed in the back by a deranged fan in April 1993. In the ensuing months, despite little change in the absolute quality of her own game, Graf's tournament winnings accumulated at almost double her 1992 pace.[1]

Reward by relative performance is the single most important distinguishing characteristic of winner-take-all markets. In the markets that economists normally study, by contrast, reward depends only on absolute performance. For instance, a production worker's pay—to the extent that it depends on performance at all—depends on the number of units he assembles each week, not on how his productivity compares with that of his coworkers.[2]

A second feature of winner-take-all markets is that rewards tend to be concentrated in the hands of a few top performers, with small differences in talent or effort often giving rise to enormous differences in incomes. Both features—reward by relative performance and high concentration of rewards—show up in economist Sherwin Rosen's description of the market for classical musicians:

> The market for classical music has never been larger than it is now, yet the number of full-time soloists on any given instrument is on the order of only a few hundred (and much smaller for instruments other than voice, violin, and piano). Performers of the first rank comprise a limited handful out of these small totals and have very large incomes. There are also known to be substantial differences between [their incomes and the incomes of] those in the second rank, even though most consumers

would have difficulty detecting more than minor differences in a "blind" hearing.[3]

As we will see in chapters 6 and 7, it is this reward-by-relative-performance feature that gives rise to many of the inefficiencies we attribute to winner-take-all markets. The fact that rewards are large and concentrated in many winner-take-all markets is of interest primarily because of its implications for income inequality. Highly concentrated rewards, by themselves, do not give rise to the kinds of inefficiencies we describe. Nor, for that matter, are winner-take-all markets the only source of income inequality. In assembly tasks for which workers are paid by the piece, for example, a small proportion of unusually productive workers may consistently earn several times more than the average worker.

Whether championship performance yields large financial rewards in a winner-take-all market naturally depends on the arena in which it occurs. In the world of sports, the most lavishly rewarded top performers are professional boxers. In 1992 alone, former heavyweight champion Evander Holyfield earned more than $28 million. There are many other winner-take-all arenas, however, in which rewards are neither large nor concentrated. In handball, for instance, Joe Durso won eight national titles between 1982 and 1992, yet had to support himself largely through his salary as a Brooklyn schoolteacher during that period. Two-sport athlete Roy Williams, Jr., has twice been bowler of the year on the Pro Bowlers Association Tour, and during the last twenty-five years has also won six world horseshoes titles. "Horseshoes are my first love, but bowling is my job," he says. "I wouldn't be able to make good money in horseshoes."[4]

Cases in which rewards depend on relative performance but are not highly concentrated clearly cannot be major sources of inequality. Such cases nonetheless often provide useful insights into the ways winner-take-all markets function, and in later chapters we will examine how many of them affect the lives of ordinary citizens. For the most part, however, our focus will be on those winner-take-all markets whose prizes are large, both in absolute terms and in relation to the rewards contestants could have earned in alternative endeavors.

Mass Markets and Deep-Pocket Markets

We see huge prizes in some winner-take-all markets because there are a multitude of buyers each with a small interest in the winner's performance. Thus, champion prizefighters earn so much more money than champion handball players because there are many more boxing fans than handball fans, and cable TV's pay-per-view makes each one an effective bidder for the champion's services. Handball fans have yet to achieve critical mass for entering the television arena.

The large incomes received by leading actors, recording stars, and best-selling authors likewise result from the willingness of a large number of buyers to pay a little more for the services of one performer rather than another. We will call markets of this type "mass" winner-take-all markets.

Large prizes in many other winner-take-all markets result from a small number of buyers who are intensely interested in the winner's performance. Examples in this category, which we call "deep-pocket" winner-take-all markets, include the markets for top painters and sculptors, for attorneys who are effective at keeping organized crime figures out of jail, and for geologists who are unusually good at finding oil.

As we will see in chapter 3, the scope of mass winner-take-all markets has grown over time relative to that of deep-pocket winner-take-all markets. But as our analysis in chapter 6 will make clear, the distributional and efficiency issues posed by these two market types are essentially the same.

We can gain additional insight into the nature of both mass and deep-pocket winner-take-all markets by examining the kinds of contestants that compete in them.

The Contestants in Winner-Take-All Markets

People and animals are not the only types of contestants in winner-take-all markets. Some of these markets, for example, involve contests between competing technologies. The rewards to different technologies typically depend not just on their absolute performance but also on how they perform relative to one another. And there are often enormous differences in rewards even when the performance differences are very small.

Consider, for instance, the struggle to come up with a zero-emissions vehicle. California recently enacted legislation requiring that at least 2 percent of all automobiles sold in the state in 1998 emit no harmful exhaust gases. Since no manufacturer can afford to abandon a market as large as California, and since the state's environmental regulations have a history of spreading to other states, this legislation has launched a frenetic search by automakers to discover the best technology for complying. Although most research has focused on electric-powered vehicles, there are still serious technical problems with this strategy. A hydrogen-powered vehicle recently introduced by Mazda has proved sufficiently promising for the ultimate outcome to remain unclear. What is clear, however, is that the manufacturer who comes up with the best technology will be a big financial winner.

History is replete with similar winner-take-all battles between rival technologies. In electric power transmission, the contest was between alternating-current methods and direct-current methods. In video recording it was between Beta and VHS. With nuclear reactors, light-water-, gas-, heavy-water-, and sodium-cooled designs were the main competitors. Unix, Macintosh, MS-DOS, Windows, and OS–2 have been the most important rival operating systems for personal computers. And digital technology battled analog technology in the race to bring high-definition television to market.

Fashions, too, often compete in winner-take-all markets. In the world of haute couture, designers often stake their survival on conflicting hunches about hem lengths and lapel widths. And executives at General Motors likewise took a financial leap of faith when they brought out their 1958 Chevrolet, the first American car in several years that lacked conspicuous tail fins. But probably no group is more vulnerable to the whims of fashion than the entrepreneurs who compete in the market for trendy nightclubs in cities like New York. They know at the outset that most of their clientele wants to patronize only the hottest club; and they know, too, that the few clubs that ever attain that status can hope to maintain it for a matter of months at most. In all these cases, the reactions of a few critical "buyers" at an early stage can spell the difference between runaway success and failure.

Various geopolitical entities also compete in winner-take-all markets. Rival political candidates are an obvious example. State and local governments engage in winner-take-all rivalries as well. When the federal government announced its decision to construct a multibillion-dollar superconducting supercollider, twenty-five states became embroiled in a competition to persuade federal bureaucrats that theirs was the most attractive jurisdiction in which to locate the facility. Local governments likewise compete to attract and retain the large corporations and government projects that are critical to their fiscal health.

Countries at war provide another obvious example of winner-take-all rivalry, but countries are also rivals in a variety of more subtle ways. For instance, as the explosive growth of international trade and commerce has made national borders more permeable, more and more of the world's most talented professionals work outside their home countries. Many of these people eventually emigrate, to the substantial economic and cultural benefit of their new countries. As one former Fortune 500 CEO put it, "Intellectual capital will go where it is wanted, and it will stay where it is well treated."[5] By all accounts the competition to attract these top professionals appears to have only just begun.

Languages, too, battle one another for supremacy in the global marketplace. And with English the almost certain victor in this struggle, the English-speaking countries have a leg up in their efforts to attract and retain the world's professionals.

Research universities are also contestants in winner-take-all markets. The winners capture the lion's share of the available research funding, the most distinguished faculty, and the most promising students. A National Science Foundation (NSF) graduate fellowship is one of the most prestigious honors that can be bestowed on an entering graduate student in the sciences, and almost two-thirds of the nearly seven hundred NSF graduate fellows in a recent year elected to study at just ten universities.[6] At the time they did the research that ultimately led to their Nobel Prizes, 49 percent of American Nobel laureates were housed in just five universities: Harvard, Columbia, Rockefeller, Berkeley, and Chicago.[7] Of course, many more than these five would be delighted to sit atop the academic pecking order. Indeed, literally hundreds of schools are striving for precisely this goal, apparently undeterred by the fact that most of them must fail. As in any other hierarchy, room at the top is limited, and the battle to achieve and maintain academic prestige is no less intense than the winner-take-all contests we see in other arenas.

Room at the top is equally limited in arts and entertainment. People who watch *60 Minutes* on Sunday evenings are unable to watch the programs that NBC, ABC, and Fox offer in the same time slot. (Some enthusiasts imagine that they escape this constraint by taping the other offerings, only to discover that they never get around to watching the tapes.) None of us has time to see all the films, plays, or concerts available in the marketplace, or to read all the books, or to listen to all the recordings. We are forced—if only reluctantly—to pick and choose. And when choose we must, we confine our attention to the best entrants in each category. Here, too, small differences between contestants often translate into large differences in economic reward.

Athletes and athletic teams are perhaps the quintessential winner-take-all contestants. In Olympic competition, only hundredths of a second separate the top performances in swimming, sprinting, downhill skiing, and scores of other events. Yet the gold medalists in these events often go on to earn millions in endorsements, while the runners-up are quickly relegated to footnotes. In team sports the differences in rewards paid to average and top performers, although generally less extreme than in individual sports, are nonetheless often substantial.

Although the contestants in winner-take-all markets are often entities other than persons, contests with high stakes almost always generate a set of closely related contests that do involve persons. During his illustrious career as a racer and breeding stallion, Secretariat earned millions of dollars. But—although he is reported to have had a very comfortable existence by equine standards—only a small fraction of his take was ever spent on the horse's care and maintenance. Most of the balance accrued to the investors in the syndicate that owned him, to the trainers who prepared him to race, to the jockeys who guided him to victory, and not least to the breeders who brokered his winning genetic mix.

The large prizes at stake in the competition among professional sports franchises tend similarly to be captured by a relatively small number of key personnel—talented coaches and athletes of high ability—who make winning more likely. When publishers stand to earn millions by bringing a best-seller to market, competing houses bid for celebrity authors, inventive publicists, and other people who enhance the odds of achieving best-seller status. Film studios hoping for a blockbuster bid for the best actors, screenwriters, directors, and producers. State and local governments trying to attract industry or federal facilities compete for the best consultants and lobbyists. Political parties compete for the most talented strategists and media advisers. Parties in high-stakes litigation compete for the ablest attorneys and private investigators. Corporations compete for the best CEOs, engineers, tax accountants, and advertising teams. Universities compete for the most prominent researchers, fund-raisers, and administrators. Clothing manufacturers compete for the most able designers. And so on.

These observations lead us to say that the ultimate winner-take-all contestants are persons, and throughout the book, our focus will be on winner-take-all contests in the labor market.

Processes for Determining Winners

Further insight into the nature of winner-take-all markets is afforded by a look at the processes used to select winners. These processes are as numerous and varied as the types of contestants. In some cases winners are chosen by lottery. The Federal Communications Commission (FCC), for example, has often used lotteries to allocate radio and television broadcast frequencies, and the Civil Aeronautics Board (CAB) once used them to allocate scarce landing and takeoff rights among commercial air carriers.

In addition to using lotteries, both the FCC and CAB have used auctions to select winners in the broadcasting and airline industries. The Department of the Interior uses auctions to allocate offshore oil-drilling leases. In the private sector, auctions are used to allocate book manuscripts, screenplays, racehorses, and a variety of other important ingredients in winner-take-all markets.

Other winner-take-all contests are decided by tests of skill, learning, or ability. Most athletic contests, for instance, are decided by comparing objective measures like elapsed times or numbers of points scored. Prestigious universities allocate slots among students partly on the basis of performance on the Scholastic Assessment Test (SAT), the Graduate Record Examinations, and the Law School Admissions Test. The NFL administers a battery of speed, strength, and leaping tests to prospective players.

But many other winner-take-all contests are resolved on the basis of considerably more subjective evaluations. Some athletic competitions are decided at least partly on the basis of judges' opinions, as in platform diving and figure skating. In entertainment, casting committees conduct screen tests, and record producers hold auditions. Committee evaluations are also decisive in the award of many government contracts and facilities, such as cable television franchises or the locations of military bases.

In the political arena, majority voting is by far the most common mechanism for settling contests. Voting is widely employed in other arenas as well. Corporate boards of directors elect their chairmen, university alumni elect their boards of trustees, sportswriters elect recipients of MVP awards, and so on.

One of the biggest single winner-take-all contests ever played out in the private sector culminated on November 19, 1985, when a Texas jury awarded Pennzoil more than $10.5 billion in damages against Texaco for interfering in Pennzoil's attempt to acquire Getty Oil.[8] Judges, juries, and other officers of the courts are increasingly the mechanism for settling winner-take-all disputes in the American economy.

Few moviegoers will ever forget the scene from *The Godfather* in which the uncooperative film producer awakens to find himself in bed with the severed head of his favorite thoroughbred. Coercion is a principal weapon in organized crime's efforts to acquire and maintain control over illicit enterprises. On a much larger scale, warfare has always been an important mechanism in the contests between nations.

For our purposes, perhaps the most important of all procedures for settling winner-take-all contests are the ordinary workings of the competitive marketplace. In the time-honored tradition, consumers vote with their wallets to determine who wins and who loses.

With any of these processes, winners sometimes emerge after a single trial, as with those who win the state lottery. More generally, however, society's biggest winners reach the top only after a long process of successive elimination or cumulation. Before even applying for their first faculty positions, for example, future Nobel laureates will generally have competed successfully for admission to the best undergraduate and graduate schools; and having landed a post at a top research institution, they must then compete for research grants and for the right to publish their findings in the leading journals. Only then does their competition begin in earnest.

We gain a clearer understanding of winner-take-all markets by seeing the kinds of contestants that compete in them and the kinds of processes used to choose winners. But to gain real understanding of how winner-take-all markets function, we must examine the various forces that give rise to them in the first place.

Sources of Winner-Take-All Markets

Most people who have ever suffered through an introductory economics course remember, at least dimly, that the prices and quantities of goods exchanged in the marketplace are governed by the forces of supply and demand. Some winner-take-all markets arise because of special conditions on the supply side—forces that influence costs of production. Other winner-take-all markets arise because of special conditions on the demand side—forces that influence the amounts buyers are willing to pay. Still others involve a combination of supply- and demand-side forces.

Production Cloning

On the supply side, the ultimate source of a mass winner-take-all market is that the services of the best performers can be reproduced, or "cloned," at low additional cost. For example, once the master recording has been made, it costs no more to transcribe the best soprano's performance onto a compact disc than it does her understudy's. Once the film is in the canister, it costs no more to make an additional print of an Academy Award winner than a B western. Once the television cameras have been set up, it costs no more to broadcast a tennis match between the first- and second-ranked players in the world than it does to broadcast a match between the 101st and the 102nd. If the best performers' efforts can be cloned at low marginal cost, there is less room in the market for lower-ranked talents.

More generally, whenever there are economies of scale in production or distribution, there is a natural tendency for one product, supplier, or service to dominate the market. The battle is to determine which one it will be.

Network Economies

On the demand side of many markets, a product becomes more valuable as greater numbers of consumers use it.[9] A vivid illustration is VHS's defeat of the competing Beta format in home video recorders. VHS's attraction over the initial versions of Beta was that it permitted longer recording times. Though Beta later corrected this deficiency and on most important technical dimensions came to be widely regarded by experts as superior to VHS, the initial sales advantage of VHS proved insurmountable. Once the number of consumers owning VHS passed a critical threshold, the reasons for choosing it became compelling—variety and availability of tape rentals, access to repair facilities, the capability to exchange tapes with friends, and so on.

IBM's MS-DOS format capitalized on a similar network economy. Its initial sales advantage gave software writers a strong incentive to write for the IBM operating system. The resulting software inventory gave people a good reason for choosing IBM-compatible products even after otherwise superior machines began to appear in the marketplace. And for many years, the density of IBM's sales and service network enabled it to withstand competition from much cheaper clones.

The attraction of a dense network of sales and repair facilities is often decisive in the auto industry as well. The French manufacturer Peugeot, for example, recently abandoned the American market because its declining dealer network made it prohibitively costly to attract new buyers.

Network economies are especially relevant in the choice between alternative modes of communication. For example, the value to any individual of having telephone service, a fax machine, or a hookup to an electronic mail system depends strongly on the number of others who possess the same technology. Network economies will also be decisive in the competitions between the disc and tape modes of digital audio recording. And technological compatibility is of such importance in the contest between digital and analog systems in high-definition TV that most governments are likely to allow broadcasting in only one format.

Network economies, however, are by no means confined to issues of technological compatibility. For example, one valuable part of the experience of reading a book is discussing it with a friend who has also read it. If a book has been widely reviewed and discussed in the media, people have more reason to read it than they would an otherwise identical book that has not received this attention. Similar considerations apply to movies, plays, music, spectator sports, and a host of other interactive consumer activities.

In all these processes, small differences at the early stages of competition can prove decisive. Whether magazines and other newspapers review a novel, for example, is sometimes influenced by whether it has already been reviewed favorably or displayed prominently in the *New York Times Book Review*:

> Many of its readers are in the business—bookstore owners, agents, editors, paperback houses, other publishers. A good part of the advertising in the pages of the *Book Review* is intended not so much for the individual reader as for these other players, and for motion-picture and TV-entertainment companies. A prominent ad in the *Times* is a way to let them all know about the existence of a "big book" or a "publishing event"; indeed, some authors insist that their contracts be written to include the promise of advertisements in the *Times*. The same people who say they fear and resent the *Times*'s authority over books thus contribute to the power of the *Book Review*.[10]

One novel may reach the best-seller list while another of equal or higher quality lands on the remainder tables just because the *Times* happened to send the second book to an unsympathetic reviewer.

Lock-in Through Learning or Investment

Economist Brian Arthur has described another process by which an initial winner is likely to have a cumulative advantage in subsequent rounds of the contest.[11] But whereas the network-economies story plays out on the demand side of the market, Arthur's story plays out on the supply side. He starts by observing that when there are competing technologies in a new industry, the rate at which each of them is improved is related to its prevalence in use. Technologies that are more widely used in the early stages thus tend to attract a disproportionate share of research-and-development efforts, and this in turn leads to even more widespread adoption. Arthur labels this process "lock-in through learning," and cites the nuclear reactor technology competition of the 1950s and 1960s and the U.S. steam-versus-gasoline-car competition in the 1890s as examples.[12]

In the same vein, Arthur offers the example of competing transport modes to illustrate how small differences in early investment patterns often produce large differences in final outcomes:

> [I]n most countries road and rail are to some degree substitutes as alternative modes of transportation. Each mode is self-reinforcing in that the more heavily it is used, the more funds become available for investment in capital improvements that attract further users. Therefore, one mode may achieve dominance at the expense of the other. But reversing this or trying to assure a balance may require a significant subsidy to the weaker mode to bring it level with the advantage accumulated by the dominant mode.[13]

Sociologist Robert K. Merton and others have pointed to similar forms of "path dependency" in the careers of scientific researchers.[14] Graduates of the best undergraduate schools are more likely to be admitted to the best graduate programs than others who are only marginally less talented; and the highest-ranked Ph.D's who emerge from those programs are more likely than their near peers to obtain faculty jobs at the best universities. The lighter teaching loads and more generous research support offered by the best universities in turn make it more likely that the initial research efforts of these scholars will succeed and attract the attention of other scientists. Success at this level breeds further success in the form of research grants, invitations to important conferences, and so on. Merton calls this phenomenon the "Matthew effect,"[15] after the verse in the Book of Matthew that reads, "For unto everyone that hath shall be given, and he shall have abundance; but from him that hath not shall be taken away even that which he hath."

Other Self-reinforcing Processes

Network economies and lock-in through learning are just two of many processes that involve positive-feedback effects—processes in which success breeds success. The competition among universities for scarce slots atop the academic pecking order is another such process. As sociologists Paul Kingston and Lionel Lewis note, "Prestige is a somewhat amorphous asset. Yet, for all the shadings of eliteness, there is remarkable continuity and consistency—among raters and over time—in the rankings of undergraduate schools."[16] A group of perhaps three dozen schools consistently dominates the rankings in college guides and news magazines. The evidence suggests that the perceived quality of a university is closely related to the achievement levels of its faculty, students, and alumni.[17] This means that any initial improvement in quality, whatever its source, will make it still easier to attract top students and faculty, which in turn will yield still further improvements in reputation. Commenting on the University of Pennsylvania's campaign to broaden its market and improve its image during the early 1980s, Provost Thomas Ehrlich noted, "The wonderful thing is that the more successful you are, the more successful you are. The more you hear Penn is the institution of choice, the more you want to come."[18]

Producers in the for-profit sector show similar awareness of how strongly perceptions of success can influence purchase decisions. Thus Ford Motor Company's 1993 Taurus was reported to have become the largest-selling car in the United States because of Ford's tactic of offering unusually deep discounts on sales to rental-car companies. In terms of sales to individual consumers—arguably a much better benchmark of a car's appeal—Honda's Accord retained top status. But that didn't prevent Ford from touting Taurus in its ads as "the number-one selling car in America."

The market value of being perceived as the sales leader is also apparent in other industries. It helps explain why the manufacturers of WordPerfect recently filed suit to prevent Microsoft from calling its rival product, Word, "the most popular word-processing program in the world."[19] And for several years now, Visa has spent millions on advertisements emphasizing that whereas its card is accepted "everywhere you want to be," many merchants "don't take American Express."

Strong positive feedback effects also influence career paths in entertainment and business. Casting directors, for example, often have little objective basis for choosing among the hundreds of talented but unknown actors who audition for a minor film role. But once a particular actor has been chosen and has performed according to expectation, directors have good reason to favor him in the future, for he has now become a known commodity.[20] Similarly, personnel committees often have little basis for choosing between applicants for entry-level management positions. But those candidates who are chosen at this early stage will often be in a much better position to move forward than their near peers who were not chosen. In all such cases a small initial advantage can eventually engender a nearly insurmountable lead.

Decision Leverage

One measure of the importance of any individual decision is the number of people who are affected by it. Thus the maxim: "When a sergeant makes a mistake only the platoon suffers, but when a general makes a mistake the whole army suffers." For the person in the top position of a large decision-making hierarchy (CEO, ship's captain, Supreme Court justice, and so on), a small difference in the quality of even a single decision can translate into an enormous difference in the value of final output. Consider a CEO who must decide which of two new products will be produced by his Fortune 100 firm. Even though the product chosen may account for only a small share of the firm's total sales, making the right choice could easily mean several million dollars of added profit. Thus, if the top contenders for the CEO position are distinguishable with respect to the quality of the decisions they are likely to make in office, then the competitively determined salary of the best candidate can be dramatically higher than for the second best, even when the estimated difference in their talents is very small.

Natural Limits on the Size of the Agenda

Some winner-take-all markets arise because of cognitive limitations on the part of buyers. In many product markets, we are either unable to, or we simply choose not to, keep track of a host of similar competing products. Psychologist G. A. Miller has surveyed evidence suggesting that people have difficulty processing lists that contain more than seven items.[21] To simplify our lives, we remember the relevant details of at most a few products in each category. As sociologist William J. Goode has put it:

> Each person's investment or concern in a given field (even his or her own) is limited. Most people are satisfied to know the names of a few baseball players, scientists, bartenders, sculptors, or political figures. Ordinary group conversations do not continue for long on any one of these topics, and all parties are satisfied in making a small number of evaluative remarks about them. If everyone admired completely different "heroes" in each activity, they could not all hold an adequate or satisfying conversation. Consensus about a few leaders is itself a source of pleasure in informal talk among friends.
>
> Indeed, if we examine the conversations of any subgroup, whether a neighborhood gathering, a family dinner, or a group of women, it is clear that only a few names come into prominence, and only those of high evaluation or notoriety are discussed at length. That is, in both a psychological and temporal sense, people do not possess sufficient time and energy—enough "shelf space"—to focus on any but the top competitors.[22]

Mental-shelf-space limitations help explain why, for example, a tennis player like Andres Gomez—for many years ranked in the top ten worldwide and winner of the 1989 French Open—earned little from endorsement contracts in the United States and Western Europe, where he was consistently overshadowed by higher-ranked players like Stefan Edberg, Boris Becker, and Jim Courier. As virtually the only member of the set of world-class Ecuadorian professional athletes, however, he was a celebrity of the first rank in his native country.

Consider the case of *Gray Eagles,* a first novel by American author Duane Unkefer that flopped in the United States but spent three months on the best-seller list in Canada. Unkefer himself was puzzled, saying that although he had written "a good book, an adventure story, a love story, a thriller," it was not about hockey or ice fishing or any other subject that ought to have appealed particularly to Canadians.[23] Although his American publisher, William Morrow, spent much more than it usually does on publicity for a first novel, the book never broke out of the flock to engage the attention of the U.S. media. The generally slower pace of the Canadian media market, however, enabled the book's Canadian publisher to arrange a five-city promotional tour with dozens of broadcast and print interviews. This tour, which could never have been set up in the United States for an unknown author, got *Gray Eagles* onto the Canadian readers' agenda. And since the book was such a good read, that was all it took.

Mental-shelf-space limitations also seem to help explain why fewer golfers than tennis players achieve celebrity status in the United States, even though television consistently devotes many more hours of coverage to golf than to tennis. Most professional tennis tournaments take place in a single-elimination format played over four to seven rounds, with the top players matched against lower-ranked players in the early rounds. Golf tournaments, by contrast, are decided by cumulative stroke totals over several rounds and are not set up to favor top players. It is thus much more likely that a lower-ranked player will win in golf than in tennis. For example, the PGA top earner, Greg Norman, won only two of nineteen tournaments in 1986, and, on the women's side, the LPGA top earner, Pat Bradley, won only five of twenty-six. By contrast, Ivan Lendl won seventy-four of eighty matches and nine of the fifteen tournaments he entered that year; Martina Navratilova won eighty-nine of ninety-two matches and fourteen of seventeen tournaments.[24] The failure of a handful of consistent winners to emerge on the PGA tour may also help explain the relative popularity of the senior men's tour, which showcases a limited number of better-known older players, such as Arnold Palmer and Jack Nicklaus.

In all cases the value of winning a spot on the agenda depends on how much effort is required to maintain that position once achieved. As in the case of political office holders, incumbents in other arenas often enjoy a clear advantage.

Habit Formation, or Acquired Tastes

Winner-take-all markets sometimes arise because of aspects of human nature that traditional economic analysis tends to ignore. A standard assumption in economics is that the more we consume of something, the less we are willing to sacrifice to obtain more of it. In many cases this assumption is well founded: A thirsty man, for instance, is willing to pay more for his first pint of water than for his third. Yet there appear to be important exceptions to this pattern. For example, a new style of music that irritates on first hearing often grows much more appealing after repeated listenings. As psychologist David Berlyne writes: "Particular harmonic or melodic practices are considered objectionable and proscribed at one period; they stir up protest when a few innovators begin to adopt them; they are then regarded as acceptable and enjoyable."[25]

Similarly, we initially dislike some foods that go on to become favorites once we get used to them.[26] Few smokers report having liked the taste of their first cigarette, and most Scotch drinkers say it took them awhile to acquire a taste for it.

Habit formation and acquired tastes often help to concentrate demand on a handful of top performers. During the early 1990s, the *MacNeil/Lehrer Newshour* almost always turned first to David Gergen and Mark Shields for commentary as major news stories unfolded. Arguably many others were just as knowledgeable about domestic political affairs. But viewers grew accustomed to hearing from Gergen and Shields on such occasions, and many were bitterly disappointed when Gergen left to join the Clinton White House.[27]

Of course, the preference for the familiar is not absolute. In his discussion of musical innovation, for example, Berlyne goes on to observe that, once they have won acceptance, many innovations wear out their welcome and in the end are regarded as "banal and insipid."[28] More accurately, then, we might say that people prefer the "familiar but not too familiar." Such a preference might help to explain the rapid turnover in those segments of arts and fashion—MTV videos, for instance—in which exposure to the top performers is intensely repetitive.

The importance of habits and acquired tastes points to another reason that history matters. It also suggests an underlying rationale for the phenomenon of brand loyalties, whose intensity often appears to transcend all narrowly economic measures of costs and benefits.

Purely Positional Concerns

Another aspect of human nature that gives rise to winner-take-all markets is our tendency to value many goods not just according to their absolute properties, but also according to how they compare with the goods consumed by others. Such goods have sometimes been called status goods, but we prefer the more neutral and general term "positional goods," coined by the late economist Fred Hirsch.[29]

Sometimes the demand for positional goods reflects pure status seeking. But positional demands are often important even when buyers are not consciously aware of any desire to keep up with the Joneses. We may find satisfaction in driving a fast car that handles well, for example, even if we have no interest in an auto race with our neighbors. Yet qualities like speed and handling are inescapably relative. Today a fast sedan is one that will accelerate from zero to sixty miles per hour in less than seven seconds. In 1925, by contrast, a car was considered fast if it would *eventually* reach sixty. No matter which era we consider, however, only a limited number of cars can attain superlative status in any category. Thus, if the elapsed times in acceleration tests were suddenly to rise by half for every automobile, the owner of a Porsche 911 Turbo would still derive the same satisfaction as before from driving one of the fastest cars on the road.

By its very nature, the demand for top rank can be satisfied by only a limited number of products in any given category. And this, together with the fact that people are often willing to pay substantial premiums for top-ranked products,[30] often gives rise to intense winner-take-all competitions between the aspiring suppliers of those products.

Even consumers who profess no interest in consumption comparisons per se will nonetheless often have much at stake in how their consumption compares with that of others. This is especially true when people care what others think of their ability. For example, attributes like intelligence or productivity are only imperfectly observable, and job seekers in particular stand to lose much if evaluators underestimate them. Hence their interest in *relative* consumption, for in competitive markets, there is a positive correlation between ability and earned income and in turn between earned income and observable consumption items like clothing, automobiles, and houses. An investment banker, for example, would be ill advised to wear a polyester suit when meeting an important client for the first time.

Gifts and Special Occasions

Similar issues arise in connection with gift giving and the celebration of special occasions. As economist Richard Layard once put it, in a poor society a man can prove to his wife that he loves her by giving her a rose, but in a rich society he must give a dozen. To celebrate a special occasion, people search not for an average restaurant meal or bottle of wine but for ones that are special. As New York restaurateur Alan Stillman describes this phenomenon: "On any given day in New York, hundreds of major business deals are closed, deals worth millions of dollars. On any given day, dozens of people get big promotions, huge law fees or court settlements. When they celebrate at a dinner or lunch, cost literally is no object. They order the most expensive wines we have."[31] A 1982 Chateau Petrus for four hundred dollars a bottle? No problem. But although every vintner and every restaurateur would be delighted to be chosen on celebratory occasions, only a limited number can ever attain that status. With gifts, likewise, the rule of thumb is that the more important the occasion, the more we plan to spend. And as before, the emphasis is on relative quality: We give two ounces of Russian caviar, not forty pounds of frozen whitefish costing the same amount; one silk undergarment, not an equivalent dollar purchase of Fruit of the Loom cotton underpants. A young man gives his fiancée a half-carat diamond, not the thirty-carat garnet that he could buy for the same money, and so on. In each of these cases, the result is to concentrate demand on a handful of top suppliers.

Avoidance of Regret

The demand for a front-rank product or service may also stem from a desire to avoid regret over possible adverse outcomes attributable to having bought less than the best. Thus when you buy the highest-rated brand of tires, you needn't second-guess yourself when you have an accident caused by a blowout. One leading manufacturer banks on precisely this motive when it spends millions on television ads showing a baby sitting atop a tire as the voice-over urges viewers to "buy Michelins because so much is riding on your tires."

Similarly, the manager who hires the blue-chip consulting firm insulates herself from the criticism she would face if a regulatory issue were decided adversely. Sometimes choosing the premium consultant may be warranted because of the high stakes of the contested issue. But even when the stakes are not high, managers will often want to be able to cover themselves by having done everything possible in the event of an unfavorable outcome. In genuinely high-stakes arenas, this pressure to hire the best can be all but irresistible:

> "Imagine yourself a producer in charge of a very, very expensive film," said a top composer connected to a network of successful producers, a freelancer who had worked with some of the biggest people on some of the most expensive films in the seventies. "You could shop around and see who's good but not expensive," he explained, "but if your picture goes down the drain, the people who are working with you, and the people in charge, say of distribution at Disney, Universal, Fox— wherever—will scream, 'Idiot, why didn't you get the best?' So there's pressure to hire a name."[32]

The pressure to "hire a name" is a demand-related source of winner-take-all markets not just in entertainment, but in many other arenas as well.

Concentrated Purchasing Power

Another important demand-related source of winner-take-all markets stems from the concentration of great wealth in the hands of a few individuals. The wealthiest 1 percent of American families holds roughly 37 percent of the nation's total wealth.[33] These people are able to bring great resources to bear on behalf of outcomes they care strongly about, and this often gives rise to what we have called deep-pocket winner-take-all markets. Speaking of high-priced lawyers, for example, economist Alfred Marshall noted that "a rich client whose reputation, or fortune, or both, are at stake will scarcely count any price too high to secure the services of the best man he can get."[34]

Concentration of wealth also yields winner-take-all effects in markets for paintings, sculpture, architecture, and other one-of-a-kind artistic productions.

Similar concentration exists in the distribution of valuations by organizations. Large corporations, for example, place a high value on limiting their tax liabilities. The most talented corporate tax attorneys are often able to reduce these liabilities by tens of millions of dollars, and their salaries are scaled accordingly. Regulated companies may be viewed as being in high-stakes contests with the government across an even broader front. These contests pit the skills of company lawyers and economists against those of the regulators, and the result is often intense bidding for the economists and lawyers most likely to influence their outcomes. Similar behavior is triggered by decisions about the locations of attractive government facilities, the recipients of broadcast licenses, tariffs and quotas on imports, and other forms of public largesse.[35]

With this picture of the forces that give rise to winner-take-all markets in hand, we are now in a position to examine how the economic environment has been changing over time.

3

The Growth of
Winner-Take-All Markets

Winner-take-all markets are hardly a new phenomenon. The renowned British soprano Elizabeth Billington, for example, earned between £10,000 and £15,000 in the 1801 London season,[1] an enviable sum indeed by the standards of her day. And yet the technology of Billington's era imposed sharp limits on her ability to reach broader audiences.

What is new is the rapid erosion of the barriers that once prevented the top performers from serving broader markets. In the music industry, the driving force was the arrival of breathtakingly lifelike recorded music. Changes in physical production technologies have been important in other industries as well, but they often explain only a small part of the picture.

More important and sweeping changes have strengthened the basic forces that give rise to winner-take-all markets. As we will see, these changes predict both an expansion, or a broadening of the scope, and an intensification—that is, an increase in the dispersion of rewards—of winner-take-all markets.

Falling Transportation and Tariff Costs

One early and continuing change, well under way even before the ink was dry on the Declaration of Independence, has been the decline in the cost of transporting goods and services to market. The turnpikes and canals of the eighteenth century, the great railroads of the nineteenth century, and modern trucking along the vast highway networks of the twentieth century have each, in turn, made it possible for the best producers to extend their offerings to ever broader domestic markets.

More recently, technological advances in ocean shipping, the growing importance of air freight, and the steady decline of tariff barriers have extended this phenomenon across international borders. With the exception of the period between World Wars I and II, internationally traded goods have grown as a share of output in Western countries since the dawn of the Industrial Revolution, more than doubling since 1960 alone.[2] To be a player in the tire market in northern Ohio it was once sufficient to be the best tire maker in that part of the state. But the well-informed consumers of northern Ohio—like their counterparts everywhere else—now choose from among only a handful of the best tire producers worldwide.

The importance of transportation costs and tariff barriers naturally varies from industry to industry. Transport costs are especially important for products that are heavy or bulky in relation to their value. Falling transport costs thus do much to help explain why the hundreds of piano manufacturers at the turn of the century have now dwindled to just a few. The cheaper a product is to transport, the more likely that a mere handful of suppliers will dominate its global market.

Goods have become less costly to ship not only because unit transportation costs have fallen, but also because goods have gotten *lighter.* In other words, there has been a general increase in the ratio of the prices of goods, adjusted for inflation, to their shipping weights. For example, roughly 80 percent of the cost of a computer in 1984 was in its hardware, the remaining 20 percent in its software; by 1990 those proportions were reversed.[3] More generally, the weight of U.S. export products, per constant dollar, fell by 43 percent from 1967 to 1988.[4]

This movement is the result of many forces, including the move toward "mass customization"—the oxymoronic term used to describe the mass production of individually customized goods and services. In 1993 Joseph Pine contrasted this movement with the mass production movement ushered in by Henry Ford:

> While the practitioners of Mass Production share the common goal of developing, producing, marketing, and delivering goods and services at prices low enough that everyone can afford them, practitioners of Mass Customization share the goal of developing, producing, marketing, and delivering affordable goods and services with enough variety and customization that *nearly everyone finds exactly what they want.*[5]

One publisher's new custom electronic publishing venture is an example of this mass customization movement. Requiring little more lead time than for supplying conventional texts and collections of readings, it allows professors to assemble books tailored to their exact specifications. For instance, chapters from one text can be combined with chapters from a second, and both then supplemented with teaching aids from a third. This flexibility naturally commands a higher price, but the premium is not large and many buyers are willing to pay more for products that more fully meet their needs. The result is to increase the worldwide demand for texts written by the publisher's authors.

In more general terms, one of the many effects of mass customization is to increase the value per pound of delivered product, thus reducing effective transport costs. And this, as we have seen, further broadens the scope of domestic and international markets, further concentrating demand for the most able producers in each category.

Computing and Telecommunications

Perhaps the most profound changes in the underlying forces that give rise to winner-take-all effects have stemmed from technological developments in two areas—telecommunications and electronic computing. Information is essential for a market to expand in scope. Sellers must be able to identify potential customers and persuade them to try their products; they must also be able to communicate with, and monitor the behavior of, their agents in remote parts of the distribution chain. Buyers, for their part, need some way to identify the offerings that best suit their needs. They must also feel confident that the local sales agent can speak and act on behalf of the manufacturer, which, in turn, requires close communication between the two. Even if goods could be transported free of charge, markets would remain highly localized unless buyers and sellers had some means to accomplish these tasks. The global communications revolution has unleashed a host of new capabilities that facilitate them.

Indeed, despite all that has been written about this revolution, it remains difficult to comprehend how quickly and profoundly it has altered the worldwide flow of information. The first transatlantic telephone cable, which could transmit no more than 36 conversations at one time, was not laid until 1956, and even as recently as 1966, only 138 simultaneous conversations could take place between Europe and all of North America.

Describing the difficulty his New York headquarters had when trying to make telephone contact with overseas branches in the 1950s and 1960s, former Citibank chairman Walter Wriston says: "There were so few international lines available that it could take a day or more to get a circuit. Once a connection was made, people in the branch would stay on the phone reading books and newspapers aloud all day just to keep the line open until it was needed."[6] Branch officers hired squads of youths, called "dialers," who "did nothing but dial phones all day in hope of getting through."[7]

The pace of change quickened in 1966 with the launching of the first earth communications satellite, and by 1976 the addition of the sixth transatlantic cable had brought total capacity to four thousand simultaneous conversations. The year 1988 saw the installation of the first fiberoptic transatlantic cable, which by itself could carry forty thousand additional conversations. And by the early 1990s there were upward of 1.5 million available voice connections, a large fraction of them carried via satellite.

These developments have been accompanied by a parallel reduction in the time required to disseminate information through other channels. Military commanders once had to wait hours or even days to learn the results of their initiatives. But with the minicam and satellite uplink feeding CNN's live coverage, both Saddam Hussein and the

Allied pilots discovered instantly whether the bombs had struck their targets. And whereas almost all television news footage is now broadcast on the same day it is taped, as recently as the 1970s more than half was at least a day old.

The changes in our ability to process information have been no less dramatic than the changes in our ability to communicate it. This manuscript was composed on a desktop computer whose capabilities, even though two generations behind current equipment, could scarcely have been imagined by the men who developed the first electronic computer in 1946. Stored on its hard disk is a commercial software program that can beat all but the world's leading chess players, a feat that experts not long ago confidently predicted would never happen.

At the frontiers of computing research lie still more impressive capabilities. The NSF-sponsored supercomputer at Cornell University, for example, can process 125 billion floating-point calculations per second. New developments in parallel processing promise to increase that capability many times over.

With our progress in data processing has come equally rapid progress in our ability to store and transmit large volumes of information. A single CD-ROM can replace two thousand conventional library card-catalog drawers, and we can now digitize and transmit in just a few minutes all of the information contained in a two-hour motion picture.

For present purposes, perhaps the most important effect of our increased capacity to collect, process, and transmit information has been to reinforce the trend toward broader markets launched by falling transportation and tariff costs. For example, electronic media have transformed local and national entertainment markets into genuinely global ones. And successful American films and television programs increasingly dominate markets worldwide.

Information technology has also been decisive in the struggle between commercial air carriers. Two of the strongest survivors of the postderegulation era in the United States, United and American, owe much of their success to the entrenchment of their computerized reservations systems among the nation's travel agents. When an agent equipped with American's Sabre reservation system punches in a request for flight schedules between Chicago and Dallas, for example, the computer screen preferentially displays American's flights, relegating competitors to the bottom of the list. So critical is this seemingly small advantage that American Airlines president Robert Crandall remarked in 1986 that if he were forced to divest either the airline or Sabre, he would keep Sabre.[8]

A second, more subtle way in which the information revolution has supported the intensification of winner-take-all markets involves the mental-shelf-space constraints we discussed in chapter 2. Although our ability to generate and process information electronically has grown rapidly, our capacity as human beings to absorb and make sense of information has changed relatively little. The amount of information we can actually use is thus a declining fraction of the total information available.

The abstracts alone of the papers presented at a recent meeting on sequencing the human genome ran to more than 350 printed pages. Richard De Gennaro, the chief librarian at Harvard, estimates that although the college's holdings will double during the next twenty years, from seven to fourteen million volumes, each year's acquisitions will continue to fall as a share of the total volumes published that year.[9] One upshot is that mental-shelf-space constraints and agenda limitations bind ever more tightly. For any given number of sellers trying to get our attention, an increasingly small fraction in each category can hope to succeed. Mental-shelf-space constraints and agenda limitations thus constitute another growing source of winner-take-all effects.

A third effect of both the information revolution and the fall in transportation and tariff costs is an enhanced capacity to match buyers and sellers in deep-pocket markets. When additional information is costly to acquire or process, searching may not be worthwhile, even when important outcomes hang in the balance. For example, the task of visually comparing crime-scene fingerprints with prints stored in card archives is so time consuming that many jurisdictions do not even attempt it except for crimes involving murder, kidnap, or rape. In jurisdictions that have computerized facilities, by contrast, these searches take only minutes.

Several decades ago it was likewise often extremely difficult for people with highly specialized interests to make contact with one another. But with the rise of electronic bulletin boards and specialty publications, this matching problem has become increasingly soluble. Witness, for example, the recent emergence of the American Gourd Society, whose 2,500 members have a shared passion for raising gourds and for crafting artifacts from them; or the Diving Dentists Society, which unites North American dentists interested in scuba or other forms of diving. There is now even a Ginger Alden "Lady Superstar" Fan Club. This organization consists of fans and friends of Elvis Presley's last girlfriend, a model and actress.[10]

Diving dentists' clubs and Ginger Alden fan clubs are clearly not organizations of great economic significance. But the existence of these organizations forcefully illustrates that a search for the right product or service is worthwhile if it can be accomplished at sufficiently low cost. Trade magazines, specialty catalogs, 800 numbers, and electronic bulletin boards each year put a growing number of consumers in touch with the producers whose products best fill their idiosyncratic demands, and for which they are therefore willing to pay premium prices. And although the size of individual premiums is often small in such cases, cumulatively they can spell large increases in producer incomes.

Consider also the related case of the hundreds of Kuwaiti oil fields left ablaze as Iraqi soldiers fled the country near the end of the Persian Gulf war. These fires confronted Kuwaitis with a multibillion-dollar problem, and for help in solving it they did not confine their search to the Middle East. As with many other high-valued services, there is now a well-organized global market for the best oil-field firemen, and this market led the Kuwaitis directly to the late Red Adair. In an earlier time, Adair would have labored exclusively in the West Texas oil fields near his home, where he originally earned his reputation as the world's premier oil-field fireman. With the global communication network in place, however, he worked on only the most valuable jobs, no matter where in the world they might be located.

The information revolution and falling transport and tariff costs have also combined to strengthen the network effects that give rise to winner-take-all markets. This change follows from what it means to be part of a network—namely, that there be some form of interconnectedness among members. Perhaps the most explosive growth has come in the most literal networks of all—electronic communications networks like telephone, fax, and E-mail.

The number of fax machines, for example, grew from just 300,000 worldwide in 1983 to more than 8 million in 1992.[11] From 1985 to April 1994 the Internet grew from some 200 networks to well over 30,000. During the same period the number of people wired into the Internet worldwide grew from roughly 1,000[12] to over 25 million.[13] In mid–1994 the number of Internet users and traffic flow over the network were each growing from 10 to 15 percent per month.[14] By forging closer communications between people, these networks push us ever closer to Marshall McLuhan's vision of the global village.

The growing influence of American television, films, and other media has created international cultural and fashion networks of a more diffuse sort. And these networks, in turn, support a variety of growing international markets, each of which serves to extend the reach of the most talented performers.

The Growing Role of English

Not even the most advanced electronic technologies can facilitate communication if people do not share a common language. The very existence of cheap means of communication appears to have accelerated the emergence of English as the de facto international language, and, with it, the further expansion and intensification of winner-take-all markets:

> When an Argentine pilot lands his airliner in Turkey, he and the ground controller talk in English.
>
> When German physicists want to alert the international scientific community to a new discovery, they publish their findings in English-language journals.
>
> When Japanese executives cut deals with Scandinavian entrepreneurs in Bangkok, they communicate in English. . . .
>
> When pop singers from Hong Kong to Heidelberg ring out their songs, the lyrics as often as not are in English.[15]

English is the native language in twelve countries and is used as a medium to conduct official government business in thirty-three others.

It is now a required or widely studied subject in the schools of at least fifty-six additional countries. More than one person in seven worldwide speaks English as either a first or second language. More than 80 percent of all information stored in computers around the world is stored in English.[16] English has already become the language of choice for the international business community; and to the great dismay of the French and others, the European Community will conduct much of its official business in English.

The growing importance of English affects the forces that give rise to winner-take-all markets in at least two important ways. First, it joins the information revolution and falling transport and tariff costs in supporting a broader scope of international markets. A second effect, also a consequence of putting more people into effective contact with one another, is to strengthen the various network relationships we have discussed.

Innovation in Production Methods

Adam Smith was the first to recognize formally the enormous gains in productivity that arise from the division and specialization of labor. He illustrated the basic idea with this classic description of work in a small Scottish pin factory:

> One man draws out the wire, another straightens it, a third cuts it, a fourth points it, a fifth grinds it at the top for receiving the head; to make the head requires two or three distinct operations... I have seen a small manufactory of this kind where only ten men were employed . . . [who] could, when they exerted themselves, make among them about twelve pounds of pins in a day. There are in a pound upwards of four thousand pins of middling size. Those ten persons, therefore, could make among them upwards of forty-eight thousand pins in a day. Each person, therefore, making a tenth part of forty-eight thousand pins, might be considered as making four thousand eight hundred pins in a day. But if they had all wrought separately and independently, and without any of them having been educated to this peculiar business, they certainly could not each of them have made twenty, perhaps not one pin in a day . . ."[17]

In addition to supporting greater productivity, the division and specialization of labor also gives rise to winner-take-all markets. To be sure, the enormous gains in productivity have meant higher incomes even for society's poorest workers. In relative terms, however, those who specialize in highly repetitive production tasks have been the losers in this process, while those who oversee the results have been the winners. Payments that once accrued to a multitude of skilled workers increasingly flow toward the much smaller number of designers, executives, financiers, and others whose efforts are responsible for the new automated processes.

Adam Smith also recognized that the division and specialization of labor is limited primarily by the scale of the relevant market. Large markets support high levels of specialization; small markets do not: "In the lone houses and very small villages which are scattered about in so desert a country as the Highlands of Scotland, every farmer must be butcher, baker, and brewer for his own family."[18]

Since the earliest days of the Industrial Revolution, growing urbanization facilitated ever finer specialization of labor and the development of complementary machinery. More recent technological forces that broaden the scope of markets have pushed this process yet another step. These same forces have thus contributed not only to the expansion of winner-take-all markets, but also to their intensification.

Before World War II, automated production equipment performed only the tasks of the least skilled workers. Strong backs continue to be displaced by machinery, but we now see programmable industrial robots that displace even highly skilled craftsmen, often doing their intricate work not only faster but to a higher quality standard as well. The result has been a reduction in demand for craftsmen and an increase in demand for the designers of the robots that replace them.

Perhaps the most significant change in production methods is that the new machines not only perform the work but also gather, record, and transmit detailed information about what they are doing. As technology analyst Shoshana Zuboff describes the change: "The same technology simultaneously generates information about the underlying productive and administrative processes through which an organization accomplishes its work. It provides a deeper level of transparency to activities that had been either partially or completely opaque."[19]

The newly available information, Zuboff argues, will have profound effects on the ways in which businesses are organized and managed. One change is that the middle managers whose job it was to monitor production will occupy fewer slots on the organizational charts. Zuboff also argues that the need to anticipate and respond to rapidly changing environmental conditions will concentrate additional power in the hands of what she calls the organization's "intellective skill base." We may thus be witnessing the emergence of a new class of winners on the industrial scene—the "symbolic analysts," to use Secretary of Labor Robert Reich's term:

> Included in this category are the problem-solving, -identifying, and brokering of many people who call themselves research scientists, design engineers, software engineers, civil engineers, biotechnology engineers, sound engineers, public relations executives, investment bankers, lawyers, real estate developers, and even a few creative accountants. Also included is much of the work done by management consultants, financial consultants, tax consultants, energy consultants, agricultural consultants, armaments consultants, architectural consultants, management information specialists, organization development specialists, strategic planners, corporate headhunters, and systems analysts. Also: advertising executives and marketing strategists, art directors, architects, cinematographers, film editors, production designers, publishers, writers, and editors, journalists, musicians, television and film producers, and even university professors.[20]

No matter what new organizational forms ultimately emerge, the cumulative effect of these changes will be to increase still further the leverage of the economy's most able performers.

The Erosion of Rules That Limit Bidding for the Best

Before there can be large and concentrated rewards in a winner-take-all market, not only must the top performers generate high value, but also there must be effective competition for their services. Yet in many markets, a variety of formal and informal rules traditionally prevented such competition.

Most major sports leagues in the United States, for example, once maintained restrictive agreements that prevented team owners from bidding for one another's most talented players. In the wake of Andy Messersmith's successful challenge of baseball's reserve clause, however, these agreements have toppled one by one. By now, players have won at least limited free agency rights in all the major professional team sports.

There have been parallel changes in the rules governing payments in individual sports. Amateur status, for example, is no longer required for competing in the Olympics. And under the rules of the new Association of Tennis Professionals (ATP) tour, players are no longer prohibited from accepting guarantees and appearance fees.

Unlike the owners of professional sports teams, business owners were never subject to formal sanctions against bidding for one another's most talented employees. But informal norms often seemed to have virtually the same effect. Under these norms it was once almost universal practice to promote business executives from within, which frequently enabled companies to retain top executives for less than one-tenth of today's salaries.

The antiraiding norms of business have recently begun to unravel. As recently as 1984, the business community expressed surprise when Apple hired a new chief executive with a background in soft-drink marketing. But since then interfirm and interindustry boundaries have become increasingly permeable, and business executives are today little different from the free agents of professional sports. Firms that fail to pay outstanding executives their due now stand to lose them to aggressive rivals.

Deregulation has provided an additional source of increased competition in the airline, trucking, banking, brokerage, and other industries in the United States. Added to that has been the increased threat of outside takeovers resulting from the introduction of junk bonds and other new sources of financial capital. These developments have increased the potential damage that could result from poor performance, making it all the more important to bid for the most talented players in key positions.

The Rise of Independent Contracting

Several factors have caused traditional employment contracts to be increasingly replaced by independent-contractor relationships. Electronic communications, for example, make it possible to work in remote sites and still remain in effective contact with other team members. Advances in information processing have also reduced the overhead costs associated with independent-contractor status. Computer software can now bill clients electronically, keep accounts in order, and file tax returns. The rising costs of health care and other fringe benefits, together with increasing exposure to tort liability, have given firms additional incentives to deal with independent contractors rather than employees.

One immediate consequence of this shift has been to tie the worker's pay much more closely to the economic value of what he or she produces. When people work as employees of large firms, their compensation is typically determined by bureaucratic personnel formulas that link pay to seniority, education, job title, and a variety of other easily measured characteristics. Within any given category, pay usually varies little among individuals, even in the face of substantial individual variations in productivity. Under this traditional system, the most productive employees in a group effectively subsidize the least productive.[21] The move to independent-contractor status eliminates this subsidy, and enables the most productive individuals to come much closer to capturing their full market value.

Changes in the Level and Distribution of Income

Although the rate of income growth has declined since the early 1970s, real per capita income in the United States was nonetheless more than 11 percent higher in 1989 than it had been a decade earlier. When income rises, patterns of demand change. Spending on some goods—necessities like food and work clothing, for example—rises less than in proportion to income. Spending on other goods, such as fine jewelry, foreign travel, and vacation real estate, goes up more than in proportion to the rise in income.

Positional goods are in the latter category. Again, these are goods whose value depends in large measure on how they compare with goods consumed by others—in brief, goods that confer status. Status matters in both rich and poor societies, but people devote a larger share of their incomes to positional goods in rich societies. As we noted in the last chapter, demands for positional goods give rise to winner-take-all markets because only a limited number of producers can credibly claim to have the best offering in any category. So as income grows and, with it, the demand for positional goods, the payoff to supplying these goods will also grow.

Reinforcing this effect have been significant changes in the distribution of income. The pretax incomes of the top 1 percent of U.S. earners, for example, grew by 104 percent from 1977 to 1989, a period during which the median income rose less than 7 percent.[22] At the same time, tax rates on the top earners have fallen since the 1960s. Whereas the marginal tax rate on the highest incomes was 91 percent when John F. Kennedy took office in 1961, it was only 28 percent when Ronald Reagan left the presidency in 1989. The tax legislation enacted in the early part of the Clinton administration has moved tax rates on top U.S. incomes slightly higher, but even with these changes, personal disposable income is now much more concentrated at the top than it was several decades ago. The effect of this distributional change is to bolster still further the demand for positional goods, and thus to concentrate demand still further on the handful of producers who supply them.

The Amplifying Effect of Social Context

In later chapters we will attempt to trace the effects on earnings of changes in the forces that give rise to winner-take-all markets. Anyone making such an effort needs to be mindful of the importance of social comparisons in pay determination. We touched on this subject briefly when we discussed the effect of independent contracting on market salaries.

There we noted that people tend to be more concerned about how their salaries compare with those of closely associated coworkers than with those of people who work outside their organizations. Yet comparisons with outsiders also matter. And they matter especially for people who occupy unique positions—for whom reference standards are therefore unlikely to be available within the firm. The only reasonable reference standard available to CEOs, for example, is the salary distribution of other CEOs. Similarly, an investment banking firm has only one chief economist, an orchestra has only one first violinist, a baseball team has but one starting catcher, a television network has only one news director, and a basketball team has just one coach.

External pay comparisons matter not only because of individual concerns about equity, but also because it is often hard to measure the value of an individual's contribution to the firm's bottom line. That Wayne Gretzky helped the Edmonton Oilers win four Stanley Cups is beyond question. Yet no one can say *precisely* how much he helped them. That Lee Iacocca rescued Chrysler from bankruptcy and greatly enriched the corporation's shareholders is likewise beyond question. Yet in his case, too, no one knows just how much he enriched them. And hence the natural tendency of compensation committees to rely on external benchmarks.

The upshot is that the pay of unique employees depends not only on direct estimates of the value of their contributions but also on the actual pay received by similarly situated outsiders. There is, in effect, an element of social construction to pay determination. Thus a change in any one individual's productivity affects not only that individual's pay but also the pay of others; and the resulting movements in their pay in turn induce additional movements in the prime mover's pay.

Self-reinforcing processes of this sort are a prominent feature of the mathematical literature on chaos. For our purposes their significance is that even small changes in the forces that give rise to winner-take-all markets may be strongly amplified through the social comparison process.

Countervailing Effects: The Boutique Movement

Of course, not all the economic changes of the past century have been hostile to lesser-ranked performers. Computerized typesetting, for instance, has enabled publishers to bring niche books to market with smaller print runs than was ever possible before. Likewise, the same information revolution that has given us the Diving Dentists Society often enables buyers to desert large firms in favor of smaller specialty suppliers. This tendency is reinforced by growth in real incomes, which historically has supported consumer appetites for greater variety. The clearest manifestation of this trend has been the flowering of the boutique movement, a process whereby specialty suppliers have stolen market share, especially among upper-income buyers, from traditional mass merchandisers.

In some cases, these countervailing forces may transform a large-scale winner-take-all market into several smaller ones—an offset, in our terms, to the intensification of winner-take-all markets that results from other forces. The boutique movement in effect compresses the gap between the top earners and others.

At the same time, however, the boutique movement is itself subject to many of the same forces that have given rise to consolidation and intensification in other areas. Once small independent microbreweries demonstrated the profitability of specialty beers, for example, large national breweries began producing and distributing similar beers under their own specialty labels. Likewise, once affluent shoppers began leaving traditional department stores in favor of independent specialty clothing shops, the national chains began to partition large portions of their floor space into in-house specialty boutiques.

Even when boutique sellers remain small, moreover, the movement makes it possible for many people with special talents to command premium rewards in the marketplace. In these cases the boutique movement itself contributes to both the expansion and the intensification of winner-take-all markets.

It is possible, too, that the growing boutique movement may provide additional competition for the top performers in existing large organizations. In television, for example, the growing number and availability of cable channels might influence the salaries of current network star performers in two offsetting ways. By fragmenting the audience, these channels might make any given performer's drawing power less valuable. Countervailing this pressure, the presence of additional players in the game, each aspiring to capture audience shares from rivals, might drive star performers' salaries even higher. The question of the extent to which these opposing forces have actually altered the distribution of economic rewards in specific industries is of course empirical.

4

Runaway Incomes at the Top

By the end of 1994, Steven Spielberg's *Jurassic Park* had grossed nearly a billion dollars, making it by far the biggest box-office bonanza in film history. Spielberg himself headed *Forbes* magazine's list of the top earners in the entertainment industry, with 1993–94 income of more than $330 million. A growing number of CEOs now earn comparable amounts and a handful of Wall Street money managers take home even larger sums. Multimillion-dollar annual paychecks have also become increasingly common in athletics, law, journalism, consulting, publishing, and a host of other domains.

These trends are consistent with our claim that winner-take-all markets have expanded and intensified. For a small group of illustrative cases, we will now argue that changes in the forces responsible for growth in these markets do indeed appear to be linked to the runaway earnings of top performers. None of these cases is meant to be definitive. Rather, our claim is that, taken as a whole, the pattern they trace is consistent with the view that winner-take-all markets are a phenomenon of growing importance.

Book Publishing

Changes in the distribution of rewards in the publishing industry have been driven in part by changes in the ways information about books is disseminated. National best-seller lists and television talk shows have become increasingly prominent in the marketing of books, with the result that publishers feel increasing pressure to invest in book tours and related promotional activities. The best-seller lists by definition, and the promotional investments in fact, are concentrated on only a small proportion of titles.[1]

Also important has been the explosive growth of chain retailing. Book retailing was once a cottage industry run by thousands of independent entrepreneurs, each with an idiosyncratic sense of what titles might interest local readers. These bookstores have increasingly given way to large conglomerate chain outlets, such as Waldenbooks and Barnes & Noble. The four largest book chains accounted for almost 40 percent of total sales in 1991, more than triple their market share in 1972. Waldenbooks, which had only sixty-nine stores in 1969, had more than twelve hundred by 1993.[2]

The chains rely heavily on high turnover of best-sellers, and tend to stock almost identical titles in shops of a given size—in contrast to the more diverse lists of the independent operators. Where it was once common to see scores, if not hundreds, of titles on display in a store window, these spaces increasingly feature only a few authors, whose latest books are displayed in stacks of fifty or a hundred copies.

Editors and publishers explicitly recognize the increasingly all-or-nothing character of the business. In the late 1970s Aaron Asher, then editor in chief at Farrar, Straus & Giroux, had this to say about the increasing difficulty of selling paperback rights to the titles of midlist authors:

> Now more and more of these books are not being bought at all by the paperback houses. It's not merely that the mass-market publisher who has laid out a million dollars for a blockbuster can't afford the additional money to buy ten middle books for five thousand dollars apiece—that's a drop in the bucket to him. The *room* isn't there. The investment, the energy, all the thinking in a paperback house are geared to the book that it can make a killing on. Everything else is secondary.[3]

Another important change in the publishing industry has been the erosion of informal norms that once bound authors to their editors and publishers for extended periods. One result of these norms was that best-selling authors received the same royalty rates as other authors, which meant that the high revenues from their work were spread, in effect, among midlist authors. Publishing houses, however, are increasingly in the hands of bottom-line-oriented conglomerates; and authors are increasingly represented by agents who shop for the most favorable contracts. The effect of these changes has been to shift rewards from midlist to best-selling authors.

Of course, not all the relevant changes in the publishing industry have worked to the advantage of best-selling authors. On the physical production side, as noted earlier, computerized typesetting helps make smaller niche books economically feasible. On the distribution side, Random House has tried to compensate for the chain stores' unwillingness to stock midlist titles by producing a catalog with annotated listings of current titles in print, any of which can be shipped within days to buyers who call an 800 number. More recently, some of the major chains, and some independents as well, have been constructing "superstores," warehouselike facilities that stock upward of 250,000 titles. As we will see, however, these countervailing forces do not appear to have prevented a sharp increase in rewards to best-selling authors.

The competitive logic of the publishing industry tells us that the lion's share of the rewards from any manuscript with a good chance of becoming a best-seller will be captured by the author. Book buyers seldom know, and even less care, which companies publish the books they read. Their primary interests are the subject, the author, and the quality of the manuscript. Any one of a large number of competing publishing houses can do the job of producing the book and distributing it. And so the well-known author with a good manuscript sits in the driver's seat.

The truth of this claim has always been evident in the paperback segment of the publishing industry. The surest prediction that a manuscript will be commercially successful in paperback form is that it has already succeeded in the hardcover market. In 1968 Fawcett paid $410,000 for the rights to Mario Puzo's *The Godfather*. In 1972 Avon paid $1,100,000 for the rights to *Jonathan Livingston Seagull*, by

Richard Bach. Colleen McCullough's *The Thorn Birds* fetched $1,900,000 from Avon in 1976. In 1978, New American Library (NAL) paid $2,550,000 for Mario Puzo's *Fools Die.*[4]

As competitive pressures intensified, large paperback auctions were consummated for manuscripts that had not yet even appeared in hardcover, and for which, therefore, there could be no reassuring market evidence. In September 1979, for example, Bantam paid more than $3,200,000 for the paperback rights to Judith Krantz's *Princess Daisy*—then the highest amount ever paid for paperback rights—even though the book was not scheduled for hardcover release until the following March.

Bantam's payment to Krantz, widely reported in the press, sent shock waves through the publishing industry. "It's revolting," said Roger Straus of Farrar, Straus & Giroux.[5] Yet given the success of Krantz's first novel, *Scruples,* which sold more than a million copies in hardcover, and the confident judgment that *Princess Daisy* was an even better manuscript, Bantam was not greatly at risk despite its $3,200,000 commitment. At a sale price of $3.50 a copy and a printing cost of only 13 cents a copy (in print runs of one million copies), Bantam stood to collect roughly $1.00 per copy after paying all distribution and royalty expenses. Bantam already had three million paperback copies of *Scruples* in print, with the prospect of an additional wave of sales once the six-hour television miniseries based on the book was aired. The paperback version of *Princess Daisy* would reap similar benefits from the release of the feature film based on the book. If the book came even close to expectations, Bantam would do fine. And in the end, Bantam came out very well indeed. *Princess Daisy* went on to sell more than seven million copies in paperback.

With Bantam's experience in mind, authors and their agents saw the prospect of even larger sums from publishers. And indeed, competitive pressures pushed the bidding well into seven figures not just for paperback rights to completed works, but for hardcover rights to manuscripts not yet even written. In January 1986, for instance, the William Morrow Company, having seen only a few draft chapters, bid $5 million for the rights to James Clavell's *Whirlwind.*

This deal also struck observers at the time as a shockingly imprudent investment. But Clavell's *Shogun* had been an enormous hit, and if

Whirlwind did as well, Morrow would make back its advance and then some. As it turned out, however, Morrow ended up losing money. Even though *Whirlwind* could have been considered an enormous success by ordinary commercial standards—twenty-two weeks on the *New York Times* best-seller list, four of them at number one—a merely "successful" book simply doesn't generate $5 million in net revenues.

Industry executives have begun to bid with greater caution. The days of the "nearly sure bet" for publishers appear to be over. Even so, authors with consistent track records have continued to receive sharply escalating advance payments. And for such authors, it has become increasingly common to sign multibook contracts involving books that have not even been outlined. In 1990 Viking gave Stephen King $40 million for the rights to his next four books, and in that same year, Delacorte paid Danielle Steel approximately $60 million for her next five novels.

Increasing concentration is evident even among authors who make the best-seller lists. For instance, the authors of only two of 1978's five top-selling titles had appeared at least once on the top-ten lists of the preceding five years—James Michener (two top-ten appearances in the last five years) and Sidney Sheldon (one). By contrast, all five of 1990's top five had: Danielle Steel (eight appearances), Stephen King (seven), Sidney Sheldon (three), Robert Ludlum (two), and Jean Auel (one). Five of 1978's ten top-selling authors appeared among the top twenty in the previous five years, compared to nine of the top ten in 1990. In the spring of 1993, John Grisham had not only the number one book on the *New York Times* hardcover fiction list, but also the top three books on the *Times* paperback fiction list. Doubleday made a profit of some $14 million from sales of his *The Pelican Brief*.[6] By April 1995 Grisham had more than fifty-five million books in print.

Professional Tennis

Professional tennis provides a clear illustration both of how technical forces have amplified the economic value of key performers and of how changes in the rules have enabled these players to capture higher salaries.[7] In tennis, as in most other sports, revenues were once generated largely by the sale of tickets to fans who watched matches in person. But since the 1970s, tennis has joined other major sports in deriving a rapidly growing share of its revenues from the sale of television rights. For example, more than three times as many hours of professional matches were televised in 1987 than just a decade earlier.

With the growing role of television, the relative earnings of top-ranked players have risen sharply. In 1980 the average earnings of the top ten players, including endorsement fees, were roughly twelve times the average earnings of players ranked forty-one through fifty. By 1987 that ratio had grown to almost thirty.

Most tennis matches shown on network television involve at least one player ranked in the top ten. The exposure received by these players has created a lucrative endorsement market, which for the top players often yields annual earnings of several times their tournament winnings. Endorsement earnings fall off sharply outside the top ten, and few players outside the top fifty receive significant cash income from endorsements.[8]

Earnings from exhibition matches are not readily available, and thus could not be included in our estimates of the returns to top-ranked players. Fragmentary information suggests, however, that exhibition earnings are even more highly skewed than endorsement earnings.

In 1990 the men's professional tour was reorganized in a way that has still further concentrated rewards in the hands of top players. Well aware that they were not capturing revenue in proportion to their economic clout, the top men's players broke away from the Men's Tennis Council, the sport's existing governing body, to form the independent ATP tour. From a distributional perspective, the most important change implemented by the new tour was the legalization of appearance fees—guaranteed payments to individual players in return for their agreement to appear in specific tournaments. This change has enabled competing tournament directors to bid openly for the handful of top players whose name recognition guarantees sellout crowds and valuable television contracts. Appearance fees are often much larger than the tournament prizes themselves. For example, Andre Agassi's two-hundred-thousand-dollar appearance fee for the 1993 San Francisco ATP tournament was almost five times the amount he received for winning that event.

Executive Compensation

Following the death of Walt Disney, the entertainment conglomerate he founded was taken over by his son-in-law Ron Miller, a former professional football player with the Los Angeles Rams. The company languished under Miller's leadership, and in the autumn of 1984 the board replaced him as CEO with Michael Eisner, then the highly regarded number two executive at Paramount Pictures.

There ensued a period of spectacular financial success for Disney. The company's earnings rose from 15 cents per share in the fiscal year just before Eisner's appointment to $6 per share in the fiscal year ending in September 1990.[9] Eisner's performance has been handsomely rewarded. As former compensation consultant Graef Crystal describes the Disney chief's pay package:

> In 1990, he received a bonus of $10.5 million in addition to his $750,000 per year base salary. But the real payoff has come from his stock option grants. . . . Calculated off a late March 1991 market price of $119.25 per share, his unexercised option gains were likely on the order of $240 million. And as of March 1991, he still had more than three years of time remaining on his 1984 option grants and almost eight years on his 1989 grants. I once asked one of Eisner's key subordinates why Eisner seemed to be interested in amassing so much money. He said he thought that Eisner wanted to amass one of America's great family fortunes, on the order of the Rockefellers, Mellons, and duPonts. He appears to be well on his way.[10]

Although Eisner has clearly done well even by the lofty standards of CEO pay, he is by no means a fraternity of one. Brookings Institution scholar Margaret Blair reports that whereas CEOs earned approximately twenty-three times what engineers earned in the early 1980s, and seven times what Supreme Court justices earned, these pay differences had nearly doubled by 1992.[11]

According to Crystal's estimates, the surge in executive compensation began well before the 1980s. He reports that whereas the typical head of a large American corporation "earned total compensation (excluding perquisites and fringe benefits) that was around 35 times the pay of an average manufacturing worker in 1974, a typical CEO today earns pay that is around 120 times that of an average manufacturing worker and about 150 times that of the average worker in both manufacturing and service industries."[12] In a sample of two hundred of the largest United States corporations, Crystal estimated current average CEO pay, including the value of stock options and other incentives, at $2.8 million per year. The top twenty CEOs on the *Business Week* tabulation for 1993 all made more than $10 million, led by Eisner with $203 million (which, the magazine reported, was nearly as large as the GNP of Grenada).

Crystal and other critics have argued that there is little economic sense to the vast increases in compensation for CEOs, claiming that the increases are the result of cozy dealing between management and directors, and thus come directly out of shareholders' pockets. Shareholder abuse undoubtedly does occur in specific cases. Under Ross Johnson's "leadership," for example, RJR-Nabisco maintained a large fleet of corporate jet aircraft (the "RJR Air Force") used to ferry executives, directors, and high-profile clients to weekend retreats in the Colorado Rockies, where they played golf with top touring professionals on seven-figure company retainers. According to one report, the only passenger on one RJR-Nabisco cross-country jet was Johnson's dog, which was listed on the flight manifest as "G. Shepherd."[13] Although Johnson's pay consistently placed him near the top of the *Business Week* rankings throughout his tenure, the market provided stark evidence of the cost of his stewardship when it pegged the price of RJR-Nabisco stock at roughly half what it eventually fetched in the fabled takeover.

In *The Cost of Talent*, former Harvard president Derek Bok argues that shareholder abuse is not the only cause of runaway CEO compensation.[14] According to Bok, prevailing market conditions are incompatible with effective competition for executive talent. Companies know that hiring the best CEO will often mean tens of millions in additional profit each year, yet hiring committees can never be truly certain which of the many attractive candidates is best.

In a world of incomplete information, the occasional conspicuous failure is of course inevitable. But this does not signal a breakdown of competition. Indeed, intense competition is what forces companies to play their hunches in the market for CEOs. Because firms share largely common expectations about the quality of talent, failure to pay high salaries will often mean losing top candidates to rival bidders. It is newsworthy when highly paid performers fail, but isolated failures do not support Bok's more general claim.

Moreover, the market imperfections that Bok cites are not new. Nor have they become more prevalent. On the contrary, improved communications and falling transportation costs have made such imperfections much *less* serious now than they were several decades ago. Buyers may not be perfectly informed, but they have more information than they used to, and this makes it more difficult for renegade sellers to outrun their bad reputations. Similarly, with increased vigilance on the part of institutional shareholders and a growing threat of hostile takeovers, the latitude for executive pay abuse should be shrinking rather than growing. Granted, mediocre executive performances are sometimes rewarded with high salaries, as in the celebrated instance of former General Motors CEO Roger Smith. But as Smith and his immediate successor, Robert Stemple, can attest, executives who fail to deliver on the corporate bottom line cannot expect to remain in command indefinitely.

The other essential element in Bok's story is the social ratification of greed he identifies with the 1980s, which made huge salaries more acceptable than they once were. According to Bok the same market imperfections that produce such large salaries today might also have done so in the past had it not been for social norms that kept inequality at bay.

Bok is surely correct that social forces influence salaries. Who would deny that a corporate board would find it easier to approve a multimillion-dollar CEO compensation package if such contracts were the rule than if theirs were the only one? But by itself this cannot explain how seven-figure salaries became common in the first place. Bok seems to assign responsibility to the free-market values of the Reagan administration. Yet similar values were celebrated during the 1920s and 1950s, and executive pay was a much smaller multiple of the average worker's salary in those decades than it is now.

We have argued that the explosion of CEO pay has resulted not from any imperfections in competitive forces, but rather from their increasing intensity. The high cost of capital during the 1980s led corporations to restructure themselves through leveraged buyouts and stock buyback programs. The corporate debt used to finance these programs was attractive because it could be serviced with before-tax dollars (unlike profits on equity). Debt also removed much of the slack in corporate finances, forcing managers to focus on enhancing net worth rather than pursuing other goals. Even though the cost of capital came down in the late 1980s, the pressure remains as corporations encounter ever keener competition in the global marketplace. In an environment of high leveraging and rapid change, the CEO's job has become more critical than ever before.

It is doubtful, however, that these pressures alone could account for the explosive growth in executive pay in the United States. After all, globalization has had similar effects on the leverage of executives in Germany and Japan, where executive compensation remains modest by U.S. standards. Crystal, who estimated that U.S. CEOs earned roughly 150 times the average worker's salary in 1990, estimated that the corresponding multiples were only 16 in Japan and 21 in Germany.[15] As the experience in those countries has clearly demonstrated, the mere fact that a top CEO contributes millions to a company's bottom line does not by itself give rise to a commensurate salary.

In order for top CEOs to capture their full economic value, a second factor must also be present—namely, there must be open competition for their services. And here, too, big changes have been occurring. Put simply, there has been a dramatic increase in the extent to which American firms compete with one another for the services of top executive talent.

In seeking the best possible chief executive, boards have increasingly searched outside their own corridors. Hiring an outsider may seem risky when things are going well, but may be necessary when a major downsizing or restructuring is required. Once relatively rare, moves of this sort have grown increasingly commonplace and now scarcely raise an eyebrow. Our own study of CEOs hired by roughly eight hundred of the largest U.S. manufacturing and service companies found a steady increase in the proportion of outside hires. Thus from the early 1970s to the early 1990s, we estimate that the number of new CEOs who had been with their companies for less than three years grew by almost 50 percent.[16]

A case in point is Eastman Kodak's decision to go outside in 1993. In the face of huge losses, the board decided to replace its chief executive, Kay Whitmore, after just three years. The company tapped George Fisher, who in his six years as head of Motorola had "engineered one of the most remarkable transformations in U.S. corporate history, turning Motorola into a worldwide leader in microprocessors and cellular telephones."[17]

IBM, another failing giant, had pursued Fisher earlier in 1993, but after he turned them down, Kodak came to him with a more enticing offer of corporate and personal opportunities. One report pegged Fisher's new compensation package at close to $70 million, which would be a bargain of the first magnitude if he proved successful. Eastman Kodak had losses of $1.7 billion during the first three quarters of 1993.

If every company were to promote from within, there would be no reason to pay the most talented senior officers what they were worth, because they would have no place else to go. This remains the current state of affairs in Germany and Japan, where CEOs are still promoted almost exclusively from within, and where, as noted, CEO pay has grown much less rapidly than in the United States.

A critically important implication of the U.S. trend toward hiring from the outside is that it effectively breaks the implicit reserve clause that once bound executives to their companies. Although it is still true that more than half of newly appointed CEOs are insiders, the game has now fundamentally changed. In the United States, leaving for an outside post has become an increasingly available option for the best performers. To hang on to its most valued senior officers, the board must now pay them enough to keep them from jumping ship. Elimination of the reserve clause in baseball was an essential precondition for the explosive growth in the salaries of top players in recent years. Increased mobility has played a similar role in the market for top executives.

The effects on executive pay of this more open system of competition will be amplified by the social forces we discussed in the previous chapter. In an environment where multimillion-dollar compensation packages are unheard of, compensation committees will be reluctant to pay that much even in the face of clear evidence that their CEO is worth it. But let some other firm try to bid that CEO away, and the compensation committee will quickly begin to see matters differently. Rather than lose their CEO, they might agree to a multimillion-dollar package, despite the fire it would draw from social critics. Once implemented, this package becomes a benchmark that makes subsequent multimillion-dollar packages much easier to justify.

Business Consulting

With businesses facing more intense competitive pressures than ever, they have increasingly turned to paid consultants for advice on how to manage. AT&T, for example, paid out almost $350 million to business consultants in 1993 alone.[18]

When the CEO of a major corporation is under fire, she cannot turn to just anyone for advice. She knows that if things continue to go wrong, her board will want to know why she didn't retain the best. These pressures have created a bonanza of late for an elite handful of consulting companies. For example, McKinsey & Co.—"the most well-known, most secretive, most high priced, most prestigious, most consistently successful, most envied, most trusted, most disliked management consulting firm on earth"[19]—had revenues of $1.3 billion in 1993, more than twice its volume only five years earlier.[20] Although McKinsey is not the largest management consulting firm, its 3,100 consultants generated an average of $387,000 in billings, the highest of any firm in the industry.[21]

McKinsey's spectacular earnings growth is by no means unique. Indeed, its three-year growth as of 1993 was the lowest among the ten largest consulting firms. (See table 4–1.)

The forces that drive the market for consultants are essentially the same as the ones that drive the market for CEOs. To the extent that these forces have increased the leverage, and hence the economic value, of CEOs at the highest levels, they will have similar effects for top consultants.

Motion Pictures and Television

The star system in the film and television industries is nothing new. But growing international markets, increased revenues from sales of video

TABLE 4–1

Revenues and Growth of Top Consulting Firms

Firm	1993 Revenues ($ Million)	3-Year Growth Rate (Percentage)
Andersen Consulting	2,876	53
Coopers & Lybrand	1,351	50
McKinsey & Co.	1,300	31
Booz Allen & Hamilton	800	54
Gemini Consulting	516	128
CSC Consulting	470	96
Boston Consulting Group	340	114
AT. Kearney	278	84
Mercer Management Consulting	134	34
Monitor	90	80

Source: John A. Byrne, "The Craze for Consultants," *Business Week,* July 25, 1994, p. 65.

cassettes and other subsidiary rights, and the unprecedented success of several blockbuster films like *Jaws* and *Star Wars* in the 1970s launched a process that has driven star salaries to new levels.

The market for video cassettes was launched in 1977 when the Magic Video Corporation released cassette recordings of 50 feature films at retail prices between $49.95 and $79.95.[22] Sales of video cassettes, which stood at only 22 million copies as recently as 1984, now exceed 250 million copies a year and generate more than $5 billion in annual revenue.[23] Sales of rights to broadcast and cable television have also been swelling rapidly. By 1981 Home Box Office (HBO) had surpassed the largest theater chains to become Hollywood's biggest single customer, with annual purchases in excess of $180 million. Foreign box office revenues grew more than 52 percent during the decade ending in 1990, more than twice the estimated growth rate for domestic revenues.[24]

These new revenue sources have helped fuel an unprecedentedly heavy round of bidding for the basic ingredients of a hit movie—a good screenplay, good actors, a good director, and a good musical score. Just as authors tend to capture most of the financial rewards in publishing, screenwriters, actors, directors, composers, and a handful of other key players tend to capture the payoffs from hit movies. As the revenues generated by the biggest hits rose, so did the payoffs to these top performers.

As Harold Vogel wrote in his 1986 book, *Entertainment Industry Economics*:

> By hiring people whose ability to attract large audiences has already been proved, a producer can gain considerable financial leverage. It may be less risky to pay a star $1.5 million than to pay an unknown $100,000; the presence of the star may easily increase the value of the property by several times that $1.5 million salary through increased sales in theatrical and other markets, whereas the unknown may contribute nothing from the standpoint of return on investment.[25]

Economic theory tells us, however, that if it is clearly better to hire a star at $1.5 million than an unknown at $100,000, then the star is actually underpriced. And there is evidence that, even at several million dollars per film, the salaries of top stars were indeed too low in the early 1980s. In an illustrative budget for a blockbuster film produced in 1979, Leedy used a figure of $2 million for the "major lead actor."[26] In 1987 Twentieth Century-Fox paid Bruce Willis, then the star of the hit television series *Moonlighting*—but an actor without a single significant movie credit—$5 million for the lead role in *Die Hard.* In 1988 Arnold Schwarzenegger received $11 million for *Total Recall,* and in 1990 Michael Douglas got $15 million for *Basic Instinct.*[27] Schwarzenegger received $15 million (plus a percentage of gross receipts) for *True Lies* in 1994; the same amount went to Eddie Murphy for *Beverly Hills Cop 3* and to Bruce Willis for *Die Hard 3.* Even child star Macauley Culkin received $8 million for his appearance in *Getting Even with Dad.* Mel Gibson and Kevin Costner now command more than $10 million per film, a sharp increase from just a few years earlier; when profit shares are included, their total compensation per film sometimes tops $25 million.[28]

Screenwriters who just a few years ago got $250,000 for a screenplay are now paid well over a million dollars.[29] For example, Shane Black, who wrote the screenplay for *Lethal Weapon,* received $1.75 million for the script for *The Last Boy Scout.*[30] Joe Eszterhas got $3 million for his screenplay for *Basic Instinct.*[31] Richard Donner, director of *Lethal Weapon,* now asks $4 million per film plus revenue sharing. James Cameron got $6 million for directing *Terminator 2.*

As in publishing, the bidding has escalated to the point where hiring the top talent is no longer any assurance of a successful project. Among some of the recent big-budget losers: *Hudson Hawk,* starring Bruce Willis; *Days of Thunder,* starring Tom Cruise; *Dick Tracy,* starring Warren Beatty and Madonna; and even the one film that seemed to have every possible ingredient for success—Warner Brothers' *The Bonfire of the Vanities,* based on Tom Wolfe's best-selling novel, starring Tom Hanks and Bruce Willis, and directed by Brian De Palma.[32]

To anyone familiar with the competitive logic of winner-take-all markets, it will come as no surprise that the ultimate winners are not the studios who produce high-profile films or the investors who back them, but the handful of personnel who attract large audiences. "As Geoffrey Holmes, a senior vice president at Time Warner Inc. puts it: 'Wall Street brought money to Hollywood by the bucket, but it all ended up at the Beverly Hills Rolls Royce Dealers.'"[33]

In television as well, the growing importance of international and syndication rights appears to have supported sharply increased demand for top performers. In the winter of 1993, shortly after NBC announced with regret that its hit series *Cheers* would be closing down after thirteen seasons, the series' lead actor Ted Danson told friends that he had refused the network's offer of $13 million to do another season.[34] Danson's 1993–94 salary alone would have been more than double *Cheers'* entire annual production budget a decade earlier. Also in the winter of 1993, CBS announced the signing of late-night talk-show host David Letterman to a three-year contract valued at more than $42 million. Small changes in Nielsen ratings translate into millions of dollars in advertising revenues, and performers who can deliver the points have enjoyed expanding economic leverage.

Film stars have received enormous salaries for many years, and so it may seem only natural that television entertainers have achieved parity. What is more surprising is the emergence in recent years of television newscasters as celebrities in their own right. The networks have long since recognized the importance of high ratings in their nightly news broadcast as a lead-in to their prime-time programming. This realization has set in motion an intense competition among the network news shows, in which the most important dimension is the anchors themselves. Their ability to attract audiences is now clearly reflected in their pay: ABC pays perennially top-ranked Peter Jennings approximately $7 million per year. At CBS, Dan Rather and former coanchor Connie Chung collectively earned almost as much, while NBC's Tom Brokaw comes in at a bargain-basement rate of $2 million.[35]

The networks have also discovered that one way to beat the rising production costs of entertainment programming is to schedule prime-time news magazines. Footage for these shows is relatively cheap and, with a celebrity reporter in front of the camera, the audience shares are comparable to those of traditional dramas or sitcoms. We should expect, therefore, that recognition of this profit opportunity should lead to increased bidding for the celebrity hosts with proven drawing power. And indeed it has. ABC, for example, now pays Barbara Walters $10 million annually for cohosting its popular *20/20.* Diane Sawyer receives more than $5 million for appearing on several ABC prime-time news magazines each week. Ted Koppel, king of the late news time slot, gets $6 million a year.[36] All these sums are far more than mere cost-of-living adjustments to the salaries once received by Cronkite and Huntley and Brinkley.

Even sportscasters have become celebrities. When CBS lost its NFL contract to the upstart Fox network, Fox and the remaining networks scrambled to sign John Madden, then the premier football analyst for CBS. After many rounds of bidding, Madden emerged with a four-year contract from Fox estimated to be worth between $25 and $30 million.[37]

Both the Madden case and Diane Sawyer's recent contract negotiations with ABC offer an opportunity to assess the strength of the countervailing forces associated with the boutique movement discussed in chapter 3. In the television industry, this movement is embodied in the growth of cable channels, which might be expected to produce two countervailing effects on the salaries of top performers. On the one hand, by fragmenting audience sizes, the new channels might make the services of any given star performers less valuable; on the other, the new channels also reduce channel loyalty and create more vigorous competition for audience shares, which may drive top performers' salaries higher than ever.

In hindsight, analysts appear to be converging on the view that the growing number of channels makes the top stars more valuable. As industry analyst Ken Auletta recently observed:

> With more channels and movies and games and home-shopping and sports and computer bulletin boards to choose from, brand names like Sawyer and Madden stand out. "Uniqueness and distinctiveness become more important as people are confronted by multiple choices," Eric Ober, the president of CBS News, says. And [ABC News president Roone] Arledge says, "If five hundred new colas were introduced tomorrow, Coca-Cola would be more important than ever"[38]

Fashion Models

In 1928 Paul H. Nystrom, then professor of marketing at Columbia University's business school, published *The Economics of Fashion,* which to this day remains the definitive economic history of the fashion industry from the late eighteenth through early twentieth centuries. Nowhere in Professor Nystrom's 521-page volume does he refer to any fashion model by name. Models of that time posed largely for artists' sketches, and although there was some glamour in the work, they were paid little and received virtually no public recognition.

Shortly after the publication of Nystrom's book, however, fashion models began to assume a more prominent public role. Increasingly they were photographed rather than sketched, and by the early 1930s, the John Robert Powers agency had organized an elite cadre of models whose faces and figures graced the covers of national publications.

But models as celebrities first came into their own with the rise to prominence of the Conover Modeling Agency, founded in Manhattan in 1938 by Harry Conover (with the help of a loan from former President Gerald Ford, then a Powers model). Conover gave his models what were thought at the time to be catchy nicknames—Lassie

Newland, Jinx Falkenburg, Choo Choo Johnson—and his agency staged elaborate publicity stunts to get their names and pictures into the media.[39] Walter Winchell and Ed Sullivan mentioned them regularly in their newspaper columns. They became known as the "Conover Cover Girls" and were the inspiration for the 1944 Columbia film *Cover Girl,* in which some of them appeared.

With this rise in public recognition came substantially greater economic rewards. The most successful of all of the Conover models was Anita Colby. Nicknamed "The Face," Colby was then the highest-paid model in the business, earning an hourly fee of $25 in the early 1940s (about $300 per hour in 1995 dollars). A few of the agency's other top models at that time earned as much as $20 per hour, but most received the standard rate of $5.

Those figures, of course, were only the beginning. Caprice Bendetti, described by the *New York Times* in 1993 as "an average model," earns between $150,000 and $300,000 yearly.[40] Her face has never appeared on the cover of *Vogue, Elle,* or *Harper's Bazaar*; and because she is approaching twenty-seven, an advanced age in fashion modeling, it probably never will. Few people outside the fashion industry know who Caprice Bendetti is, but Cindy Crawford, Elle Macpherson, Claudia Schiffer, Kate Moss, and Kristen McMenamy are household names—or, at any rate, household faces—and command daily fees well into five figures. Schiffer, for instance, was reportedly paid $25,000 for "a couple of laps on the runway at Macy's Passport fashion show" in October 1992.[41] She and a handful of other supermodels dominate the fashion magazine covers, earning between two and three million dollars each year in modeling fees alone. Their earnings from workout tapes, MTV series, and endorsements add considerably to these totals.

Modeling is a winner-take-all market of the most extreme sort. Contrary to the pronouncements of the *New York Times,* however, an average model does not come close to earning $150,000 a year. In fact, the annual income of most models, now as in the 1940s, is zero—even negative, if allowance is made for money spent on portfolios and modeling schools by the many thousands of aspiring models who never land a professional booking. But the winners in this business are paid ever more handsomely.

College and Professional Team Sports

The infusion of television revenues during the past several decades has substantially increased the revenues that accrue to the best college athletic programs, especially those that make it to one of the prestigious postseason football bowl games or to the final four of the National College Athletic Association (NCAA) basketball tournament. In 1988, for example, the NCAA paid more than $28.6 million to the 64 teams in its Division I men's basketball tournament—including $1,153,000 to each of the final four teams.[42] By 1990 the NCAA was paying out $64 million to member conferences and schools under its basketball television contract. Under the current contract, signed in December 1994, the television rights to the tournament will cost CBS an average of $216 million each year, 51 percent more than under its previous contract.[43] The lure of such sums has caused the athletic budgets of major colleges and universities to escalate sharply. For example, the University of Michigan's athletic budget, which stood at around $3 million in 1968, had grown to approximately $20 million by 1988.

Where large prizes are at stake, whether in college athletics or in any other arena, contestants face powerful incentives to bid for the key resources that will enhance their chances of winning. The administrators of Texas A&M University were clearly thinking along these lines in 1982, when they paid the then-unprecedented salary of $375,000 to lure football coach Jackie Sherrill to their campus. Sherrill had demonstrated in his previous posts the ability to create a winning program, and he went on to do the same at A&M, winning three Southwest Conference titles in seven seasons.[44]

In short order other schools saw the logic of this move, and the salaries of elite coaches escalated sharply further. In 1990 Rick Pitino, the University of Kentucky men's basketball coach, was paid more than $800,000; the late Jim Valvano, North Carolina State University's men's basketball coach, got $750,000; and Lou Holtz, head football coach at Notre Dame, was paid between $500,000 and $700,000.[45]

Indeed, athletic directors think that having just the right coach is so important in big-money sports that many have now taken to buying out the contracts of coaches who have failed to produce winning records. In December 1992, for example, the University of Pittsburgh announced that it was paying Paul Hackett $500,000 to step down after he had compiled a 13–20–1 record during his previous three years as head football coach. At the time, Hackett had three years remaining on his contract. The University of Arkansas fired head football coach Jack Crowe in the fall of 1992 after a loss to The Citadel—only one game into his five-year contract. Crowe got a $600,000 severance payment. His replacement was Danny Ford, who had himself gotten a $1 million payment in 1990 to stop coaching the Clemson Tigers.[46]

Evidence of the bidding for critical inputs is even more fierce in the realm of professional sports, where players' salaries have escalated dramatically for the past two decades. These soaring salaries have led critics to denounce franchise owners for their stupidity and players for their greed. But as the logic of competition in winner-take-all markets makes clear, neither of these attributions is necessary to account for the observed changes in compensation levels.

For most of their history, major professional sports leagues enforced agreements that prohibited franchise owners from bidding for one another's players. Former St. Louis Cardinal outfielder Curt Flood challenged the major league baseball reserve clause in 1970, and although the courts ruled against him, they characterized the clause as an "aberration."[47] Further challenges ensued and, in the wake of the celebrated Andy Messersmith and Dave McNally cases in 1975 and 1976, baseball became the first professional sport to abandon its reserve clause. In the years since then, we have had a chance to witness the effect of free-market incentives on players' salaries.

These salaries rose relatively slowly in the years prior to 1976 but have escalated sharply since then. (See Figure 4–1.) The average salary was more than 2,000 percent greater in 1993 than it was in 1976. It is now more than fifty times the average per capita income in the United States, up from only eight times in 1976.[48] Although the pace has slackened a bit in the wake of a recent decline in national television revenues, bidding for the most talented players remains intense. On November 28, 1989, Oakland Athletics outfielder Rickey Henderson signed a four-year contract at an average of $3 million per year, making him the highest-paid player in the game at the time. But between then

FIGURE 4–1

Average Salaries in Major-League Baseball

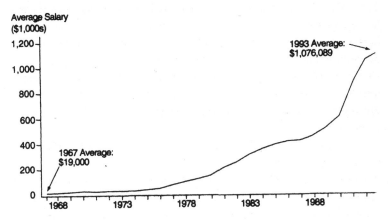

Source: Major League Baseball Players Association, as reported in *The Sporting News,* August 8, 1994, p. 15

and the 1993 season, 122 other players signed contracts at even higher salaries.[49] By 1994, there were 362 players earning more than $1 million.[50]

Because free agency has existed much longer in baseball than in other team sports, baseball salaries tend to be the highest. Indeed, baseball salaries have escalated to the point where even relatively weak players receive million-dollar annual salaries. Los Angeles Dodger shortstop Alfredo Griffin, for example, received $1 million in 1990 despite ranking eleventh among National League shortstops in batting (at .211) and being tied for first in fielding errors (with twenty-six).[51]

But other team sports are rapidly generating their own stables of multimillionaire athletes. Thus twenty-seven players in the National Basketball Association earned at least $2 million in the 1990–91 season.[52] James Worthy of the Los Angeles Lakers was the highest paid NBA player during the 1994–95 season at $7.2 million,[53] but will soon be surpassed by the Knicks center Patrick Ewing, whose contract calls for $9.5 million the following year.[54] Larry Johnson's current contract with the Charlotte Hornets will pay him $84 million over twelve years.

NFL players have long been the lowest-paid among the three major

U.S. sports. But the players and owners agreed on a limited form of free agency in 1993, and player salaries have begun to escalate accordingly. John Elway, for instance, signed a four-year, $20 million contract with the Denver Broncos in March 1993; and Dallas Cowboys quarterback Troy Aikman became the highest-paid player in the NFL in 1994 with an annual salary of $6.25 million.

Even hockey, which until recently lacked a network television contract, has a growing group of millionaire athletes. Its highest-paid star, Wayne Gretzky, earned more than $8 million in 1993–94.[55]

Prices of Luxuries

As noted in the preceding chapter, one consequence of growing income inequality is that a growing share of the national income is spent on the goods and services demanded by the rich. This predicts a change in spending patterns: A smaller share of the national income will be devoted to necessities like food, and a growing share to luxuries like vacation homes. In turn we should see a rise in the prices of luxuries relative to other goods, and a corresponding rise in the incomes of those who produce luxuries.

It is difficult to track movements in the prices of luxuries and other positional goods because the goods that confer status in one period are often completely out of fashion in another. There are a handful of items, however, whose ability to signal high rank has endured for considerable periods. Russian caviar, for example, has long been a staple of the very rich, and although the sports cars manufactured by Jaguar may have lost some of their luster in recent years, they remain powerful symbols of status in many countries. In late 1992 *The Economist* published a study of price movements for these and several other luxury goods. The Jaguar two-seater is included for the sake of continuity despite its poor market performance in recent years. The study's findings, summarized in table 4–2, conform to the predicted pattern of price increases well in excess of the rate of inflation.

Oil paintings by past masters are perhaps the quintessential positional goods. The prices of such paintings move erratically, with occasional episodes of sharp increase or decline followed by extended periods of stasis. Over the long run, however, prices not only have

TABLE 4–2

The Rising Prices of Positional Goods

| | *Price (year)* | *Price (1992)* | *Average Annual Percentage* |
Item		*(in 1992 Dollars)*	*Increase*
Russian caviar (2 oz.)	20.37 (1912)	129.00	2.3
Most expensive Jaguar two-seater	11,143.00 (1932)	73,545.00	3.2
Parker Duofold fountain pen	60.00 (1927)	236.00	2.2
Top-of-the-line Purdey shotgun	7,312.00 (1901)	38,380.00	1.8
Dunhill "Rollagas" cigarette lighter	92.00(1958)	205.00	2.4
Louis Vuitton suitcase	422.00 (1912)	1,670.00	1.7
Cartier Tank watch	1,223.00 (1921)	4,180.00	1.7
Index of all goods and services	1.00 (all years)	1.00	0.0

Source: Adapted from *The Economist,* December 26, 1992, p. 96.

trended substantially upward, but have done so at an accelerating rate. In a recent book, Peter Watson has meticulously documented the evolution of art prices since the early 1700s.[56] Some sample points on his estimated trend line for the most expensive painting ever sold: in 1715 Nicolas Poussin's *The Seven Sacraments* brought $121,680 in 1992 dollars; Raphael's *The Alba Madonna* fetched the equivalent of $1,381,613 1992 dollars in 1836; and on a May evening in 1990, before a hushed crowd at Christie's in Manhattan, van Gogh's *Portrait of Dr. Gachet* became (and remains) the most expensive painting ever sold, at $82,500,000 ($88,533,285 in 1992 dollars). Watson estimated that growth in the prices of the most expensive paintings accelerated in the mid–1800s and again sharply around 1980.

The market for art has always been and probably will always remain a winner-take-all market. The biggest winners in this market have usually been dead for many years. But there are also winner-take-all markets on an only somewhat smaller scale for the works of the best living painters in every era. For example, Jean Meissonier's *Friedland,* which sold for £13,500 in 1887 ($1.5 million now), made him the most expensive living painter of his day, and a wealthy man even by current standards.[57]

The evidence we have examined is fragmentary, and much of it is anecdotal. But as we are about to see, its general pattern is consistent with more systematic evidence on how incomes have changed over time in specific occupations.

5

Minor-League Superstars

For all the attention that has been focused on the explosive growth in multimillion-dollar salaries in recent years, the number of people who earn such salaries remains relatively small. By themselves superstar salaries have thus contributed little to rising inequality. The really important new source of inequality has been the escalating earnings of the near rich—the salespeople, administrators, accountants, physicians, and millions of other "minor-league superstars" who dominate the smaller niche markets of everyday life.

Why have the earnings of these people been rising so rapidly? Despite all that has been written on this phenomenon, it remains largely unexplained. Traditional economic theories focus on differences in the education, training, experience, and other attributes that people bring to their jobs—important factors, to be sure. Yet growing inequality has not resulted from significant changes in these factors. Indeed, the top earners today have skills that are little different from the skills top earners had fifteen years ago.

The real changes have been not in people but in the way the environment translates skill differences into earnings differences. This transformation has resulted from the same forces that give rise to celebrity labor markets. The process has been further enhanced, as in those markets, by institutional and social trends that have led to more open competition for top performers. The best performers are simply worth more now, and they're getting it. Although the winner-take-all phenomenon is most conspicuous in celebrity labor markets, its aggregate importance is far greater in the ordinary labor markets that employ most readers of this book.

Trends in Inequality

Despite its social and political turmoil, the Vietnam era provided a favorable economic climate for most workers. The sustained growth in productivity and wages during that period continued a trend that began just after World War II. The broad-based upward movement in earnings provided an ever larger group with the trappings of the American dream—a house in the suburbs, two cars, a college education for the kids.

All this came to an end with the Arab oil embargo of 1974. Since then, wages and salaries have generally lagged behind inflation, especially for males of average skills and education. So accustomed had most of us become to steadily rising living standards that it remains something of a shock to realize that the all-time peak in the average wage rate occurred more than two decades ago. Since then the increase in labor force participation by women has mitigated the loss in male earnings, but despite this, median family income has grown little since the early 1970s.

Yet while members of the middle class have struggled to hold their own, the rich have grown considerably richer. The increasing polarization of household incomes is a trend every bit as troubling as the lack of growth in the middle. Economist Paul Krugman has estimated that the top 1 percent of households claimed 70 percent of overall growth in personal income between 1977 and 1989.[1] By the end of the Reagan presidency, this elite had average income nearly twenty times as large as that of the median household.[2]

These trends in household income are largely the result of corresponding movements in wages and salaries, which constitute roughly 70 percent of personal income. During the 1980s the ratio of hourly earnings between the ninetieth and tenth percentile of full-time workers increased sharply, by approximately 20 percent for men and 25 percent for women.[3] The real earnings of the median worker held roughly constant during that decade. "The country's future as a middle-class society is in jeopardy," warned journalist Robert Kuttner in 1983, when the first hints of earnings polarization were coming to light.[4] Things have gotten worse since then.

Many explanations have been offered for these trends in earnings. Trade unions have declined, as has employment in manufacturing, with the concomitant loss of "good" blue-collar jobs paying wages that could support a middle-class lifestyle. As trade barriers have fallen, American manual workers have increasingly found themselves competing with their low-wage counterparts in the Second and Third Worlds to determine who will produce the goods sold by global corporations. Another important cause of increased inequality has been technological change, associated in large part with the computer revolution.[5] Employers in both service and manufacturing industries have had increasing need for more educated workers with problem-solving skills. This led to a sharp rise in the relative earnings of college graduates during the 1980s.[6]

Still, much of the increase in inequality of earnings remains a mystery. In a recent review of research on earnings trends, economists Frank Levy and Richard Murnane concluded that the "most important unresolved puzzle" is the steady increase since 1970 in the "residual variation" in earnings—the variation left after education and other observable characteristics of workers, such as occupation and demographic characteristics, are accounted for.[7]

Our own work, which we will summarize presently, documents the considerable increase in inequality even *within* the white-collar professions. The number of high-paid workers has increased rapidly even as the average white-collar job was barely keeping up with inflation.

Jobs That Pay Well

What do you have to earn in a year to make it into the top 1 percent? In 1989 the answer was about $120,000. Just 1.07 million U.S. workers earned that much.[8] Let's call this elite group the "Centurion Club." Using census data,[9] we can identify the occupations that contribute most to club membership, and track their growth over the decade since the previous census. Fortunately for our purposes, 1979 and 1989 were at similar points in the business cycle, both being peak years.

Do some occupations supply disproportionately many Centurions? It is hardly surprising that doctors and lawyers are well represented in the club. Forty percent of the full-time physicians were Centurions in 1989, and 20 percent of the lawyers. Together they constituted almost 30 percent of club members.

Another group of relevant occupations, including sales and executive positions, had far lower average earnings. In each of these, fewer than one in twenty workers earned as much as $120,000 in 1989. But these occupations are so large that they still make a major contribution to Centurion membership. Most notable are the executive and administrative positions, making up 34 percent of the Centurions; sales supervisors and representatives, 19 percent; and management-related professions such as accountants and consultants, 7 percent.

Other occupations figure less prominently in our elite but are still of interest. For example, in the arts and entertainment—including all writers, actors, musicians, artists, and athletes—only about 2 percent (16,000 people) earned $120,000 or more in 1989. And only 1.4 percent of our fellow college professors—5,800 in all—made that much.

Back in 1979 an income of $70,000 had the same purchasing power as $120,000 in 1989.[10] Using $70,000 as our cutoff point, the number of Centurions in 1979 was only 538,000. That this number nearly doubled by 1989 is due partly to expansion in the number of people employed in the relevant occupations. A second factor behind the growing number of Centurions was growth in median earnings (after adjusting for inflation). This factor made a substantial contribution in law and a few other professions. But by far the most important cause of the increase in Centurions was growth in earnings inequality. Earnings became more concentrated at the top in every relevant occupation.

Consider dentists, whose membership in the Centurion Club expanded by fully 78 percent between 1979 and 1989. The number of full-time, practicing dentists actually fell slightly in the 1980s, so overall growth cannot explain this dramatic increase. Nor was there any significant growth in the inflation-adjusted median earnings of dentists.

What changed for dentists in the 1980s was a dramatic shift in the distribution of their earnings about the median. Whereas fewer dentists earned incomes in the moderately high range of $60,000 to $120,000, the numbers increased sharply at both the low and high ends of the earnings spectrum.

We looked at all the white-collar occupations in this fashion, and in each category found the same general pattern. For all these occupations combined, we found this striking result: 63 percent of the growth in the Centurion Club between 1979 and 1989 resulted from increased inequality of earnings.[11]

Finally we checked to see if some of the growing inequality was the result of changes in the age and experience profile in these occupations. But when we confine the analysis to full-time male workers aged thirty-five to fifty-four with a college education, our conclusion is much the same as before. Even for this more narrowly defined group, the increase in earnings inequality was dramatic during the 1980s, and accounts for almost half the increase in high-paid workers.

Explaining the Growth in Inequality

The growth in earnings inequality for dentists, lawyers, and others indicates that the market is placing a higher value on the services of the top performers. But why are these people being paid so much more? Our claim is that it is largely because of the strengthening forces that give rise to winner-take-all markets. This explanation differs sharply from the prevailing explanations of inequality. And because inequality is a subject of such pressing policy concern, it is important to scrutinize the competing explanations with care.

Economists have tried to explain growing earnings inequality by asserting that the best performers have somehow gotten "better" relative to their colleagues in recent years (in the sense of having acquired more of whatever attributes the market values). This view follows naturally from human capital theory, the reigning economic theory of wage determination. Human capital theory explains differences in wage rates by differences in education, training, experience, intelligence, motivation, and other human factors that influence productivity.

These factors add up to an amalgam that economists call human capital, which is analogous to financial or physical capital. Human capital commands a price in the labor market, just as financial capital commands a price in the capital markets. Thus, a worker with twice as much human capital as another will earn twice the wage, just as someone with $10,000 in the bank will earn twice as much interest as someone with only $5,000.

Human capital theory has explained many important features of the labor market. People who invest more in schooling, for example, earn more, on average, than people who invest less. But despite its surface plausibility, the theory has always left a great deal unexplained. For instance, Christopher Jencks, in his book titled *Inequality,* found that schooling and other indicators of human capital account for only 15 percent of the variance in individual earnings. Thus it should not seem surprising that changes in the distribution of human capital have been unable to explain the sharp increases in inequality of recent years.

The human capital story directs our attention to the worker rather than the job. Yet a person who embodies a certain level of human capital will realize its full value only if placed in a position with adequate scope and opportunity. This principle is evident to Westerners who visit Eastern Europe, where the legacy of Communist rule is a highly educated populace with remarkably low earnings. For example, physicians in Romania are paid just $100 a month. Some end up supplementing their earnings by cleaning house for Western expatriates in Bucharest at $10 a day. Many Romanians and other Eastern Europeans would qualify for jobs paying twenty to one hundred times as much in America as they currently earn.

Similar observations apply to the comparison of workers *within* the U.S. economy. Here, too, we find people with similar accumulations of human capital earning vastly different incomes.

To understand such large differences, the winner-take-all perspective urges us to look first to the nature of the positions people hold, rather than to their personal characteristics. Organizations have hierarchies of positions, with pay scales that reflect the level of responsibility or scope of each position. High salaries are associated with positions that entail a great deal of leverage on the worker's efforts. In these positions small differences in performance translate into large differences in the profitability of the venture. Corporations seek the ablest candidates for these highly leveraged positions, and are willing to pay a hefty price for them.

An economist under the influence of the human capital metaphor might ask: Why not save money by hiring two mediocre people to fill that position instead of paying the exorbitant salary required to attract the best? Although that sort of substitution might work with physical capital, in does not necessarily work with human capital. Two average surgeons, CEOs, novelists, or quarterbacks are often a poor substitute for a single gifted one.

The result is that for positions in which additional talent has great value to the employer or the marketplace, there is no reason to expect that the market will compensate individuals in proportion to their human capital. For these positions—ones that confer the greatest leverage or "amplification" of human talent[12]—small increments of talent have great value, and may be greatly rewarded as a result of the normal competitive market process. This insight lies at the core of our alternative explanation of growing earnings inequality.

Of course, there are circumstances under which even the most talented do not enjoy unusually high earnings. Military officers have always been in the same bind as baseball players were under the reserve clause. Since there is no effective competition among employers for their services, even the most senior officers are paid rather modest salaries.

In other arenas bidding up the salaries of the most able is constrained by law, custom, or internal politics. Members of the president's cabinet, for example, are paid only six times as much as recent college graduates hired into the management track of the federal service as GS-7s. This modest spread is virtually unchanged from what it was in 1974. For some nonprofit agencies, similarly, the charitable ethos forbids lavish compensation for the top officers, no matter how valuable they might be to the organization—witness the uproar when it was revealed that the head of United Way was being paid $450,000 in 1992.

But when market forces are given free play, the talented individual who has a choice of employers (or of becoming self-employed) has the chance of ending up a big winner.

Jobs in Which Success Breeds Success

At first glance careers in such occupations as sales or dentistry might not seem to involve winner-take-all payoffs. Within a given sales group, for example, an individual salesperson's commissions are typically proportional to the number of sales he or she makes. Likewise, among practicing dentists, someone who fills three cavities per hour would appear to generate billings at roughly three times the rate as someone who fills only one.

These observations are misleading, however, because they focus too narrowly on productivity differences for individuals performing the same tasks. Within any specific occupation, a far greater proportion of the variability in lifetime earnings is explained by differences in the kinds of tasks individuals actually do. In virtually every occupation except the most menial ones—and even in some of those—a successful career evolves in a series of "trials." As in Jesus' parable of the talents, the financial analyst (or lawyer or manager) who does relatively well in a position of small responsibility is then promoted to a position with greater scope.

In the sales profession, for example, employers monitor performance and award the more lucrative sales territory to those who demonstrate their effectiveness. In his book *Liar's Poker,* Michael Lewis illustrates this point with an account of his initiation as a bond salesman in London for Salomon Brothers: "I couldn't help noticing that [my customers] were different from the customers of established salesmen. Mine were small institutional investors, defined as those with less than one hundred million dollars each who, on each trade, would commit only a few million."[13] As a result of a combination of luck and skill, Lewis performs well with these small clients and is quickly promoted. As he puts it: "Success bred success. Pretty soon Salomon management was leading me to the clients of other salespeople in hopes that with larger customers I could do gargantuan pieces of business. By June 1986, six months into the job, I was plugged into several of the largest pools of money in Europe."[14]

Lewis's success at Salomon was thus explained not by the fact that he sold more than his colleagues to the same kinds of clients they served; rather, it was because management realized that his unusual selling talents would yield the highest payoff if he were assigned to the firm's high-volume clients. There are only so many of these clients to go around, and Lewis gained access to them by outperforming his immediate rivals, who in this case were other Salomon Brothers salespeople.

Self-employed persons go through a comparable process. The scope for the talents of private-practice professionals depends on the market for their services. The demand for the services of an accountant, lawyer, chiropractor, or dentist typically stems from his or her reputation in the relevant community, which engenders referrals and word-of-mouth advertising. Competence is perhaps necessary, but certainly not sufficient, for developing a strong reputation and enough leverage to earn a Centurion-level income.

Consider two clinical psychologists with similar skills and training who decide to establish private practices. One acquires clients early as a result of referrals from physicians and therapists who have the impression that she is competent, based on a casual knowledge of her training and personality. Since most of her clients feel good about their sessions with her, they eventually begin to refer their friends to her as well. Success breeds success: As she gains experience, her skill as a therapist increases, and as her base of current and former clients grows, the market for her services expands. Ultimately she is able to maintain a full practice with high fees.

The other psychologist, with equal skills as a therapist but slightly fewer connections to referral sources in the community, gets off to a slower start. Although his clients have high regard for him, he does not attract enough of them initially to achieve self-sustaining growth in the demand for his services. Eventually he is forced to give up trying to build a lucrative career in private practice and accept a position with a mental health clinic at a modest salary.

As these examples make clear, the development of professional careers is shaped by a variety of self-reinforcing processes that translate human capital into actual productivity. This process is uncertain. Ability and know-how matter at every step along the way. But the distribution of earnings within a group of experienced dentists, psychologists, accountants, or technical salespeople is far more diffuse than suggested by the initial distribution of measurable ability, and reflects the vagaries of chance events along the career path. Winners will tend to be selected from among the most able. And given the importance of reputation in the markets for professional services, the top tier of providers will likely do far better than the second tier—even if the objective differences between them, as measured by their human capital, are small.

Applying the Winner-Take-All Perspective

So why have we seen greater concentration of workers at the highest earnings level? What is the solution to this "mystery" of "residual variance" described by Levy and Murnane? The human capital perspective suggests the existence of a pervasive but unmeasured change in the distribution of economic talent. The winner-take-all perspective, by contrast, focuses on changes in the leverage or scope afforded human capital in the top positions. Comparing 1989 with 1979, we find that changes in technology and other factors under-pinning the winner-take-all phenomenon do indeed afford greater scope for talent at the top. And in many cases, the increasing value of talent has been accompanied by greater market freedom for individuals to claim that value in the form of high earnings.

The quintessential industry of the 1980s was investment banking, in which securities traders and salespeople enjoyed a modern gold rush. Total revenue for this industry nearly quadrupled between 1980 and 1989 (to $77 billion). Michael Lewis, in his autobiographical account of the vast growth and volatility of the bond market during the early 1980s, notes: "Nothing changed within Salomon Brothers that made the traders more able. Now, however, trades exploded in both size and frequency, A Salomon salesman who had in the past moved five million dollars' worth of merchandise through the traders' books each week was now moving three hundred million dollars through each *day*."[15] The skills of any given salesman in this environment were suddenly given much greater leverage, so that one with exceptional flair and persuasiveness with customers was worth millions of dollars per year to the investment house. Lewis notes that when Salomon balked at paying bonuses in line with this value, rivals First Boston and Drexel Burnham were quick to step in with better offers. Although the bonanza may have slowed since then, the average salary of securities salesmen in the New York firms remains well into six figures.[16]

As we saw earlier, earnings in sales professions became considerably more unequal, with the number of Centurions more than doubling between 1979 and 1989. This growth has not been limited to the financial markets. In other asset markets that enjoyed a boom during the 1980s, notably real estate, there were new opportunities for the brokers working with wealthier clients to earn high incomes by collecting their fixed percentage of ever larger transactions. And in real estate brokering as in other areas, technical changes increased the productivity of sales agents.

One text reports that the major trends in sales technology during the 1980s involved an increased use of personal computers and telephones.[17] PCs facilitate order taking, accessing inventory information, lead tracking, communication, and time management. Declining telephone tolls, combined with the dissemination of answering devices and the introduction of affordable cellular phones, caused the cost and inconvenience of communicating with customers and prospects to decline rapidly. The telephone became increasingly acceptable as the medium for calling on small accounts, filing orders, and following up on initial contacts. At a number of large companies (including IBM), many of the sales staff do not even have offices anymore. They stay in touch with headquarters through various electronic means and spend their time in the field, working with clients and potential clients.

These changes have had the obvious effect of increasing the potential productivity of salespeople: They can make more contacts, and are freed from the necessity of relying on extensive staff support. The result is to increase the size of the territory that can be effectively serviced by any one agent. Hence the most persuasive and skilled members of the sales staff will do more business, while those with less ability must struggle to find a niche.

In sales, as in other areas, the earnings of the top performers are not necessarily proportional to their value. Some companies cap the commissions of their salespeople to keep their earnings in line with other employees'. Of course, such firms often lose their top salespeople to rivals that are less sensitive to pay equity.

Sometimes the solution is to go outside the company for at least part of the sales effort. One text suggests that over half of all manufacturers make use of independent sales organizations, a practice that has been increasing since the mid 1970s.[18] High commissions paid to independent sales representatives cause less envy and concern than those same commissions would if paid internally.

Sales is one of the occupations that experienced the greatest growth in inequality at the top of the earnings range during the 1980s. But what of dentists, for whom the growth in inequality was nearly as great? What forces were at work there? As it turns out, there is virtually no recent economic literature about this particular profession,[19] so we are forced to speculate on the basis of fragmentary information. One relevant change is a move to greater specialization, similar to what took place in the medical profession. According to Chester Douglass of the Harvard School of Dental Medicine, the size of the entering class in dental schools in the United States shrank from about 6,000 in 1982 to about 4,000 in 1994. During this same period, the number of slots for residencies in oral surgery, orthodontics, periodontics, and other specialties remained constant at 1,250 per year. Thus the fraction of graduates who train in one of these highly paid areas has increased significantly. This would explain why a higher proportion of dentists might be Centurions in 1989 than in 1979, but it cannot account for the absolute number of Centurions increasing so dramatically.

A more promising explanation lies in the overall growth in the demand for dental services. Part of this growth has stemmed from expansion in dental insurance coverage, but an even more important source is the aging of the population. As the baby boomers move increasingly into middle age, more and more people are at the stage of life when the demand for dental services tends to be highest. Adding to this is the fact that older people keep their teeth longer than ever before. One study of New England residents, for example, found that although the average seventy-year-old had only seven of his or her own teeth in the early 1970s, that number has now grown to seventeen.

Jim Bader, editor of the *Journal of Dental Education* at the University of North Carolina, notes that although the demand for primary dental services has declined slightly as a result of fluoride use, there has been strong growth in the demand for cosmetic, consumer-oriented dentistry—procedures to whiten teeth, adult orthodontia, application of porcelain jacket crowns to improve the appearance of front teeth, and so on. The growth of cosmetic dentistry is fueled in part by the emergence of new computer technologies that can generate porcelain restorations of teeth. Dentists with the right software can even show their clients in advance what their new, custom-designed smiles will look like.

Bader also mentioned the lifting of the Federal Trade Commission ban on advertising as yet another factor behind the growth of cosmetic dentistry. To this must be added the effect of rising incomes for top professionals in all fields, which might be important for two separate reasons. First, these incomes make elective procedures like cosmetic dentistry more affordable. And second, the corresponding growth in competition for top positions may have increased the value of taking steps to improve one's appearance.

Taken together these changes appear to have created ample opportunity for self-reinforcing processes, like the ones that have characterized competition for top positions in other fields, to have expressed themselves in dentistry as well. Although we cannot measure the precise extent to which growing inequality among dentists is the result of these processes, this much seems clear: The available data rule out changes in human capital as a significant explanation.

Winner-take-all effects also appear to explain the growth of top incomes in the legal profession. Thus economist Sherwin Rosen recently had this to say about the market for lawyers in the United States:

> Some evidence suggests that changes in the organization of practice—the growth of large partnerships, more frequent use of contingent fees, class action suits—have resulted in extremely large earnings among a relatively small, elite group of lawyers. This "star quality" hardly is new, but its size and frequency may have become more important than in the past. . . . Furthermore, increasing litigiousness and demand for legal services might have increased scarce ability rents in law, at least in the short-run.[20]

The explosion of tort litigation in the United States has been well documented.[21] Plaintiff attorneys typically litigate tort cases on a contingent-fee basis, claiming from 30 to 50 percent of all monetary damages awarded to their clients. Tort-related earnings of attorneys thus depend on the number of suits filed, the probability of winning, and the average damages awarded. The years since 1960 have seen large increases in all three.

Thus cases in which products were blamed for injuries increased fourfold between 1976 and 1986, and in the decade ending in 1987 more medical malpractice suits were filed than in the entire previous history of American tort law. Damage claims against cities doubled between 1982 and 1986. Between 1984 and 1985 alone, claims filed against the federal government grew by 30 percent. The plaintiff's probability of winning, which was between 20 and 30 percent for product-liability cases in the 1960s, had grown to more than 50 percent by the 1980s. Monetary judgments have also grown sharply. In real terms the average tort judgment rose from $50,000 in the early 1960s to more than $250,000 in the early 1980s.

Just as there are a limited number of positions in which talent is highly leveraged in the other professions, so too there is an exceptionally high payoff to legal talent in a limited number of positions atop the litigation pyramid. Houston plaintiff attorney Joe Jamail, for example, earned at least $450 million, possibly as much as $600 million, in 1988 alone.[22] A 1989 *Forbes* survey identified sixty-two other plaintiff attorneys who made at least $2 million in both 1987 and 1988, and another 50 who made between $1 million and $2 million.[23]

In chapter 4 we discussed similar growth in earnings inequality in corporate management, consulting, fashion, journalism, publishing, sports, entertainment, and other areas. In each case we identified changes in the economic environment that have increased the value and compensation associated with the positions that have relatively great scope or leverage. The census data suggest that this phenomenon is at work not just in celebrity labor markets but also among top performers in the labor markets of everyday life. This is important, for it is the latter group that has accounted for most of the growth in earnings inequality of recent decades.

Our claim is that the growth of inequality has stemmed largely from the spread of winner-take-all markets. The most important competing explanation is that inequality has grown because of some underlying change in the distribution of human capital. Yet no one has managed to identify such a change.

Despite the apparent failure of the human capital model, the evidence we have examined does not rule out the possibility that growing inequality has been, at least in part, the result of other forces unrelated to winner-take-all markets. But here, too, no one has specified clearly what these other forces might be. At minimum we can say that the data are largely consistent with the winner-take-all explanation, but largely inconsistent with competing explanations.

If winner-take-all markets have, on balance, grown more important over time, then the issues we raise in the coming chapters assume greater significance than if they have not. But even if winner-take-all markets have not become more pervasive, they surely do play an important role in contemporary economic life. And this alone makes it important to know more about their consequences.

6

Too Many Contestants?

In 1994 the combined membership of the Actors' Equity Association, the Screen Actors Guild, and the American Federation of Television and Radio Artists was more than 150,000. Hundreds of thousands more who do not qualify for membership in these professional entertainers' unions nonetheless aspire to careers on stage, screen, and television. Although many of these people undoubtedly are driven by the sheer love of performing, countless others seek the unique combination of fame and wealth the entertainment industry can bestow. Yet only a handful will ever achieve even modest recognition, and fewer still will earn even a subsistence wage. In a recent year, for example, only 12 percent of Screen Actors Guild members were paid for appearing in films, and 90 percent of them received less than five thousand dollars for their efforts.[1] After supporting themselves by waiting tables or driving taxis for several years, most aspirants eventually become discouraged and move on to other pursuits.

As we have seen, the winner-take-all payoff structure of the entertainment industry has increasingly permeated other sectors of the economy. Our claim is that, as in the entertainment industry, this payoff structure has led too many people to abandon productive alternatives in pursuit of the top prizes. In this chapter we will explore why, exactly, the market goes astray.

Overcrowding Defined

Perhaps the most important single task facing any economy is to assign each of its workers to the job in which his or her talents add the greatest value. From a narrowly economic perspective, the ideal assignment is the one that maximizes the total value of the goods and services produced. This assignment also maximizes the total income earned by all workers in the economy. So when we assert that winner-take-all markets attract too many contestants, what we really mean is that society's total income would be higher if fewer people competed in these markets and chose other occupations instead.

To forestall possible misunderstanding, let us emphasize that, in making this claim, we are *not* saying that winner-take-all markets are an unmitigated economic disaster or even, on balance, a negative force. After all, when there is an important or highly valued job to be done, and when the identity of the person who can best perform that job is not known at the outset, we need *some* mechanism for finding out who that person is. In capitalist economies winner-take-all markets accomplish this task. Without such markets, or their functional equivalents, the enormous economic gains of the past two centuries could never have been realized. When we say that winner-take-all markets attract too many contestants, all we mean is that we could do even better if the least talented aspirants were diverted into other career channels.

Even this more limited claim is by no means self-evident. For instance, the mere fact that more than 90 percent of all actors never make a living at their craft is not, by itself, clear evidence that we have too many aspiring actors. The more people trying to become actors, the more likely it is that we will enjoy inspiring performances. Indeed, it is possible to imagine a society with too *few* aspiring actors. If, for example, there were only as many aspirants as needed to fill available parts, we would surely end up suffering through many dismal performances. In that case most people would gladly pay a little extra to generate better entertainment.

At the other extreme, however, it is equally clear that a society can have too many aspiring actors. Suppose, fancifully, that the entire population chose acting as a profession. We would then end up with an extraordinary constellation of stars, to be sure; but we would also be woefully short of health care, transportation, shelter, and other essential goods and services. At that point we would happily settle for lower entertainment quality in order to have more of the other things we value.

Between these two extremes lies the proper balance—the mix of career choices that maximizes the combined value of entertainment and all other goods and services. Our claim is that, in comparison to this optimal mix, market incentives typically lure too many contestants into winner-take-all markets, and too few into other careers. One reason involves a well-documented human frailty—namely, our tendency to overestimate our chances of prevailing against our competitors. We will discuss this issue next. But as we will go on to show, too many contestants would enter winner-take-all markets even if everyone were perfectly informed about the odds of winning.

The Overconfidence Problem

The decision to compete in a winner-take-all market is akin to buying a lottery ticket. If you win, you earn many times more—possibly even hundreds or thousands of times more—than you would have in a less risky career. If you lose, however, you earn much less.

Needless to say, an intelligent decision about whether to take such a gamble requires knowledge of the odds of winning. In a large modern economy, however, people are unlikely to know even the number of other contestants in each arena, let alone any detailed information about their relative strengths and weaknesses.

But even if people were told exactly how many others were competing, and also provided with objective evidence on the capabilities of each contestant, it is by no means clear that they would assess their odds correctly. On the contrary, our tendency grossly to overestimate both our abilities and our luck has been recognized for centuries. As Adam Smith described it:

> The over-weening conceit which the greater part of men have of their own abilities, is an ancient evil remarked by the philosophers and moralists of all ages. Their absurd presumption in their own good

fortune, has been less taken notice of. It is, however, if possible, still more universal. There is no man living who when in tolerable health and spirits, has not some share of it. The chance of gain is by every man more or less overvalued, and the chance of loss is by most men under-valued, and by scarce any man, who is in tolerable health and spirits, valued more than it is worth.[2]

Worst of all, for present purposes, overconfidence seems to peak at precisely that point in the life cycle when it does the most harm. As Smith put it, "The contempt of risk and the presumptuous hope of success, are in no period of life more active than at the age at which young people choose their professions."[3]

Smith's characterization of human nature is no less accurate today than when he made it two hundred years ago. A recent news clip, for example, reported that more than 60 percent of NCAA Division I college basketball starters believe they will eventually start for a National Basketball Association (NBA) team, whereas the actual proportion is less than 5 percent. Possibly the surveyed players exaggerated their true beliefs. But there is systematic evidence from a variety of other sources that overconfidence is pervasive.

Studies have found that most people think they are more intelligent[4] and better drivers than the average person.[5] Workers asked to rate their productivity on a percentile scale relative to their coworkers responded with an average self-assessment of being in the 77th percentile, and more than 90 percent felt they were more productive than the median worker.[6] More than 70 percent of one million high school seniors reported in a survey that they had above-average leadership ability; only 2 percent saw themselves as below average. When asked about their ability to get along with others, virtually all of those same students said they were above average; 60 percent thought they were in the top 10 percent, and 25 percent thought they were in the top 1 percent.[7] Another survey revealed that 94 percent of university professors thought they were better at their jobs than their average colleague.[8] People also see themselves as more likely than their peers to earn a large salary, and less likely to get divorced or suffer from lung cancer.[9] A recent survey found that although only 25 percent of the population thought the economy would do better in the coming year, more than half thought that they personally would do better.[10]

Psychologist Tom Gilovich has called this the "Lake Wobegon Effect," after Garrison Keillor's mythical Minnesota town "where the women are strong, the men are good-looking, and all the children are above average."[11] The phenomenon has most often been explained in motivational terms by authors who note that the observed biases are psychologically gratifying.[12] Thus, since it is unpleasant to think of oneself as below average, a cheap solution is simply to think of oneself as above average. Consistent with this view, one study found that a sample of clinically depressed patients had remarkably accurate assessments of their various abilities and social skills—this in sharp contrast to a group of ostensibly normal subjects, who had significantly inflated self-assessments.[13]

But the Lake Wobegon bias clearly has cognitive dimensions as well. Thus psychologists Amos Tversky and Daniel Kahneman have shown that when people try to estimate the likelihood of an event, they often rely on how easily they can summon examples of similar events from memory.[14] Yet, although ease of recall does, in fact, rise with the frequency of similar events, it also depends on other factors. Events that are especially salient or vivid are easily recalled even if they happen only infrequently. Wall Street money manager George Soros is not quite a celebrity, yet there is no denying the power of his $1.1 billion 1993 income to capture the imaginations of ambitious college students.[15] It is easy to think of examples of the relative handful who have made it big, but much harder to summon individual examples from the multitudes of anonymous individuals who have not; and hence, in part, the biased perception in favor of success.

The invisible-hand theory says that we get socially optimal career choices when people make well-informed, self-serving decisions on the basis of market incentives. But it also says, by implication at least, that if people generally overestimate their prospects in winner-take-all markets, the resulting career choices will not be socially (or even individually) optimal. Whatever its ultimate source, the Lake Wobegon effect describes just such a bias, for it makes participation in winner-take-all markets seem misleadingly attractive.

A Simple Winner-Take-All Economy

Free marketeers will not be surprised that we get inefficient outcomes when people make career choices on the basis of inaccurate information. Our claim, however, is that even in a world of complete foresight and full rationality, too many people would still compete in winner-take-all markets.

To grasp the reasoning behind this claim, we find it helpful to examine the career choice that confronts people in a very simple hypothetical economy. Indeed, this economy is so simple it may strike some readers as a whimsical abstraction with no possible relevance to a complex modern economy. Yet, for all its simplicity, it captures the essence of the difficulty that winner-take-all markets pose for economies like our own.

In our hypothetical economy, there are only two occupations, and you must choose one or the other. In one, people make pots out of clay; and in the other, the best singer from a field of contestants is chosen for a lucrative recording contract. The potter's market is a labor market of the traditional sort: People are paid a fixed wage from the sale of pots in the world market. The recording market, on the other hand, is a winner-take-all market. If you compete and win, you get much more than a potter's wage. Precisely how much more you get depends on sales of your recording, which in turn depend on the quality of your voice. But if you lose, you earn nothing, even if you are the runner-up and your voice is of only marginally lower quality than the winner's. Thus, unlike your reward in the potter's market, which depends only on absolute performance, your reward in the recording market depends on both absolute *and* relative performance. Singers and potters pursue their respective careers for the duration of their working lives.

Suppose there were an omniscient observer who could scan the population of this hypothetical economy at a glance and identify the individual with the best voice. The best possible allocation of talent (that is, the income-maximizing allocation) would be simply to send that one individual to the recording industry and let all the others make pots. In real life, however, no one knows at the outset who is the best singer. That is why people who aspire to the recording contract must compete for it. For each contestant this means devoting time to a singing competition that could otherwise have been spent making pots. The question therefore is: If our goal is to maximize society's total income, how many should compete for the recording contract?

In general, the more contestants there are, the better—and hence more valuable—the winner's performance will be. The logic here is simple, akin to the reasoning behind the claim that the best singer from a school of 1,000 students is likely to have a better voice than the best singer from a school of only 500. But, in most cases, there comes a point where the gain from having additional contestants diminishes. For example, the expected improvement in the winning singer's voice will generally be smaller when we move from 1,000 contestants to 1,100 than when we move from 500 to 600.

The cost of adding contestants, however, does not diminish with the number of contestants: Each time we add a contestant, we lose what that person could have earned as a potter. If our goal is to maximize the expected total income earned in both markets, we should keep adding contestants as long as the gain we expect in the winning singer's income is at least as large as the income that could have been earned making pots. Thus if people can earn, say, $10,000 as potters, and if adding an extra contestant is expected to increase the value of the winning singer's contract by $11,000 (because, with an extra contestant, the winner's voice will be worth that much more, on average), then we should add that contestant—the $11,000 gain in expected recording income will more than compensate for the $10,000 loss in potter's income. Conversely, if adding another contestant is expected to increase the value of the winning singer's contract by only $9,000, it would be better to have that person become a potter. The socially optimal (or income-maximizing) number of contestants is thus the largest number for which the effect of adding the last contestant is to increase the expected value of the winning singer's income by at least $10,000.

Unfortunately, however, this is not the number of contestants we get when individuals choose the careers that will maximize their own expected incomes. Rational contestants will focus not on how much their presence affects the expected value of the winning singer's contract but on how much they, as individuals, can expect to earn.

Suppose, for example, that there are already ninety-nine singers competing and that the entry of the hundreth will raise the expected value of the winner's contract by only $1,000—say, from $1,999,000 to $2 million. If the hundredth contestant enters, she will have a one percent chance of winning $2 million—in effect, a lottery ticket worth $20,000, or twice what she could have earned as a potter. If she is willing to accept a fair gamble, she will definitely compete for the recording contract. From the perspective of the economy as a whole, however, it would have been better if she had become a potter, for society's expected total income would then have been $9,000 higher.[16]

The dramatic nature of the waste from overcrowding becomes clear when we note that if people choose careers with the highest expected incomes, society's total income will be the same as it would have been if the recording opportunity did not even exist. This follows from the fact that contestants enter the recording contest until their expected income is just what they could have earned by making pots. (If it were higher, additional potters would enter the contest; if it were lower, some of the existing contestants would switch to potting.) In effect, the losses from overcrowding completely offset the winning singer's prize.

The difficulty is analogous to the celebrated "tragedy of the commons" problem, in which villagers send too many cattle to graze on commonly owned pastureland.[17] An extra steer becomes more valuable because of the weight it gains from eating the grass on the commons. But much of the grass it eats would otherwise have been eaten by the steers already there. Since most of the existing steers are owned by others, an individual villager considers only the weight his own steer will gain when deciding whether to send an additional steer. Because he ignores the cost to others, the prospect of sending an additional steer seems more attractive to him than it is, in fact, to the village as a whole. Similarly, when an additional singer enters the recording contest, she makes each existing contestant less likely to win, and because she ignores that cost, entry into the recording contest is misleadingly attractive.

The tragedy of the commons—and, by extension, the overcrowding problem in winner-take-all markets—is also analogous to the problem of environmental pollution. When people respond only to individual market incentives, too much pollution results because people ignore the costs of the pollution they impose on one another. Similarly, we get too many aspiring actors and rock musicians—and too many aspiring Wall Street lawyers—because people ignore the fact that their entry reduces everyone else's chances.[18]

If the least talented contestants were to drop out and become engineers, teachers, or production workers, the performance levels of the top performers in winner-take-all markets would not fall by much, if at all. In return, we would get additional output of much greater value. In short, private market incentives lead too many contestants to enter winner-take-all markets, often at high cost in terms of forgone output in other markets.

A More Realistic Economy

Our hypothetical winner-take-all economy is obviously a stick-figure caricature. Its simplicity is useful, however, insofar as it enables us to see more clearly the forces that give rise to overcrowding in winner-take-all markets. With this picture in mind, we can now flesh out the example to see how career decisions might play out under conditions more like the ones that exist in complex modern economies.

Future Opportunities

Perhaps the most patently unrealistic aspect of our hypothetical economy was that aspiring singers had to devote their whole careers to the singing contest before discovering whether they had won. How would things be different in an economy in which the contest consumes only a small part of a worker's life? We are long-lived creatures after all, a fact that essentially eliminates the need to choose once and for all whether to be a singer or a potter. One can try singing for a while and see how it goes. Those who feel they aren't making progress after a few years can then switch to pottery. In our example competing for the recording contract would entail not a lifetime of lost potter's wages but only a fraction thereof, and the cost of overcrowding would thus decline.

Yet a cost would remain. In many winner-take-all markets, it takes years to discover whether one has what it takes. More important, the decision to compete will often entail outright forfeiture of other valuable opportunities. A student who passes up math and science classes to practice his jump shot, for example, cannot easily go back and obtain the credentials for admission to engineering school once he discovers he is not going to make it in the NBA. The costs of such forgone opportunities will accumulate for as long as one lives. Having a long life span alleviates some of the efficiency losses stemming from winner-take-all markets, yet significant losses remain.

The Loser's Pay

In our hypothetical economy, the losing contestants for the recording contract got nothing. This may seem like an exaggeration, but in many winner-take-all markets it is not. Indeed, the music industry currently requires aspiring rock musicians to bear the full cost of producing and distributing their first albums. These costs often run to several hundred thousand dollars, only a tiny fraction of which is ever recovered in most cases. If the losers actually lose money, participation in the winner-take-all market obviously becomes less attractive, from both the individual and collective perspectives. Fewer people will compete, and, since the cost of competing is higher than in our hypothetical economy, fewer *should* compete.

In many other winner-take-all markets, by contrast, losing contestants receive some modest payment. People in the arts, for instance, often support themselves by moonlighting as waiters or taxi drivers. In these cases more people will compete than in our hypothetical economy, and since the cost of competing is smaller, *more should* compete.

Thus the existence of either positive or negative losers' payments alters not only the actual but also the socially ideal number of competitors in winner-take-all markets. Such payments, however, do nothing to alter the underlying tendency of winner-take-all markets to attract too many contestants.

Given the familiarity of the "starving artist" syndrome, it is easy to see that the losers in many winner-take-all markets—failed actors, painters, writers, and musicians, to name a few—do worse than they would have done in other careers. In at least some winner-take-all markets, however, it may seem as if even the losers do better than they could have elsewhere.

Consider high-stakes litigation. Opponents in a big lawsuit have strong incentives to bid for the services of the most talented attorneys, and the attorneys chosen for these tasks are handsomely rewarded. But even ordinary lawyers don't fare poorly, and indeed the *least* well-paid lawyers appear to earn more than most other people. Popular culture makes little reference to a "starving lawyer" syndrome.

Suppose that, in our hypothetical economy, even the losers in the recording industry earn more than they could have earned as potters. (Perhaps a foreign advertising agency will pay them for singing in commercials.[19]) What happens then? The answer clearly is that *everyone* will now compete in the recording industry. Moreover, everyone *should* compete, if our goal is to maximize society's income. After all, if one can earn a higher wage for work that is no less pleasant than potting, why should anyone make pots?

In practice, however, market forces make it unlikely that the loser's payment could remain higher than what contestants could have earned in other careers. The inexorable workings of supply and demand virtually guarantee that as more people leave alternative occupations to compete in a winner-take-all market, two things will happen. First, the loser's wage in the winner-take-all market will be driven down; and second, the wage in the alternative occupations will be driven up. If expected monetary compensation is all people care about, these movements must continue until the loser's wage falls below that in alternative jobs.

And in fact, even though the loser's wage in law, consulting, finance, and corporate management is often high, most of the "losers" in those careers could have achieved more attractive combinations of pay and working conditions in other, less risky occupations. In many cases they could have done better elsewhere even in purely financial terms. The students competing for admission to the nation's leading law and business schools are, after all, extremely talented and hardworking.

More important, when nonmonetary aspects of the job are factored in, the losers' rewards in the high-risk fields often become much less attractive. A talented and energetic person, for example, will derive little satisfaction from the routine processing of wills and divorce complaints, or from the daily details of managing a small section in a business going nowhere.[20]

In sum, then, even though the losers in some winner-take-all markets do reasonably well financially, these markets are essentially no different from the winner-take-all market in our hypothetical economy. They, too, will attract too many contestants.

The Status Motive

In our example we assumed that money was the sole motive for competing in the winner-take-all market, and in many cases this may be so. But in many others, especially those in the public eye, nonpecuniary motives may matter even more. The lure of fame, for example, appears to drive many aspiring athletes, actors, authors, and musicians. And although great public notoriety is less often achieved by corporate executives, lawyers, consultants, and investment bankers, the most successful performers in these occupations also enjoy considerable social status.

The status motive reinforces our conclusion that winner-take-all markets attract too many resources. Suppose that the contestants in our hypothetical economy cared not only about the monetary payment they would receive from winning the recording contract, but also about the public recognition. The effect in our example would be the same as if an additional cash payment were added to the expected reward of each contestant—and this, in turn, would stimulate additional entries.

But whereas the status motive increases the number of people who choose to compete in winner-take-all markets, it does nothing to alter the number who should compete on efficiency grounds. The criterion for efficiency is that contestants should keep being added as long as the *increase* in the winner's income (including the implicit value of his or her status) is at least as large as the amount contestants could have earned in the potter's market. Since adding a constant premium for status does nothing to alter the *rate* at which the winner's reward increases with the number of contestants, it does nothing to alter the socially efficient number of contestants.

The status motive thus lends a zero-sum flavor to the winner-take-all struggle. The reigning Wimbledon champions bask in the world's adulation each July, and this is surely a big part of what motivates aspiring professionals to spend endless hours on the practice courts. But the champions will have their moment in the spotlight whether ten thousand players compete on the professional tennis tour or only a thousand.

We might be tempted to object, however, that the winners' moment in the spotlight will surely be a little brighter the more competitors they have to defeat on their way to the top. To be sure, winning in a big arena confers greater prestige than winning in a small one. But suppose the number of contestants in *every* arena were suddenly to fall by half. Even if the absolute quality of play were to fall a bit, the World Cup, the Super Bowl, the Tour de France, the World Series, the U.S. Open, and the NBA finals would still be major media events. Although the recognition that accompanies a winning performance depends on the importance of the arena in which it occurs, importance is measured in relative, not absolute, terms—hence our claim that the status component of the tournament is a zero-sum contest.

How big a factor is the status motive? Studies have increasingly shown that concerns about status often have a substantial influence on wages.[21] Introspection alone should persuade most people that the recognition and approval of others is a profound source of human satisfaction. Imagine being assured that, in return for two years of intense preparation at a subsistence wage, you would win a standing ovation at Carnegie Hall, an Olympic Gold Medal in the hundred-meters, an Academy Award, a Pulitzer Prize, the Cy Young Award, or any other accolade of your choice—but no additional monetary compensation. Would you pay the price? That most people apparently wouldn't hesitate suggests that status is a big-ticket item. The more people value it, the greater the inefficiencies that result from the winner-take-all payoff structure.

Other Nonpecuniary Motives

Of course, status is not the only nonpecuniary motive that might influence the decision to compete in a winner-take-all market. Many aspiring musicians, for example, report being driven simply by the joy of playing, and happily put in long hours of practice even though they realize that the odds of becoming a star are prohibitively small. Likewise, many athletes find the stimulus of competition reward enough for the long hours they log on the practice fields.

The intrinsic rewards from playing music well or competing intensely in sports are like the status motive insofar as they draw more people into winner-take-all markets than would enter if money were all that mattered. But unlike status, these other rewards are not zero-sum. Only a handful of athletes can enjoy the esteem of being stars, but all can take pleasure in being fit and competing effectively.

In terms of their effect on the overcrowding problem, these other nonpecuniary motives are thus functionally equivalent to a positive loser's payment. They lure more contestants into winner-take-all markets, but they also enlarge the number who should compete on efficiency grounds. Unlike the status motive, these motives do not make the overcrowding problem worse; but neither do they mitigate it.

Observable Talent Differences

Another unrealistic feature of our hypothetical two-career economy was that potential contestants had no information about their relative odds of winning the recording contract. Contestants in any real winner-take-all market will differ in numerous observable ways that affect their chances of winning. In tennis, for example, one can observe at a glance whether another player has a stronger serve and more penetrating ground strokes.

Yet observable talent differences clearly do not uniquely predict the outcome of most important contests. In addition to having a strong serve and penetrating ground strokes, a winning tennis player must possess a variety of other attributes that are not easily observed in oneself, let alone in others. Observable talent differences matter a great deal in many arenas, but they are almost never fully determinative.

On the other hand, where we *can* observe potential contestants' talent differences, we will get a more efficient allocation of resources because only the most talented will find it worthwhile to compete. The quality of the winning contestant will be higher, and the number of contestants smaller. Both differences cause total income in the economy to rise.

But although observable talent differences mitigate the efficiency losses resulting from winner-take-all markets, they do not eliminate them. As we have shown elsewhere, overcrowding persists.[22]

Arenas in Which Relative Performance Is What Really Matters

In some arenas absolute quality is all that buyers really care about. The buyer of a machine tool, for example, is willing to pay 10 percent more for a machine that yields 10 percent more profit than competing machines.

In many other arenas, however, relative performance is what matters to the buyer. The larger purses made possible by pay-per-view television have led to an enormous increase in the number of aspiring prizefighters, with the result that today's leading heavyweights are at least a little faster and stronger than the champions of earlier years, Yet it is unclear that this increase in absolute quality has meant greater value for fans. What most fans really care about is seeing the best fighters in the game go all out for the title. Neither Gene Tunney nor Jack Dempsey would be a serious contender in today's much larger field of heavyweights, yet fans old enough to know insist that there has never been a more exciting bout than their 1927 title rematch.

Indeed, there may even be arenas in which an increase in absolute quality causes a *reduction* in delivered value. In men's tennis, for example, weight and fitness training, high-tech racquets, and the generally larger field of contestants have produced players who would completely overpower the champions of earlier eras. Yet as far as many fans are concerned, the result has been a game that is less fun to watch, at least when played on grass or other fast surfaces. In the 1994 men's final at Wimbledon, for instance, only one of the several hundred points played between Pete Sampras and Goran Ivanisevic lasted even as many as four strokes.

The focus on relative performance is most evident in sports, but it exists in varying degrees in other arenas as well. Perceptions of quality, after all, tend to be highly context-dependent. A buyer's satisfaction with his color television set, for example, depends not only on the absolute quality of its picture but also on how that quality compares with other sets in use. Even the most technically inferior of today's sets project a much sharper and brighter image than sets made thirty years ago. In the context of that earlier era, many buyers would have been thrilled to pay an enormous premium for one of today's lowest-quality sets. Yet buyers in today's market take the very same picture quality for granted.

A buyer's satisfaction with the performance of her newly purchased sports car likewise depends not only on the absolute quality of its performance but also on how it performs relative to other cars. Consider, for example, this reaction of *Motor Trend*'s reviewer to the non-turbocharged version of Toyota's award-winning Supra: "[W]e can't help considering, perhaps unfairly, the [non-turbo version] to be a domesticated version of the conquering Supra Turbo; a super sports car after a turbotomy. (How fickle our feelings: This naturally aspirated Supra claws the eyes out of the previous-generation Supra *Turbo* in *every* parameter, and yet we think of it as a purring kitten.)"[23]

If relative quality were the only thing that mattered to buyers, the social ideal would be to keep the number of contestants in each winner-take-all market to a bare minimum. Expanding the number of contestants would increase the absolute quality of what gets produced in winner-take-all markets, but if relative quality is all buyers care about, that would be a waste.

In reality, of course, most buyers care about both absolute *and* relative performance. The balance of these concerns will vary both from buyer to buyer and from market to market. Other things being equal, the losses from overcrowding will tend to be greatest in those winner-take-all markets where relative performance matters most.

Aversion to Risk

In our hypothetical example of the singers and potters, people made career choices to maximize their expected incomes. This amounts to saying that they were willing to take fair gambles—or, in the economist's parlance, they were "risk-neutral."

Are people in fact risk-neutral? Unfortunately, the behavioral evidence concerning people's attitudes toward risk is riddled with contradictions. On the one hand, many people purchase insurance against a broad range of contingencies, indicating an apparent aversion to risk. Yet people fail to insure against many of life's most important and conspicuous risks. People who live on floodplains, for example, often do not buy flood insurance even when it is offered by the government at heavily subsidized rates.[24] In 1992 some forty million Americans had no health insurance—some because they were unable to afford it, but many others who simply chose to spend their money in other ways. Even more people, many of them with high incomes, go through life without disability insurance, content apparently to trust their earning power to the whims of fate. Few people have comprehensive liability insurance commensurate with their assets at risk. Many, if not most, people appear to enjoy gambling, even when the odds of winning are considerably less than fair. Skydivers, hang gliders, bungee jumpers, rock climbers, and white-water rafters spend considerable time and money pursuing activities that, if not actually risky, have many of the trappings of risk. In sum, the behavioral evidence concerning attitudes toward risk is a muddle.

How do these attitudes influence participation in winner-take-all markets? Someone who dislikes risk will find participation in a winner-take-all market less attractive than will his risk-neutral counterpart. And a risk-neutral person, in turn, will find participation less attractive than will a risk seeker, someone who is willing to gamble even when the odds are against him. In sum, then, economies populated by risk seekers will see more contestants in winner-take-all markets than will economies populated by people who are risk-neutral, which in turn will see more contestants than in economies populated by people who are risk-averse.

Attitudes toward risk affect not only the number of people who *will* compete in winner-take-all markets, they affect also the number who *should* compete on efficiency grounds. In comparison with the socially optimal number of contestants if people are risk-neutral, the optimal number will be larger if people like to gamble, and smaller if people prefer not to.

With all these factors to sort out, it might seem hopeless to try to discover whether the actual number who compete in winner-take-all markets is greater or less than socially optimal. There is one thing, however, that we can say with confidence: Private entrepreneurs can stimulate entry into winner-take-all markets when it is insufficient, but they cannot prevent entry when it is excessive.

Suppose that because of a general aversion to risk, too few people compete in a particular winner-take-all market. Someone could organize a cooperative in which all contestants shared the payment generated by the winning contestant, thus converting the gamble into a certain payoff. We would then, as before, be left with too many contestants, despite each person's aversion to risk. The ability to form a cooperative in such cases is tantamount to the ability to eliminate risk. Such cooperative arrangements are often seen in the case of scientific researchers, many of whom cede rights to future discoveries in return for a guaranteed salary.

By contrast, if there are too many contestants in an unorganized winner-take-all market, there is no comparable step a private entrepreneur can take to limit entry. The World Boxing Association, for example, has neither the power nor the motive to prevent inner-city youths from dropping out of school to compete for the heavyweight title.

The upshot: Winner-take-all markets will attract too many entrants even when people are averse to risk taking.

Partitioning Winner-Take-All Markets

In our example, we spoke of an economy with only a single winner-take-all market. But at least some of the technological forces we have considered might permit a winner-take-all market once served by a single supplier to be broken into several smaller winner-take-all markets, each served by a slightly different kind of supplier. Thus the availability of additional cable television channels might change the market for stand-up comedy from one served by only a few comedians, each performing similar material, to a more highly fragmented market with perhaps a dozen performers, each aiming for a narrower market niche.

What happens if instead of one large winner-take-all market we have, say, ten smaller ones, each with a prize equal to one-tenth of the original? If people are willing to take fair gambles, contestants will enter each of these smaller winner-take-all markets until the expected return in each is the same as could have been earned elsewhere. The efficiency losses will thus be exactly the same as in the single winner-take-all market. The entire value of the services generated in the larger number of smaller winner-take-all markets will be dissipated by excessive entry into those markets.

Although partitioning a large winner-take-all market into many smaller ones does not affect the overcrowding problem, it may have significant effects on the distribution of incomes among contestants. By replacing one big winner with many smaller ones, partitioning will generally lessen income inequality.

The change will naturally run in the opposite direction when several small winner-take-all markets are combined into a single larger one. The total amount of overcrowding will not be affected by consolidation, but there will be an increase in inequality.

Divergence Between Price and Social Value

In our hypothetical economy, we took the payment received by the winning singer to be an accurate measure of the value of his or her services. This is a standard premise behind Adam Smith's claim that free market exchange yields the greatest good for the greatest number, and most contemporary economists continue to regard price as a reasonable measure of the social value of a good or service. There are some markets, however, in which price and social value differ significantly. The following examples from law and scientific research illustrate two ways such divergences might arise.

Imagine for a moment that Ford has filed a $10 billion lawsuit against GM for infringing some patent. And let's assume that, on purely substantive grounds, it is not clear that GM has really done anything improper, and that the odds that Ford will prevail in its suit are exactly 50–50. In other words, suppose that, from society's perspective, it makes no difference who wins the suit.

To the participants themselves, however, it obviously matters a great deal. With the substantive issues equally favoring each side, the relative skill and forcefulness with which opposing counsel present their respective cases will be decisive. Now suppose there is one lawyer in the profession—call her Jones—who is better than any other. In fact, she is only slightly more able than Smith. But the difference between the two is sufficient that, in a case this close, the side that hires Jones is sure to win. Accordingly, if Ford and GM act independently, the bidding for Jones's services will be intense. If Ford offered Jones a $5 billion fee, for example, it would be in GM's interest to bid still higher, since its failure to retain Jones would mean a sure loss of $10 billion. (Smith will not be of much value in this particular suit, since any party that hired him would be sure to lose anyway; he is thus likely to end up working for some other client with a lot at stake.)

As a result of the high-stakes bidding for the most talented litigators, some of the ablest people in the economy—people like Jones and Smith who could have made substantive contributions in other areas—are drawn into activities that add little or nothing to our gross national product. The legal fees in lawsuits of this sort dramatically overstate the social value of the corresponding legal services. In such cases the inefficiencies will be much larger than those we identified in our hypothetical economy, where the winner's payment was the same as the social value of his or her performance.

In at least some other cases, by contrast, the social value of the winner's payment will understate the social value of what he or she produces. Consider, for example, the case of John Bardeen and Walter Brattain, the Bell Labs physicists who invented the transistor. Their innovation formed the basis of the information revolution discussed in chapter 3. It has led to literally hundreds of billions of dollars worth of expanded world output. Bardeen and Brattain themselves were not the patent holders for the transistor. But even if they had been, they could have captured only the most minuscule fraction of their product's value. As economist Partha Dasgupta observes, "Patents and secrecy offer only partial protection to inventors and discoverers. Imitative research is a pervasive phenomenon."[25] Economist Edwin Mansfield and his colleagues have estimated that innovations can be imitated for an average of only 65 percent of their original cost, and that 60 percent of patented innovations are imitated within four years.[26]

Because innovation often generates significant external benefits, we might expect market forces to call forth too little innovation. But markets for innovation also tend to have winner-take-all payoff structures, and this, as we have seen, tends to generate excessive activity. The net effect thus depends on which of these opposing tendencies is larger. If, as may often be the case, the divergence between price and social value dominates, then research and innovation may constitute an important exception to our claim that winner-take-all markets attract too many resources. It was to emphasize the potential importance of this exception that we ended the title of this chapter with a question mark.

Winner-Take-All Markets and the Variability of Income

One characteristic feature of winner-take-all markets is that they translate small differences in performance into large differences in economic reward. The growing importance of winner-take-all markets thus implies a change in the pattern of incomes observed in the economy. More specifically, it implies that even if we control for age, education, experience, ability, and other individual characteristics thought to influence productivity and hence income, we should see greater income variability now than in the past. In chapter 5 we saw evidence of just such a change in income variability in the American economy.

Implications for Tax Policy

The similarity between winner-take-all markets and the tragedy of the commons suggests a straightforward way of reducing the efficiency losses associated with excessive entry into winner-take-all markets. In the tragedy of the commons, recall, the problem was that individual market incentives called forth too many steers onto the commonly owned pastureland. If the problem is that the individual market rewards for an activity are too high from a social perspective, the simplest solution is to tax that activity, thus making it less attractive. A simple tax, or grazing fee, for each steer sent onto the commons will do the trick.

In our singer-potter economy, suppose we levy a tax on the earnings of the winning singer. The individual will now compete for the recording contract as long as the expected *after-tax* payoff is at least as large as the potter's wage. With the effective reward to the winning singer thus reduced, the number of competing singers will fall. Of course, taxation is not the only way of curtailing an activity that is misleadingly attractive to individuals. An alternative solution to the tragedy of the commons is to auction a limited number of grazing permits to the highest bidders. Here, too, an alternative solution would be to auction licenses to compete for the recording contract. In a world of perfect capital markets and no transaction costs, the tax and auction alternatives would be equivalent.

In practice, however, the tax solution is likely to be more attractive. The auction approach assumes that potential contestants have resources to bid the expected value of a singing license. If they do not, and if capital markets are imperfect, then the license auction will be inefficient. Moreover, in a world in which the administrative machinery for collecting income taxes already exists, it may be cheaper just to use this machinery rather than incur additional costs to set up an auction.

We should note that any policy that limits the number of contestants in winner-take-all markets entails an element of risk, A large contestant pool would be likely to contain the best performers, but since contestants don't know how good they are until the contest has been concluded, there is a small chance that the best singers will have remained behind. A policy that makes entry less attractive therefore entails at least the possibility of discouraging the best performers. Thus, although we are likely to gain more than we lose by limiting the number of contestants, the possibility remains that making the tournament less attractive might discourage someone like Luciano Pavarotti from entering.

This possibility becomes more remote once we allow that talent differences are at least partially observable before the contest begins. For in this case the effect of a tax is selectively to discourage the least talented potential entrants, those who were least likely to win in the first place. By reducing the number of wanna-bes and directing them to alternative pursuits, the effect of the tax is thus to reduce the cost of the winner-take-all tournament (the output that contestants could have produced in other sectors), without at the same time significantly reducing its central benefit (the identification of the best performer).

Equity vs. Efficiency: An Illusory Trade-off ?

It is to the economics profession that people of the world owe the notion that the quest for distributive justice comes always and everywhere at the expense of efficiency.[27] The idea that progressive taxation weakens economic incentives is hardly new. But in recent decades, it has achieved growing currency. Whereas Milton Friedman and his followers at the University of Chicago waged a lonely battle through the 1950s and 1960s to persuade policy makers that taxation impedes economic growth, by the time Ronald Reagan assumed office in 1981, the sale had been closed. Indeed, Reagan administration officials went so far as to embrace the "Laffer curve," a relationship claiming to show that reductions in tax rates would so stimulate the economy that total tax revenues would actually rise.

Events of the past decade have cast doubt on the empirical validity of the notion that tax rate reductions cause enduring economic growth. Our analysis of the allocative effects of winner-take-all markets suggests that, on theoretical grounds, the equity-efficiency tradeoff ought never to have been expected in the first place. For the effect of taxing the highest incomes in winner-take-all markets is to reduce the allocation of labor to such markets; and this, we have seen, tends to increase society's total income.

This is not to say that sufficiently high tax rates would never discourage effort and risk taking in the ways emphasized by supply-side economists. But at the very least, the standard claim that progressive taxation comes at the expense of economic efficiency deserves reexamination. In economies in which winner-take-all effects are important, output not only need not fall with increases in the tax rates on high incomes, but it may very well rise sharply.

Although our focus has been on the inefficiencies that result from winner-take-all markets, we must again emphasize that there can be great social gains when the best performers serve wider markets. But even the most carefully conceived social institutions cannot identify the best performers free of charge. When we say that winner-take-all markets tend to be inefficient under market incentives, what we mean is that these incentives tend not to minimize the cost of identifying the best performers.

7

The Problem of Wasteful Investment

Decades ago many American cities hosted annual soapbox derbies. Fathers and sons would build small, unpowered four-wheel vehicles, which the sons would then pilot in races held on specially constructed ramps. Whichever car rolled to the bottom of the ramp in the shortest time was the winner.

Although significant monetary prizes were seldom at stake in these contests, people took them *very* seriously. Contestants often went to great lengths to seek out even the tiniest competitive advantage. The key to victory was to achieve an aerodynamically sleek vehicle with as little rolling resistance as possible. Special fiberglass resins replaced plywood in the construction of body panels. Stiffer rubber tires provided an additional advantage. But most of all, attention focused on the quest for better bearings. There was almost no limit to what one could spend for a bearing with only a marginally lower coefficient of friction.

As construction expenses continued to escalate, soapbox derbies were more and more likely to be decided by the size of one's bank account rather than by one's skill and determination as an amateur engineer. Realizing this, the organizers of these contests eventually began to impose spending limits. And although there were obvious enforcement problems, the general result was to restore the contests to a semblance of their earlier form.

Soapbox derbies are winner-take-all contests. We will describe how such contests almost invariably summon mutually offsetting, and socially wasteful, patterns of competitive investment that reinforce the inefficiencies we identified with overcrowding in chapter 6.

The Prisoner's Dilemma

The basic difficulty here is that the incentives to invest in performance enhancement confront contestants in winner-take-all markets with the familiar prisoner's dilemma, one of the most powerful metaphors in modern social theory. Many credit it to mathematician A. W. Tucker, who is said to have been the first to employ the anecdote from which it draws its name. As the story goes, two men are being held in separate cells for a crime they did, in fact, commit. If convicted, each will serve twenty years in jail. The district attorney's problem is that he has hard evidence sufficient to prove them guilty of only a minor offense, for which the penalty is just one year.

To get around this difficulty, the DA makes the following offer to each prisoner: "If you confess and your partner remains silent, you will go free. But if your partner confesses while you remain silent, you will spend twenty years in jail. If both you and your partner confess, you will each spend five years in jail." From the collective perspective of the two prisoners, the best outcome is for each to remain silent, for in that case the DA can convict them of just the minor offense and each will spend only one year in jail. Yet imagine yourself in a cell thinking over the DAs offer, and note the almost compelling incentive to confess. If your partner remains silent, you will go scot-free by confessing. Alternatively, if your partner confesses, you will get five years by confessing, compared to the twenty you would get by not confessing.

Since you know your partner faces the same incentives, you know that he, too, will be strongly tempted to confess (if only because he suspects that *you* will be). But no matter what you expect your partner to do, you will always get a shorter sentence by confessing. And yet when you both confess, you each get five years, rather than the one year you would have gotten had you both remained silent. Hence the dilemma.

The prisoner's dilemma captures the essence of an important class of problems in which actions that seem compellingly attractive to individuals yield results that are unattractive to the group as a whole. The military arms race is a prisoner's dilemma. Both antagonists do better if neither invests in armaments than if both do. Yet each side faces compelling temptations to invest, for it knows that the worst of all possibilities is for its rival to invest while it does not.

The Positional Arms Race

In winner-take-all markets, contestants compete in a tournament in which rewards depend not only on absolute performance, but also on one's rank ordering. In the examples we considered in chapter 6, the outcomes of these contests depended only on the talent and other personal characteristics of the contestants. More generally, however, the outcomes will also depend on the contestants' investments in performance enhancement.

In a lawsuit, for example, each side's chances of winning depend in part on the amount of time its lawyers spend researching the histories of related cases. If the contestants are evenly matched to begin with, a small investment by any one of them can substantially improve his or her chances of winning. Yet the same logic applies to all the other contestants as well. And it is a mathematical impossibility for *each* contestant's chances of winning to rise with investment, no matter how much he or she might invest. The lawsuit will have only a single winner no matter how many hours opposing counsel spend on legal research. Contestants in winner-take-all markets— indeed, the participants in virtually any contest—confront either a two-person or a multiperson version of the prisoner's dilemma described above.

The extent to which investments in performance enhancement increase the market value of the winning contestant's performance will vary from case to case. In some cases—our soapbox-derby example is one—individual investments will have virtually no effect on the value of the final product. The aims of these competitions, after all, are equally well met whether all contestants spend one hundred dollars on materials or all spend one thousand dollars.

In other cases investments in performance enhancement translate into a more valuable product. The sopranos who compete for the handful of recording contracts issued each year spend thousands of dollars on voice coaches and other forms of music instruction. Such efforts translate into greater clarity, dynamic range, and other performance characteristics that yield additional listener satisfaction.

In cases like these, society has an interest in performance enhancement, but only up to a point. People who invest in performance enhancement naturally turn first to the most effective investments— those that raise value the most for a given outlay. Having exploited their best opportunities, they turn next to investments with smaller returns. If our goal, as before, is to maximize society's total income, we should keep investing in performance enhancement as long as the last dollar invested yields at least a dollar's worth of extra performance. (If the last dollar invested had yielded *less* than an extra dollar's worth, it would have been better to invest less.)

Does an invisible hand lead contestants to invest in accordance with this criterion? Unfortunately, the answer seems to be no. The difficulty is that whereas from society's point of view we want investments to be driven by their effect on the value of the final product, the primary concern from each contestant's point of view is their effect on who will be the winner.

Some insight into how individual incentives drive competitive investments is afforded by experiments involving a simple auction called the entrapment game. First described by economist Martin Shubik, this game is like a standard auction, but with a diabolical twist. The auctioneer announces to an assembled group that he is going to auction off a $20 bill to the highest bidder. After someone opens the bidding, each successive bid must exceed the previous one by some specified amount—say, $.50. The twist is that once the bidding stops, not only the highest but also the second-highest bidder must give their respective bids to the auctioneer. The highest bidder then gets the $20 bill and the second-highest bidder gets nothing.

For example, if the highest bid were $9.00 and the second-highest bid were $8.50, the auctioneer would collect a total of $17.50. The highest bidder would get the $20.00, for a net gain of $11.00, and the second-highest bidder would have a loss of $8.50. Players in this game face incentives like those that confront contestants considering investments in performance enhancement. In both cases, by investing a little more than one's rivals, one can tip the outcome in one's favor.

Although the subjects in these experiments have ranged from business executives to college undergraduates, the pattern of bidding is eerily almost always the same. Following the opening bid, offers proceed quickly to $10.00, or half the amount being auctioned. There is then a pause, as the subjects appear to digest the fact that, with the next bid, the two highest bids will total more than $20.00, thus taking the auctioneer off the hook. At this point, the second-highest bidder, whose bid stands at $9.50, invariably offers $10.50, apparently thinking that it is better to have a shot at winning $9.50 than to take a sure loss of $9.50.

In most cases all but the top two bidders drop out at this point, and they quickly escalate their bids. As the bidding approaches $20.00, there is a second pause, this time as the top bidders appear to be pondering the fact that even the highest bidder is likely to come out behind. The second-highest bidder, at $19.50, is understandably reluctant to offer $20.50. But consider the alternative: Dropping out means losing $19.50 for sure. But if he or she offers $20.50 and wins, the loss will be only $.50. So as long as there seems to be even a small chance that the other bidder will drop out, it makes sense to continue. Once the $20.00 threshold has been crossed, the pace of the bidding quickens again, and from then on it is a war of nerves between the two remaining bidders. It is quite common for the bidding to reach $50.00 before someone finally yields in frustration.

One might be tempted to think that any intelligent, well-informed person would know better than to become involved in an auction whose incentives so strongly favor costly escalation. But many of the subjects in these auctions have been experienced business professionals; many others have had formal training in the theory of games and strategic interaction. For example, psychologist Max Bazerrnan reports that during the past ten years he has earned more than $17,000 by auctioning $20 bills to his MBA students at Northwestern University's Kellogg Graduate School of Management, which is consistently among the top-rated MBA programs in the world. In the course of almost two hundred of his auctions, the top two bids never totaled less than $39, and in one instance totaled $407.[1]

The incentives of the entrapment game constitute an extreme case in the sense that, by bidding just a little more than others, a contestant can be sure of winning. We might expect such incentives, for example, when a city council announces its plans to award a cable television franchise to whichever applicant gives most generously to favored local charities.

More generally, however, we would not expect the highest investor to be sure of winning. Alternatively, suppose that each contestant's probability of winning is equal to his share of total investment in performance enhancement. We call this the "lottery game" because of its resemblance to the way in which the odds in some state lotteries are determined. In such a lottery someone who buys three-quarters of all tickets sold has a 75 percent chance of winning. Likewise, in a lottery game with two identical contestants, someone who invests three times as much as his rival has a 75 percent chance of being the winner.

The difference between the lottery game and the entrapment game is that the incentives to escalate investment are weaker under the lottery game. In the entrapment game, either of two candidates with equal investments to begin with could tip the outcome decisively in her favor by making only a small additional investment. In the lottery game, by contrast, a slight increase in investment means only a slight increase in the odds of winning.

The lottery model of investment has been much studied.[2] It is well known that when there are two identically situated contestants investing independently for a fixed reward, each will invest ¼ of that reward on performance enhancement. Together they will thus squander ½ the total reward on mutually offsetting investments in performance enhancement. If there are not two contestants but one hundred, each investing independently under the incentives of the lottery model, the total amount spent on performance enhancement will be 99/100. As the number of contestants in a winner-take-all market becomes large, the level of total investment quickly approaches the value of the reward being sought. So, even under the weaker incentives posed by the lottery game, mutually offsetting investments in performance enhancement remain substantial.

In practice, contestants' investments in performance enhancement often result in a more valuable final product for end users. Thus when singers compete by investing in vocal coaching, consumers end up hearing better music. But, as careful theoretical analysis of this case has shown, the resulting levels of investment in performance enhancement, though smaller than when the final product's value is independent of investment, remain excessive.[3]

Common sense, empirical observation, and theoretical analyses of investment incentives thus lead to the same conclusion: In winner-take-all contests in which investments in performance enhancement affect the individual contestant's odds of winning, there will be mutually offsetting, socially inefficient investments in performance enhancement.[4] Because of the obvious structural similarity of these investments to the purchase of armaments in the classic military arms race, we call this pattern the "positional arms race." Let us look at some illustrative examples.

Athletics

Training for the Olympics is a serious business, with six hours a day of grueling workouts the norm for serious competitors in track and field. And as everyone knows, the difference in payoffs for very small differences in performance can be enormous. For many years the face of Mary Lou Retton, the 1984 gold medalist in gymnastics, peered out at millions of Americans each morning from the front of their Wheaties boxes. Her endorsement contracts have earned her several million dollars in the years since her medal. But although Retton's victory over the 1984 silver medalist came by only a slim margin, today almost no one can even remember the runner-up's name.

With such large differences in return hinging on such small differences in performance, it is hardly surprising that athletes seek any possible edge they can get. As the financial stakes have risen, athletic training regimens have grown significantly more grueling. Indications to this effect are especially vivid in women's sports like swimming, figure skating, and gymnastics, where peak performance often comes well before the age of twenty.

Consider the gymnast Kristie Phillips, once thought to be a sure bet to become the next Mary Lou Retton. At the age of eight, she left home to live in Houston and train with Bela Karolyi, who had coached Retton and, before her, the Romanian gold medalist Nadia Comaneci.[5] Phillips describes how Karolyi pressed her and other gymnasts to take laxatives, thyroid pills, and diuretics to lose the weight brought on by puberty. She also suffered from bulimia, which is apparently common among female gymnasts under constant pressure to control their weight. "I weighed 98 pounds and I was being called an overstuffed Christmas turkey," she recalls.[6]

Then there was the pain from injuries invariably brought on by intensive training. Phillips took twelve Advil capsules and six anti-inflammatory Naprosyns a day for the pain in her fractured left wrist, "which she trained on for three years because she felt she couldn't afford the time off to let it heal." For all that, Phillips failed even to make the 1988 Olympic team. A few months later she slashed her wrists in a suicide attempt.

Of course, hard, even punishing work has always been an acknowledged price of athletic excellence, and there is a certain rough justice in that. After all, the rewards of victory are great, and it would hardly seem fair to win them without having had to lift a finger. What is more, if Phillips had won the gold medal as expected, we may be sure that she would have felt the price well worth it.

Yet the toll exacted by modern training methods is not limited to a handful of elite athletes with clear chances for a gold medal. Among a large group of female college athletes interviewed in a recent study, 32 percent engaged in at least one form of "disordered eating" (bulimia, anorexia, or the use of laxatives, diuretics, or diet pills). Among female college gymnasts, the figure was 66 percent. One study estimated that two-thirds of female college athletes suffer from amenorrhea (irregular or nonexistent menstrual periods). Amenorrhea is associated with a loss of bone density that renders athletes susceptible to stress fractures, premature osteoporosis, and curvature of the spine. "We find women in their 20s with the bone density of postmenopausal 50-year-old women," said Pepperdine

University's Dr. Aurelia Nattiv, who has studied amenorrhea in female college gymnasts.[8]

In extreme instances, of course, the consequences of eating disorders can be much more serious, even fatal. On July 26, 1994, Christy Henrich, a former Olympic gymnastics hopeful, died at age twenty-two from complications arising from anorexia and bulimia. "I would say 99 percent of what has happened to Christy is because of the sport," her mother told reporters during an earlier hospitalization when her daughter's weight had dropped to just sixty pounds. "All the focus is on the body."[9]

Whatever the stakes of the competition involved, the fact remains that, from a collective perspective, extreme training measures are wasteful. *Someone* is going to be the Olympic gold medalist or the conference champion, after all, whether athletes train eight hours a day or only four; whether they take painkillers to train through injuries or take time off to let them heal; whether everyone takes laxatives and diuretics or no one does.

The consumption of anabolic steroids is another widespread method for gaining a competitive edge in athletics. Although one occasionally hears claims that anabolic steroids do not enhance athletic performance, few experienced athletes question that these drugs provide an advantage.

For years specialists in sports medicine in the former East Germany conducted systematic experiments to measure the effects of steroids on performance. Professor Helmut Bohl estimated that steroids provide a half-second advantage for a 100-meter sprinter, a three-second advantage for an 800-meter runner, and an extra meter's distance for a shot-putter.[10] These advantages are 8.33, 75, and 1.35 times the respective differences between the gold- and silver-medal performances in the 1992 Olympic Games.[11]

And so we are not surprised that consumption of anabolic steroids has become so common among world-class athletes. Just how common is difficult to say, because sophisticated masking techniques make steroid consumption almost impossible to detect. When detection does occur, it is often only by a fluke. For example, although credible evidence of his long-term steroid use later emerged, Canadian sprinter Ben Johnson is said to have forfeited his

1988 100-meters Olympic gold medal only because someone sabotaged his urine sample. Likewise, the German sprinter Katrin Krabbe, the world champion in the 100-meter in 1990, failed a drug test only because it could be shown that urine samples ostensibly from her and two other athletes had in fact come from only one of them. Yet despite the difficulty of detection, we know that at least six different Olympic gold medalists consumed steroids through much of the 1980s.[12]

There is also indirect evidence that steroid use is widespread. From time to time, for example, a technical advance in detection techniques is announced, causing athletes to discontinue steroids until a new masking technique can be developed. At the 1990 World Weightlifting Championship in Budapest, the recently introduced "steroid profile" detection method apparently had this effect, as lifters in that competition "attempted weights far below what they had put up in the past, and only one athlete even tried for a world record."[13]

In addition to enhanced athletic performance, the short-term medical consequences of steroid use include hair loss, skin disorders, heightened aggressiveness, and even severe psychosis. There is insufficient evidence to support confident predictions about the long-term consequences of steroid use. But at least fragmentary evidence links steroid consumption to a variety of circulatory disorders, testicular atrophy, abnormal sperm morphology, and higher risks of some cancers.[14]

Steroid use thus entails at least the potential to cause serious medical harm. And since there is no evidence that steroid use enhances the value of athletic competition from a spectator's perspective, a strong case can be made that the collective consequences of this particular form of the positional arms race are uniformly negative.

Growing financial incentives have led to a variety of other positional arms races that now compromise the financial health of our colleges and universities. Before television transformed college football and basketball into big-time entertainment industries, college athletic programs had relatively modest budgets that were financed largely through revenues from ticket sales, so that programs that did not generate a modest profit at least did not impose a heavy burden on their institutions. But this, as we will see, is no longer the case.

There is no denying that the top prizes in college athletics have proved compellingly attractive. A successful college athletic program generates not only large revenues (see chapter 4) but also many indirect benefits. One is that these programs seem to attract more and better students. After winning the NCAA basketball championship in 1983, for example, North Carolina State University experienced a 40 percent rise in applications for admission.[15] Boston College applications went up from 12,500 in 1984 to 16,200 in 1985 after Doug Flutie won the Heisman Trophy for the 1984 season.[16] With more applicants, a school can be more selective. One study has shown that the SAT scores of a school's entering freshmen rise when the school's within-conference winning percentage rises.[17]

But viewed from the perspective of higher education as a whole, the private incentive to invest in athletics in order to attract better students is clearly too large. After all, for every football or basketball team that wins an extra game, some other team must lose one. There are only so many good students in the total applicant pool, and no clear social purpose is served by reallocating them to schools with successful athletic programs.

But if the gains from better applicants are illusory for higher education as a whole, the increased revenue flows to individual colleges are not. And with all these added revenues, it might seem natural to suppose that college athletic programs have been making ever-larger contributions to the institutions of higher learning that sponsor them. In fact, however, college athletic programs have been an increasing financial burden on their sponsoring institutions. As journalist Murray Sperber described the financial picture in his recent book:

> If profit and loss is defined according to ordinary business practices, of the 802 members of the NCAA (the National Collegiate Athletic Association), the 493 of the NAIA (National Association of Intercollegiate Athletics), and the 1050 nonaffiliated junior colleges, only 10 to 20 athletic programs make a consistent albeit small profit, and in any given year another 20 to 30 break even or do better. The rest—over 2300 institutions—lose anywhere from a few dollars to millions annually.[18]

Note that this seemingly contradictory state of affairs is precisely what ought to have been expected on the basis of the logic of positional arms races. Where large prizes are at stake, in college athletics or in any other arena, contestants face powerful incentives to spend money to enhance their prospects of winning. And although a few winners will come out ahead, most contestants will fare worse than if they had not invested.

Athletes are of course the primary ingredient in a successful program, so it is no surprise that expenditures on recruiting have escalated sharply. Whereas most programs once focused their recruiting efforts on states close to home, a major program must now recruit nationwide, a task that often consumes the energies of several assistant coaches. The average 1985 expense budget, of which recruiting was a major component, for Division I schools with football teams was 286 percent higher than in 1973.[19]

Increasingly frequent violations of NCAA rules provide further indications of the pressures of the positional arms race in college sports. Reports of illegal side payments to athletes have grown more common in recent years.[20] Some programs even employ the lure of romance, arranging "dates" to enhance the athletes' campus visits:

> Often these dates belong to a special club, organized by the athletic department, and they receive some sort of compensation for their services. The University of Florida's "Gator Getters" was one of the first of these groups but now most big-time programs have similar organizations. At the University of Texas at Austin, a Texas Angel often follows up her date with a football recruit by writing to him as often as once a day to try to convince him to sign with the Longhorns.[21]

Some organizations abandon all pretense that the dates are local coeds. "A Texas Christian [University] booster took a prospective player to a local motel, where, the [NCAA] report said, the athlete was provided with lodging, meals, and prostitutes until the signing date."[22]

The deficits generated in pursuit of the top prizes in college sports have spawned an energetic search for new sources of revenue. Corporations have contributed handsomely for the right to sponsor postseason college bowl games, which now bear their corporate logos. Thus we now have the USF&G Sugar Bowl, the John Hancock Sun Bowl, and the Sea World Holiday Bowl.

Universities have also turned to students for additional revenues to cover athletic budget deficits. The University of Maryland athletic department, for example, collects almost one-third of its total receipts in the form of a mandatory athletic surcharge on students.[23] After a 1982 audit showed an athletic deficit of $3.4 million at the University of Houston, the athletic department's share of student fees rose from $400,000 to approximately $2 million, "despite protests from Houston students, 70 percent of whom were part-time or evening students, and not interested in a high-powered college sports program."[24]

Universities have even turned to the state for help. In 1985, for example, the athletic departments of Division I football schools received an average of more than $736,000 in public funds. More than two-thirds of all public colleges in the NCAA received taxpayer dollars for their athletic programs.[25] Indirect sources of public support—as when an athletic coach at a public university draws his salary from the physical education department—add to these totals.

But the logic of positional arms races dictates that each new source of revenue is consumed by a pressing new investment to maintain competitive position. And so athletic budget deficits have continued to grow. For example, a survey by the College Football Association revealed that the cost of running an athletic department grew by 36 percent between 1983 and 1988, while revenue from all sources was growing by only 27 percent.[26]

Even large schools with traditionally successful programs are increasingly plagued by athletic budget deficits. The University of Michigan, a long-time powerhouse in both football and basketball, lost $2.5 million in 1988–89.[27] And imagine the dismay of the Fighting Irish at the spectacle of a South Bend newspaper headline proclaiming: NOTRE DAME WILL NOT MAKE MONEY ON ATHLETICS THIS YEAR.[28]

University administrators have begun to appreciate the structural forces responsible for their dilemma. For instance, Lansing Baker, president of Utica College, had this to say in 1988 about the burdens of participation in the NCAA's Division I (the most competitive of the NCAA divisions): "[It] is like being in a poker game where you have the second- or third-best hand, but they keep bumping up and bumping up, until you have trouble staying in."[29] Indeed, some schools have decided that the stakes have simply grown too high. Citing increased financial pressure from mounting athletic budget deficits, the University of Santa Clara (California) dropped its football program in January 1993.[30]

Earnings Forecasting

The stock market is the cornerstone of the American capital market. Together with retained earnings, loans from commercial banks, and proceeds from the sale of corporate bonds, revenues from the sale of stock are the principal means of purchasing and maintaining the machinery and equipment that drive the American economy.

Ownership of a share of stock in a given company is, in effect, an entitlement to a share in its present and future earnings. Thus, other things being equal, a share in a company expected to have high future earnings will sell for more than one in a company expected to have low future earnings. From the perspective of overall economic efficiency, this is just as it should be. It is the mechanism by which the market makes capital available to those firms that are expected to produce "what the public wants at prices it can afford."

Since a company's future earnings are always uncertain, the price of its stock will necessarily depend on the market's considered judgment about what those earnings will be. This means that someone who can forecast earnings more accurately than others can reap enormous financial rewards. Consider, for example, an investment analyst who discovers that the future earnings of a given company are sure to be 20 percent higher than the market's current estimate. This means that if the company's stock is currently selling for $100 per share, it will rise to $120 once this information becomes generally known. By being the first to have this information, the analyst and his clients are thus in a position to make a financial killing. Their best strategy is to buy as much stock as they can finance as quickly as they can. For example, if they can buy just fifty thousand shares at the current price, they stand to make a million dollars in a matter of hours or days.

The catch is that reliable new information about future earnings is extremely difficult to come by. For one thing, nonpublic information obtained through an official of the company is ruled out, because the law prohibits trading on the basis of insider information. So the information must come from an analysis of publicly available data. But with so much at stake, thousands of other analysts are also feverishly picking over the same data. If Salomon Brothers spends hundreds of thousands of dollars on a computer forecasting model that yields results just a few days after those obtained by Morgan Stanley, Salomon gets nothing. Under these conditions, each firm faces powerful incentives to invest not only in more accurate but also in faster earnings forecasting methods.

For society as a whole, however, both the timing and quality of earnings forecasts are considerably less important. Granted, quicker and better earnings forecasts are socially beneficial to the extent that they speed the flow of capital to the companies that can make the best use of it. But relatively little is lost, from society's perspective, by small delays in the timing, or marginal declines in the accuracy, of earnings forecasts. Society's scarce capital resources would still be allocated to the right companies even if all current forecasts were delayed by a few days.

Given the gains that can be had by trading large blocks of stock at favorable terms, it is not surprising that the earnings forecasting industry confronts a positional arms race of the first magnitude. In the United States alone, the financial industry now spends billions each year on earnings forecasts. Many more dollars are allocated to the same purpose through less formal channels. Unlike the investments in steroids in athletics, not all these resources constitute social waste. Yet it is certain that expenditures on forecasting could be cut substantially without compromising the efficiency of the capital market.

Advertising and Promotion

The potential of television talk shows to promote the sale of books first came to light with the publication of Alexander King's *Mine Enemy Grows Older* in 1959.[31] King, a former editor and artist as well as a gifted raconteur, had for many years been a frequent guest on NBC's *Tonight Show,* then hosted by Jack Paar. King's memoir chronicled his recovery from drug addiction, and in the wake of his lengthy on-the-air discussion *of Mine Enemy* with Paar, the book shot onto the *Times* best-seller list. King's second book, *May This House Be Safe from Tigers,* which he also promoted during appearances on *Tonight,* was a big hit as well, selling more than 150,000 copies in hardcover.

Art Linkletter's *Kids Say the Darndest Things* further demonstrated what television promotion could do for the sale of a trade book. Inspired by this example, Bernard Geis, who had been Linkletter's editor at Prentice-Hall, broke away to form his own company, specializing in the publication of books "that would be readily promotable by the hosts or guests of television shows, not excluding shows being run by the financial backers of Bernard Geis Associates."[32]

Following the strategy of signing celebrity authors whose regular television appearances could be used to plug their books, Geis published a string of successful titles between the late 1950s and mid–1960s. But it was not until 1966 that his firm had its first runaway best-seller: Jacqueline Susann's *Valley of the Dolls,* a novel about three women who come to New York in search of romance and success. Geis published *Dolls* against the advice of several of his editors, who even by the forgiving standards of Geis books condemned it as "literary trash." Unlike other Geis authors, Jacqueline Susann was not a celebrity when the book was published. But she became one in the course of an unprecedentedly intense cross-country campaign to publicize her book through television, radio, and print interviews, appearances at bookstores and shopping malls, and more. As Geis put it, Susann appeared on so many radio and television shows that "someone said then that the only thing you could turn on without getting Jacqueline Susann was the water faucet."[33]

The results were spectacular. *Valley of the Dolls* stayed on the hardcover best-seller list for almost eighteen months, selling 350,000 copies. In 1967, another whirlwind publicity tour launched Bantam's release of the paperback edition, which went on to sell more than 22 million copies.

The lesson that intensive, sustained media exposure could make a big best-seller out of even a questionable manuscript was not lost on publishing executives. Today every major house maintains a large, aggressive staff of publicists who constantly search for new ways to bring books to the media's attention. Each year thousands of authors embark, full of hope, on national media tours, armed in many cases with booklets provided by their publishers that instruct the authors how to be self-confident, charming, charismatic, spontaneous. . . .

Print advertising adds to the resources consumed by publicity departments. For example, a full-page ad in the *New York Times Book Review,* which reaches no more than two million readers, now costs upward of fifteen thousand dollars.

Yet no matter how much publishers spend on advertising and promotional tours, an inescapable mathematical constraint remains. The *New York Times* best-seller list includes only fifteen works of fiction and fifteen nonfiction each week. Efforts on behalf of any one book—in terms of their effect on its likelihood of making this critical list—thus come entirely at the expense of others. If each publisher invested a little less on publicity, authors and publishers would have a larger pie to divide. And yet the simple logic of the positional arms race works against such cutbacks: In the quest for elusive best-seller status, failure to pull out all the stops in promoting a given title all but consigns it to the remainder tables.

Of course, publishing is not the only sector in which firms vie with one another for a share of the buyer's limited attention. Procter & Gamble spends more than $2 billion a year to advertise its various toothpastes, soaps, and detergents. The Philip Morris companies spend nearly as much advertising their different brands of cigarettes. Kellogg spends more than half a billion dollars a year plugging its breakfast cereals and other products. And Anheuser-Busch spends almost the same amount to promote its various brands of beer. Altogether, the top one hundred U.S. advertisers spent a total of almost $50 billion in 1991 alone.[34]

Social critics have long identified advertising as perhaps the largest and most conspicuous example of pure social waste in a market economy. This is an extreme view that ignores the many potentially beneficial effects of advertising, such as providing useful product information and helping to finance radio, television, and print media. But even the most enthusiastic proponent of advertising must concede that the private incentives to engage in it are larger than the social ones.

When, for example, Congress enacted a law in 1971 prohibiting cigarette manufacturers from advertising on television, total tobacco advertising expenses fell by 20 percent the next year, while the industry's profits rose sharply. In the years since, however, the inexorable pressures of the positional arms race have led cigarette manufacturers to discover new ways to promote their products. By 1991 Philip Morris alone was spending more on advertising in real terms than the entire industry had spent during the year before the television ban.

If advertising and promotional expenditures were curtailed in every industry, there would be both costs and benefits. But, as the logic of the positional arms race makes clear, the collective gains from such a cutback would almost surely exceed the collective losses.

The Overworked American

The positional arms race plays itself out not only in such high-stakes arenas as investment banking, entertainment, publishing, and sports, but also in the everyday competition to maintain or improve one's position in the distribution of income. As abundant evidence from the natural and social sciences has shown, relative income is an important determinant of both psychological and physical well-being.[35] As we discussed in chapter 2, even people who do not care about relative income per se have powerful reasons for caring where they stand in the distribution of income. If a parent's goal is to educate her children as well as possible, for example, then she can further that goal by having higher relative income, which permits her to purchase a house in a better school district.

In chapter 2 we discussed how small initial differences are often decisive in many winner-take-all labor markets. In these situations people have a variety of options available for attempting to get ahead of their rivals. They may invest in more or better education (our subject in the next chapter). They may accept riskier or otherwise less pleasant jobs, which tend to pay more, or they may work longer hours. Our focus here is on this last option.

In the standard economic calculus, we decide whether to work another hour by weighing the value of what can be bought with the extra income against what we lose by giving up an hour of leisure. This cost-benefit test presumes that the value of what can be bought with extra income is independent of what others buy, which implies that the private and social incentives regarding work are one and the same. But when satisfaction—or the likelihood of promotion—depends not only on absolute but also on relative effort, the invisible hand breaks down. At the individual level, for example, each worker's goal may be to enhance her odds of promotion by working a little longer. The logic of this strategy, economist Lotte Bailyn explains, follows from the fact that it is much easier for the employer to measure and reward a worker's hours than to measure the amount she actually produces.[36] But if all workers pursue this strategy, they are destined to be frustrated, for no matter how much they work, there are only so many slots for promotion.

And yet the option of cutting back is hardly attractive either. "People who work reduced hours pay a huge penalty" in career terms, says economist Juliet Schor. "It's taken as a negative signal" about their commitment to their employer.[37] Thus, when relative performance is an important determinant of reward, private incentives lead people to work too much.[38] This helps explain the attraction of collective measures—overtime laws and national holidays, for example—whose effect is to reduce the number of hours people work. We will discuss such policies in more detail in chapter 11. For the moment, we observe only that the growth in income and the increased income inequality of recent years—both of which foster demands for positional goods—increase private incentives to work longer hours. In her recent book, Schor has estimated that Americans do indeed work many more hours than they did two decades ago. The increases have been substantial for both men and women, but particularly for women, who worked an average of 22 percent more hours in 1987 than they had in 1969.[39]

Needless to say, if we worked less than we currently do, we would have less income. But then if *everyone* worked less, we would *need* less income, because the amount of income we "need" is in part determined by the amount that others have. Of course, individuals do not face a collective choice between all working more and all working less.

We must each choose individually, since we have no control over what others do. And it is for this reason that private incentives favor excessive work.

Cultivating the Aura of a Winner

The top performers in many winner-take-all markets consume in a manner that befits their incomes: In the walk-in closet in the Hollywood superagent's master bedroom, a rack of Armani suits; for his commute to the office, a Ferrari Testarossa; to keep track of time, a gold Rolex; for his evening meal, dinner at Spago; at day's end, a wooded estate in Brentwood; and for weekends, a Malibu cottage and a chalet in Aspen.

Material possessions like these confer an almost tangible aura of success on their owners. They are effective signals precisely because the vice-president of a small-town bank cannot afford them.

Social circles are highly stratified, and the various layers have their own symbols of success. Someone from the bottom layer cannot mimic the lifestyles of those in the top layer, but within each layer there is at least some room to maneuver. By saving less or borrowing more, a person can buy a more fashionable suit or a better car, and thus alter his apparent position within his circle.

The irony is that, from the individual's point of view, doing so may actually be a good investment. There *is* a link, after all, between a person's ability and the amount of income he earns, which is why there is also a link between the kind of goods he owns and outsiders' estimates of his ability. As clothiers never tire of reminding us, we never get a second chance to make a good first impression. The job applicant who arrives for his interview dressed for success is more likely to be chosen than his rival whose clothes are merely clean and mended.

The more important the job, the more important—and the more expensive—it is to look the part. An aspiring Hollywood agent is ill advised to show up for lunch driving an eight-year-old Ford Escort. In one sense, he cannot afford to buy the new Porsche Carrera; but in another sense, he cannot afford not to. In many winner-take-all markets, the task of creating a favorable impression requires major capital investments.

As compellingly attractive as such investments are from the individual contestant's point of view, however, they contribute virtually nothing to the welfare of contestants as a group. The problem is that in the effort to create a good impression, it is relative, not absolute, performance that counts. When all contestants escalate their expenditures on cars and clothing, no one fares any better than before. The quest to create a good impression is a positional arms race, pure and simple.

Investing in one's own performance is not the only way to forge ahead. Since reward depends on relative performance, an alternative strategy is to sabotage the performance of one's rivals. The assault on skater Nancy Kerrigan by compatriots of rival Tonya Harding is a vivid case in point.

Many forms of sabotage are illegal, of course. But many others are well within the letter, if not the spirit, of the law. A corporation, for example, may impose costs on its rivals by filing antitrust suits accompanied by burdensome information requests.

Many investments in performance enhancement at least have the redeeming feature of resulting in a product or service that is more valuable to buyers. Sabotage clearly lacks this feature, with the result that positional arms races involving sabotage generate even greater welfare losses.

Some Exceptions

A word of caution is in order here. All we are saying is that whenever market incentives would otherwise lead individuals to invest optimally in performance enhancement, rewards that depend on relative performance will lead to excessive investment. This clearly does not imply excessive investment in *all* cases—even those where reward depends on rank. After all, a variety of other factors might cause people to invest *too little* in performance enhancement.

Take, for example, the general problem of shirking by employees, about which there is a large literature in economics.[40] People dislike work, the conventional theory goes, and will expend effort only if their performance can be monitored and rewarded effectively. Thus, when monitoring is costly, workers will tend to devote too little effort to their jobs. In such cases a winner-take-all reward structure that stimulates additional effort might actually result in greater efficiency, not less.

Indeed, firms may sometimes deliberately construct tournament pay schemes for precisely this reason. A bonus may be awarded, for example, to the agent who sells the most units each quarter. Our own focus, by contrast, is on instances in which tournament pay schemes are a natural feature of the market structure, not an artifact imposed for the sake of stimulating extra effort. In these cases, and especially when the rewards to top performers are extremely high, shirking is unlikely to be a serious problem. On the contrary, the same incentives that led Olympic gymnast Kristie Phillips to swallow painkillers so she could keep practicing with a broken wrist are likely to call forth similar levels of effort in other domains as well.

A second qualification to our general claim needs to be taken more seriously. Our argument implies that investment in performance enhancement will be excessive from the point of view of the global economy, but not necessarily from the perspective of individual nations within it. Citizens of the world at large, for example, might fare better if we spent more dollars on food and health care, and fewer dollars on improving the picture clarity of HDTV. But to the citizens of the nation that developed the winning HDTV technology, things might look very different. The winner's rewards from capturing the world market are likely to be more than sufficient to compensate for its own investments in R&D. This observation will be especially important when, in chapter 11, we examine policies for dealing with winner-take-all markets. Individual nations will often have little interest in curtailing arms races in which they have a good chance to win.

8

The Battle for Educational Prestige

As college professors for more than two decades, we have witnessed a steady shift in the career aspirations of our most able students. Whereas these students once tended to favor careers in science, engineering, and other academic disciplines, increasingly they have responded to the lure of six-figure paychecks in law and finance. Thus the number of new lawyers admitted annually to the bar, which stood at 19,000 in 1969–70, had risen to 47,000 in 1989–90.[1] During that same period, the ratio of doctorates to bachelor's degrees granted by American universities fell from 0.064 to less than 0.04.[2]

As the financial rewards in law and finance have grown, so has competition for the top jobs in those professions. Imagine the problem confronting the hiring officers of Wall Street investment banking firms, which attract literally thousands of ostensibly well-qualified applicants for each entry-level position. According to one account, almost half of Yale's 1986 graduating class interviewed for a position with First Boston.[3]

Given the costs of sorting through the deluge of resumes, it was inevitable that firms would come to rely heavily on educational credentials. By now few students can have missed the message that without an elite degree, access to the professional fast track has become increasingly difficult. Elite educational credentials have also become increasingly important in the quest for admission to the nation's leading graduate and professional schools. Recall, for example, our account in chapter 1 of the student from a small Florida college who was rejected by Harvard in spite of a straight-A record and the unqualified praise of her academic advisers.

Many of the nation's most prestigious employers have an interest in hiring the graduates of elite institutions quite independently of how they perform on the job. Consider the CEO of a floundering Fortune 500 company faced with the task of hiring a management consulting firm. He interviews the consulting teams from two firms and finds that they are indistinguishable in terms of their ability to respond to his concerns and formulate initial strategic plans. One team, however, consists of graduates of Stanford, Harvard, and Chicago, while the other is made up of graduates of less distinguished institutions.

With nothing more to go on, the CEO will have a compelling interest in choosing the former team. He wants, after all, to tell his board that he got the best advice available, and because the quality of advice is inherently difficult to evaluate, educational credentials can sharply increase the likelihood of a favorable assessment. McKinsey & Co., the nation's leading management consulting firm, has disproportionate access to the most lucrative consulting contracts in the industry, and elite educational credentials are the "sine qua non for membership in this outfit—filled as it is with Baker Scholars from the Harvard Business School, Rhodes scholars, White House Fellows, nuclear physicists, and Ph.D.s in the hard sciences."[4]

Students are remarkably sophisticated about these matters. If access to the top jobs depends more and more on educational credentials, we would expect them to do everything in their power to improve their credentials, and indeed they have. Education's growing role as gatekeeper has given rise to increasingly intense competition for admission into the nation's leading colleges and universities. Whereas it was once common for the brightest high school students to attend state universities close to home, increasingly they matriculate at a small handful of the most selective private institutions of higher learning.

The universities that have been losing top students have not given up without a fight, however. Elite educational status is what these students want, and one way a university can provide it is to hire faculty with visible and influential research records. The increased bidding for these faculty, we will see, has given rise to winner-take-all markets even in the hallowed halls of academe. The salaries of star professors have grown substantially, both in absolute and in relative terms, even as they have experienced significant reductions in their teaching duties.

These competitive pressures have confronted universities with an increasingly painful dilemma. Bidding for academic superstars places greater strains on budgets that are already stretched thin; and yet failure to maintain their place in the academic hierarchy can lead to still more daunting costs. Most schools have attempted to remain competitive, and in the process, tuition costs have escalated sharply.

Determinants of Educational Status

There is no mystery about which colleges and universities constitute the elite in American higher education. As noted by the sociologists Paul Kingston and Lionel Lewis, "prestige is a somewhat amorphous asset. Yet, for all the shadings of eliteness, there is remarkable continuity and consistency—among raters and over time—in the rankings of undergraduate schools."[5] Some three dozen schools consistently place at the top of the rankings in college guides and news magazines. The eleven institutions identified by one study as best in the nation in 1940 have appeared at or near the top of most of the rankings published since then.[6]

What factors govern membership in this elite? A reputation for a long tradition of academic excellence is clearly important—indeed, perhaps too important in some instances. Respondents in one survey, for example, are said to have listed Princeton as one of the ten best law schools in the country even though Princeton has never had a law school. Yet it is equally clear that reputations cannot be sustained indefinitely in the face of objective evidence to the contrary. The schools at the top of the academic totem pole do in fact consistently score higher than others on objective measures of faculty and student quality, the two most important components of academic prestige.[7]

Student quality is measured in part by grades and test scores, but includes other less formal criteria as well. For example, elite schools strongly favor applicants with significant achievements outside the classroom, such as having published a story in *The New Yorker* or having won a figure-skating title. Their ability to attract such students, and the high visibility these students often achieve after graduation, further enhances the institution's reputation.

How about the faculty? Direct measures of the quality of a faculty's research focus primarily on the quantity and influence of its publications. The influence of research is measured in a variety of ways, including the selectiveness of the journals in which it is published, the frequency with which it is cited by other scholars, and the extent to which it is singled out for such academic awards as the Nobel Prize.

The faculty and students of elite institutions thus coexist in a relationship in which each helps to determine the status of the other. Students acquire enhanced academic status merely by attending schools in which top faculty are known to teach; for their part, faculty members gain status by teaching in schools that are known to attract top students.

Changes in the quality of either group are thus likely to set in motion a chain of self-reinforcing processes.[8] For example, a direct consequence of adopting a more generous financial aid policy for gifted students would be to increase the number of such students who choose to attend. But there would be indirect effects as well. Having better students would make it possible to attract better faculty, and having better faculty would, in turn, make it still easier to attract better students.

For that matter, merely having better students makes it possible to attract better students. For example, one survey found that top high school students tend to judge college quality primarily on the basis of the achievements of the student body.[9] A second study found that applicants tend to prefer colleges that matriculate students abler than themselves, the optimal choice being a school whose students' average combined SAT score exceeded their own by roughly one hundred points.[10] Unlike Garrison Keillor's mythical Lake Wobegon, Ideal U. is apparently a place where all the students are below average.

Benefits of High Academic Status

No matter how it is measured, academic status is of critical importance for the distribution of resources, both within academia and beyond. Thus forty of the most prestigious institutions received more than half of the $3.4 billion donated by private foundations and corporations to institutions of higher learning in the 1989–90 academic year.[11] The top ten universities alone received more than 20 percent of these funds.[12]

Governmental research and fellowship support is similarly concentrated among the nation's leading universities. In 1981, 28 percent of the $4.4 billion in federal funding for academic research and development went to just ten universities.[13] And as we noted in chapter 2, some two-thirds of the nearly 700 recipients of the prestigious National Science Foundation Graduate Fellowships chose to attend one of just ten universities in 1988.

Academic prestige benefits not only the high-ranked institutions themselves but also the faculty and students who populate them. From the perspective of a faculty member, an appointment at a high-ranked institution confers both the intrinsic satisfaction of high status and a variety of other, more tangible rewards. Consider identical twins with identical academic records except that, by some twist of fate, one teaches at an elite institution, whereas her sister teaches at a lower-ranked school. The first twin's papers are more likely to be accepted by leading professional journals.[14] Her books are more likely to be discussed in the *New York Review of Books*. Her applications for research grants are more likely to be funded. She is more likely to enjoy lucrative consulting opportunities. If she writes a textbook, it will sell more copies. She is more likely to be invited to give lectures and be asked to join other leading scholars at professional conferences. And she is also more likely to enjoy the stimulus of working with gifted colleagues and students.

Her twin faces considerably less attractive prospects. Noting the cumulative-advantage process of academic careers in science, the sociologist Robert Merton offered this bleak portrayal of the conditions confronting scholars who fail to land at a top-ranked institution:

Absent or in short supply are the resources or access to needed equipment, an abundance of able assistance, time institutionally set aside for research, and, above all else perhaps, a cognitive microenvironment composed of colleagues at the research front who are themselves evokers of excellence, bringing out the best in the people around them. Not least is the special resource of being located at strategic nodes in the networks of scientific communication that provide ready access to information at the frontiers of research.[15]

The individual student at a high-ranked university enjoys a similar constellation of benefits. He is more likely to be granted admission to a leading graduate or professional school, and more likely to land a top starting job. And no matter what career path he chooses, the network of faculty and student contacts he develops in school will enhance his opportunities for a lifetime.

A 1990 survey by *Fortune* documents the extent to which graduates of elite schools hold the top positions in the business world.[16] *Fortune* obtained responses from nearly 1,500 current and former CEOs of Fortune 500 and Service 500 companies ("service" companies are those in banking, insurance, and so on). Almost all these top executives (93 percent) had graduated from college, and the seven schools that led the list were Yale, Princeton, Harvard, Northwestern, Cornell, Columbia, and Stanford, all elite private universities. These seven schools claimed 166 CEO-respondents as undergraduate alumni. The author notes: "The dominance of the Ivy League is, if anything, increasing: Whereas 14 percent of the former CEOs surveyed hold Ivy League undergraduate degrees, nearly 19 percent of the current CEOs do."[17]

Of course, only relatively few alumni from any school, elite or otherwise, become CEOs of Fortune 500 companies. But taken as a whole, graduates of elite schools are much more successful in the labor market than are graduates of other colleges and universities. This is no surprise, given that students at elite schools are selected for many personal qualities that also predict success on the job.

The best evidence of the value of an elite degree comes from an unusually rich data set, the National Longitudinal Study of the High School Class of 1972, which followed this cohort through 1986. Economist Estelle James and her coauthors report their analysis of a sample of males who had graduated from college and who worked for an employer in 1985. The authors found that even after controlling for the individual worker's academic performance, the overall selectivity of his alma mater (as measured by average SAT scores of its freshman class) had a considerable effect—each additional one hundred points of average combined SAT scores increased earnings by about 4 percent. And alumni of private eastern schools earned a few percent more than others even after controlling for this measure of selectivity.

With these benefits in view, it is not surprising that the best students have always been concentrated in the top-ranked colleges and universities. And as we will presently see, they have become increasingly so in recent decades.

Trends in Concentration of Top Students

One way to identify the most able college-bound seniors is to use the lists of winners of national merit-based prizes. For example, the Westinghouse Science Talent Search, begun in 1942, identifies high school seniors talented in science, mathematics, and engineering. Just forty finalists are selected each year nationwide. For the period 1960–89, fully half of these finalists matriculated at just one of seven universities: Harvard alone attracted one-fifth of all finalists, followed, by MIT, Princeton, Stanford, Yale, Cal Tech, and Cornell.

Presidential Scholars have also typically chosen one of the elite universities. The Presidential Scholars Program was established in 1964 "to recognize and honor our nation's most distinguished graduating high school seniors." Two winners are selected from each state, and up to fifteen winners are chosen at large. We obtained data for scholars selected during 1987–89, and found that, as in the case of the Westinghouse finalists, the top seven choices accounted for half of the total. Harvard alone matriculated 18 percent, followed by Princeton, Stanford, Yale, MIT, Duke, and Michigan. Note that five of these schools appear on both lists of the top seven.

Although the reputational ranking of colleges and universities is nearly the same now as it was several decades ago, there is evidence that the importance of reputation in the competition for top students has increased in recent years. For the Westinghouse Science Talent

Search, we found that the top seven universities attracted 59 percent of the finalists in the 1980s, more than ten percentage points higher than in the 1970s.

Further indications of rising concentration are evident in the college choices of the much larger group of high school seniors who have not necessarily won one of these prizes but have credentials sufficient to gain admission to the most selective schools. One method for identifying members of this group (albeit with a large number of errors of both inclusion and exclusion) is the SAT, taken by all but a few students who intend to apply to a selective college.

Peterson's Guide to Four-Year Colleges reports the fraction of each freshman class that scored above 500, 600, and 700 on each of the SAT tests (verbal and math). The most selective of these six categories consists of students who scored above 700 on the SATV. In 1989 only 9,510 (less than 1 percent) of the 1.1 million seniors who took the SAT scored this high. Of this group, we estimate that 4,075 (42.8 percent) matriculated at one of the thirty-three colleges and universities designated as "most competitive" by *Barron's*.[18] Since these schools matriculated only 2.4 percent of the seniors taking the SAT in that year, this result demonstrates an extraordinary degree of concentration.[19]

If anything, this measure tends to be an understatement because some of the seniors with a high SATV were not qualified for admission to an elite school. If it were possible to exclude them from our tabulation, the resulting measure of concentration would be still higher. The top four universities (Harvard, Princeton, Stanford, and Yale) had a combined freshman class equal to only 0.5 percent of all those who took the SAT, but included 17.5 percent of all those scoring above 700 on the SATV

Between 1979 and 1989 students scoring over 700 on their SATV who chose one of the "most competitive" colleges on the *Barron's* list increased from 32 to 43 percent, even though the number of matriculants at these schools increased only slightly during this period.[20]

The trend toward increased concentration of top students in at least some leading universities began well before the 1980s. For example, the median combined SAT score for entering freshmen at Harvard, which stood at 1191 in 1952, had already risen to 1388 by

1965. The relative quality of Harvard students (as measured by SATs, prizes, and other indicators) has improved still further since then.

The increase in concentration of top students at Harvard and other elite schools does not appear to be the result of a change in relative prices of private and public education. On the contrary, because the relative price of attending an elite private school has been increasing over the last two decades,[21] the observed increase in concentration must have resulted from an increase in demand for elite universities.

Economist Charles Clotfelter argues that demand has grown in part from the substantial increase in the income and wealth of households in the top fifth of the income distribution,[22] which supply a disproportionate share of the students who attend elite schools.[23] He notes, for example, that between 1977 and 1987 the average income of households in the top quintile increased in real terms by 12.5 percent. Stock market and real estate values also increased sharply during this period, and there were two cuts in the top rate of the federal income tax.

But affordability is not the whole explanation. A recent study by Princeton University vice-president Richard Spies[24] finds a large increase in recent years in the probability that a student with given characteristics, including family income, would apply to an elite private school.[25] Using his results, we estimate that the likelihood that a student with a combined SAT score of 1400 applied for admission to one of a group of thirty-three elite schools increased from 50 percent in 1976 to 72 percent in 1987.

Although the elite schools that Spies studied were all selective, private, and expensive, a number of public schools also have strong academic reputations. We have made some preliminary attempts to check whether demand has also shifted toward relatively more prestigious public institutions. Thus we studied the distribution of students among the eight campuses of the University of California, finding that Berkeley, the flagship campus, dramatically increased its share of the best U.C. students during the 1980s. For example, the percentage of U.C. freshmen with SAT verbal scores above 750 who chose the Berkeley campus rose from 36.1 percent in 1980 to 71.7 percent in 1988. The corresponding figures for U.C. freshmen with SAT math scores above 750 were 40.2 percent and 50.0 percent, respectively.

In sum there is considerable evidence that students who are qualified for admission to an elite school were more likely to choose such a school in the late 1980s than they were a decade earlier. There is also evidence that the trend toward increased concentration began well before the 1980s. These changes cannot be accounted for by trends in tuition and other costs, and they did not result solely from changes in the income distribution.

Of course, there are other possible explanations. Colleges and universities spent more on recruiting students during this period because of concerns about the declining population of eighteen-year-olds, and this effort may have encouraged college-bound seniors to consider schools that they would otherwise have ignored. We also know that college applicants as a group invested more in "shopping" for the right option: In 1988, 37 percent of college freshmen said they had applied to three or more colleges, a higher percentage than ever before.[26] Only 15 percent applied to that many in 1968.

Numerous social commentators have described the 1980s as a time of increased materialism, conspicuous consumption, and brand-name consciousness. The colleges with the most prestigious brand names may have been the beneficiaries of this general cultural shift. The proliferation of publications offering national rankings of colleges and universities may be one quantifiable aspect of this shift.

On-Campus Recruiting

Another possibility is that the shift in concentration may be related to trends in the job market for entry-level managers and professionals, including greater emphasis on educational credentials and a relative decline in preference for graduates of local colleges and universities. For example, top students should find a university more attractive if favored employers actively recruit there. And elite employers, for their part, have an obvious incentive to focus on universities that attract top students. Thus the choices of students and recruiters tend to reinforce one another: As top students become more concentrated in elite universities, elite firms will concentrate more of their recruiting in those universities; and this makes elite universities still more attractive to top students.

In an attempt to learn more about the behavior of recruiters, we conducted a survey of past, current, and expected future recruiting practices of a sample of firms that recruit at Cornell University, an Ivy League school that is consistently among the most selective in the nation. Firms in the sample indicated that almost half of the colleges they visited in the last year consistently rank among the top twenty-five nationwide.[27]

We asked respondents to report whether the ratio of top-ranked campus visits to total campus visits had increased, decreased, or remained the same over the past ten years. Thirty-five percent reported an increase, only 13 percent a decrease. (The remaining 51 percent reported no change.) When asked how they expected their proportion of visits to elite universities to change in the future, 22 percent expected an increase, whereas only 10 percent expected a decrease. Sixty-eight percent expected no change from the current ratio.

In a further analysis of our survey data, we found that it was the "elite" firms that were most likely to report an increased focus on the top universities. "Elite" was defined for this purpose to mean that the firm conducted at least 70 percent of its campus visits and total interviews at top-twenty-five universities, and was either one of the largest firms in its industry grouping, or appeared on the Levering list of the 100 most attractive companies as viewed by employees. This definition gave us a subsample of about half (thirty-nine) of the firms in our survey.

The observed pattern of changes is the one we expected. Forty-one percent of elite firms had increased their proportion of visits to top-ranked universities during the last decade; only 8 percent had decreased that proportion. The corresponding figures for other firms are 30 percent and 19 percent, respectively.

Cornell's undergraduate placement director, Thomas Devlin, told us that he has observed a steady trend toward more targeted recruiting over the last two decades. He reports that firms have become less likely to choose campuses on the basis of geographic proximity, and more likely to choose on the basis of student characteristics. His impressions are thus consistent with the responses of the firms we surveyed. Both lend support to the more general claim that top students have more to gain than ever by attending an elite university.

The increased focus of elite corporate recruiters on elite campuses may often generate large costs that would otherwise be avoidable. For example, a top student might once have found it attractive to attend a nearby state university because the presence of other top students there meant that it would be worthwhile for elite recruiters to visit the campus. But once sufficiently many top students migrate from state universities to elite schools, this is no longer a safe assumption. By going to the nearby state university, the top student may be much more likely to be overlooked by elite employers and graduate schools.

The elite university's higher tuition and greater distance from family represent painful sacrifices for many top students. When Jim Besaw was a top senior at John Marshall High School in Rochester, Minnesota, in the spring of 1994, he was offered a full scholarship to Carleton College, a small, highly selective liberal arts school in his native state. Even though his father is retired and his mother earns only $8,000 a year, Besaw passed up the Carleton scholarship to enter Yale's freshman class. "I'm willing to lose some money now, and take out a loan, because I feel I might get a better job if I go to one of the more prestigious schools,"[28] he explained. Many other students apparently agree, as Yale's applications posted a 21 percent increase in 1994.

The Educational Tracking Debate

What has been the effect of this increased concentration of top students on the overall quality of educational services? There are clearly many benefits. For example, the most gifted and scholastically motivated students are placed on a fast track, where they are challenged by their course work and each other to realize their full intellectual potential. Later in life they will form a network with the other alumni, many of whom will be in a position to help them in their careers. Thus those with the most to offer in this information-age economy will be given the greatest opportunity.

Another advantage to the current arrangement is that the obvious advantages of attending an elite school will help motivate some of our most gifted high school students. In an effort to establish a record that will pass muster at Stanford or MIT, they will study harder, sign up for more difficult course work, do volunteer work, and seek to excel in sports or drama or the mastery of a foreign language.

But increased concentration of top students also entails costs. Most notably it has resulted in socially wasteful cram courses aimed at boosting performance on the SATs. And the loss of top students from the second- or third-tier schools deprives the remaining students at those schools of whatever personal or organizational benefits derive from additional contact with top students. Among other things, it diminishes the value of the honors curriculum that many large state universities offer to their best students. Economists Michael McPherson and Morton Schapiro, for example, discuss evidence that the beneficial effects of associating with talented peers taper off beyond some point, and suggest that our brightest students might contribute more to overall educational achievement if they were less concentrated in the elite institutions.[29] And to the extent that outstanding faculty are drawn to an elite school by the effects of tracking, students in the nonelite schools lose the benefit of their services.

Another cost of tracking is that it diminishes the opportunities for late bloomers—those whose true high academic potential becomes apparent only after they begin college. As Alan Gregg has described this problem:

> By being generous with time, yes, lavish with it, Nature allows man an extraordinary chance to learn. What gain can there be, then, in throwing away this natural advantage by rewarding precocity, as we certainly do when we gear the grades in school to chronological age by starting the first grade at the age of six, and so college entrance for the vast majority at seventeen and a half to nineteen? For, once you have most of your students the same age, the academic rewards . . . go to those who are uncommonly bright for their age. In other words, you have rewarded precocity, which may or may not be the precursor of later ability. So, in effect, you have unwittingly belittled man's cardinal educational capital—time to mature.[30]

The burdens imposed on late bloomers by the current system are even more troubling in light of Robert Merton's suggestion that the penalty for being a late bloomer is considerably heavier for students whose socioeconomic status was low to begin with.[31]

The efficiency gains from increasing the concentration of top students in elite schools thus come at a cost. Among the losers are the late bloomers and other gifted students who, for whatever reason, have been left behind in the shift to elite schools. We know of no way to assess the relative magnitudes of these gains and losses.

The allocation of students among universities has implications not only for efficiency but also for equity. Several studies report, for example, that family income is an important predictor of who applies to and attends an elite school, even after controlling for high-school grades, standardized-test scores, parents' education, and other personal characteristics.[32] This is true even though postwar admissions policies at elite private schools have become largely meritocratic. Upper-income students are thus able to take advantage of the high returns on an investment in an elite education, whereas middle-class students of equal ability are often forced to settle for less.

Is the trend toward higher concentration likely to change? Although the brochures of elite schools emphasize their commitment to enhanced "diversity" in the composition of their student bodies, we speak from experience in saying that these schools perceive no particular virtue in diversity with respect to academic ability. The late Sen. Roman Hruska (R., Neb.) was ridiculed when he argued for G. Harrold Carswell's nomination to the Supreme Court on the grounds that people of mediocre intellect also deserve representation on the nation's highest court. The admissions committees of elite schools would likewise ridicule any suggestion that students of modest intellectual ability be admitted simply to create a class that is more representative of the population (rather than, say, to make possible a better football team).

Existing social and economic forces thus all but assure that the nation's best students will continue to become more concentrated in the elite schools. We share in the general perception that this implicit tracking system makes sense pedagogically, but only up to a point. Whether we have passed that point remains an open question. But even if we have not, there are still grounds for concern about the implications of current trends for social mobility and fairness.

Consequences of the Race for Academic Prestige

Bad Moves That Work

For as long as universities have been granting formal degrees, there have been committees whose task it has been to rule on the curriculum requirements for those degrees. The theory behind these requirements is simple enough: Students between the ages of seventeen and twenty-two are often in a poor position to know what courses will be of greatest value to them later in life; and even when they do know, they will sometimes lack the necessary motivation to take certain challenging courses.

Of course, degree requirements also entail costs. At the very least, they deny students flexibility even when students have the necessary wisdom, maturity, and self-discipline to make good use of it. And so most systems entail compromises: Many courses are required of all students; many others are required only of students who elect to major in a given subject; and a large block is left as free electives. The system is far from perfect, but in view of the multiple and often conflicting objectives that shaped its design, it works well enough.

In 1969 Brown University launched a radical new approach by essentially abandoning conventional degree requirements. Students became largely free, under Brown's policy, to design their own courses of study. Since all policies regarding degree requirements are the products of compromise, Brown's new policy was obviously not completely without merit. Yet it is fair to say that educational experts were at the time, and remain, highly skeptical about it.

Student reaction to the new policy was a different matter. The very thought of attending an Ivy League university without degree requirements seemed almost too good to be true. Brown's applications shot up sharply. And with so many additional students to choose from, the university could afford to be pickier. Always selective, Brown soon became the most selective school in the nation in terms of the SAT scores of its entering freshmen. In a word, Brown got hot.

This raises an interesting and paradoxical issue. Suppose, for the sake of argument, that Brown's new curriculum policy was academically ill advised. On that view, it might seem that the quality of education at Brown was destined to suffer as a result. But curriculum policy is only one of many ingredients that govern quality of education. Having a brighter freshman class meant that professors were able to set a more challenging pace in the classroom, and that students had richer opportunities to learn from one another. In the now-familiar success-breeds-success pattern, having brighter students also made it easier to attract more of the same, as well as more highly qualified faculty.

All things considered, then, it simply does not follow that the quality of education declined at Brown in the wake of its questionable curriculum policy. On the contrary, a good case can be made that the quality of education at Brown is higher now than ever.

However, the mere fact that the policy change may have worked well for Brown does not imply that such changes would be a good move for higher education generally. As in other arms races, policies that are compellingly advantageous for each side are often transparently harmful for people as a whole. Brown's policy helped it to attract good students and faculty who otherwise would have ended up elsewhere. If other institutions match Brown's move (which, to varying degrees, some have), the initial distribution of talent may eventually be restored. But to the extent that there were sound reasons for having curriculum requirements in the first place, there is every reason to suspect that the new situation will be worse than the old. Brown's policy may have been a bad move that worked for Brown. If so, it puts pressure on other institutions to make the same bad move.

Catering to the Rankings

Published national academic rankings have become increasingly important in determining students' decisions about where to apply. This is especially true for the nation's business schools, where most applicants pay full tuition themselves and are therefore extremely focused on getting maximum career advantage. It is a rare business student who fails to matriculate at the most highly ranked school that accepted him.

Over time the *Business Week* poll has emerged as the leading arbiter of business school rankings. Every two years, the magazine's staff surveys students, corporate recruiters, and others who are associated with the nation's most prominent MBA degree programs. The magazine also considers the selectivity of each school's admission process, together with various measures of student-body achievement, such as test scores, and salaries before and after graduation. Results are assigned weights and combined to produce an overall score, which is then used to rank the schools. The special autumn edition in which the results are published every other year has become one of *Business Week's* biggest sellers.

When a school moves significantly upward or downward in the *Business Week* rankings, there ensues a large and almost immediate change in its number of applications, and ten months later, a corresponding change in the quality of its entering class. Since business school budgets are driven largely by student tuition payments, the *Business Week* rankings have become very important—so important, in fact, that schools have begun to alter their behavior in an effort to achieve higher scores.

It would obviously be a good thing if these changes were designed primarily to boost the quality of the schools' educational programs. But, although some changes may have had that effect, many others seem designed only to influence the numbers. For example, since *Business Week* interviews graduates only in alternate years, some schools have begun to reallocate resources with this in mind. Where possible, the best instructors are assigned to teach classes taken by students in the *Business Week* cohort. Rather than increase the resources devoted to teaching generally, the survey thus rewards schools that shift resources from one class to another. And in general, the more unequally resources are distributed, the less effective overall teaching will be.

Students in the *Business Week* class often get preferential treatment by the placement office; and they are often the beneficiaries of special receptions, orientation sessions, and other attempts to curry favor. Professors experience increased pressure not to give poor grades or take other steps that might make students unhappy, lest their angry comments cost the school points in the *Business Week* poll. Having received harsh comments from its graduating class in one *Business Week* survey, a leading school was said to have written a letter to its next *Business Week* class pointing out to them that their evaluations would have direct repercussions on the economic value of their degrees.

As troubling as these steps are, attempts to "game" the *Business Week* survey may have only just begun. For example, a school might gain ground in the rankings by simply waiving its normal application fee. This would encourage more students to apply, and since *Business Week* measures selectivity as the ratio of the number accepted to the number who apply, this would boost the school's selectivity score. In the area of recruiter ratings, *Business Week* tries to compensate for the fact that recruiters tend to have less knowledge about smaller schools by boosting the recruiter ratings by 50 percent for schools with entering classes smaller than two hundred. It is easy to imagine some schools near this threshold cutting their enrollments deliberately to qualify for the bonus.

Of course, the *Business Week* poll also helps match the most talented students with the top-rated programs, which, as noted earlier, can have productive consequences. Whether the growing prominence of published rankings is, on balance, a good thing thus remains an empirical question. But it would surely be worthwhile to look for less costly ways to solve the assignment problem.

Financial Implications

When a student who would have gone to the University of Texas decides instead to matriculate at Harvard, his parents swell with pride. But the same decision is viewed very differently by state legislators and university administrators in Texas. Legislators worry about the "brain drain." They know that when top students go to college out of state, they are much less likely to live and work in Texas after graduation—and therefore much less likely to pay taxes. Moreover, their absence makes it much harder for the state to attract employers who offer skilled jobs at high wages. University administrators worry that the loss of top students makes it harder to attract other top students, which, in turn, makes it harder to attract and retain top faculty.

These fears undoubtedly do much to explain why in 1983 the University of Texas offered Harvard physicist Steven Weinberg, a Nobel laureate, a salary of $110,000—an unprecedentedly high salary at the time—to join the Texas faculty. In the years since, however, six-figure salaries have become increasingly common in academia, as universities have attempted to woo the handful of leading scholars in each field whose presence brings instant recognition to their home departments.

There is growing anecdotal evidence of this tendency to spend large sums in order to attract highly visible lecturers, even some who lack traditional academic credentials. The University of South Carolina, for example, paid Jihan Sadat, widow of slain Egyptian President Anwar Sadat, more than $300,000 to teach a single course on Egyptian culture for three semesters.[33] South Carolina also paid Howard Simons, former managing editor of the *Washington Post,* $45,000 for lecturing on campus once a week for a single semester.[34]

We were able to obtain one crude measure of the salary growth of the nation's most distinguished research faculty by examining data supplied to us by the Center for Advanced Study in the Behavioral Sciences. Each year, the center invites a group of distinguished scholars in the social and behavioral sciences to spend their sabbatical leaves in its idyllic, parklike setting in the hills above the Stanford University campus. Because the center provides most of its fellows with one-half their previous academic year's salaries, it is a uniquely valuable source of information on how the salaries of leading researchers have changed over time. The average salary of the five most highly paid center fellows each year grew at an annual rate of more than 7 percent between 1986 and 1992. By contrast, average faculty salaries nationwide grew at an annual rate of only 4.3 percent.[35]

Another consequence of the increased bidding for distinguished faculty has been reduced teaching loads. Whereas in the 1970s it was common to see teaching loads of four semester courses a year in the leading research universities, in the years since it has become increasingly common to see three-course loads. And a growing number of top researchers now have positions that require no teaching at all.

All these changes have put university budgets under increasing pressure and have led to steady increases in tuition. Indeed, except for medical care, the cost of higher education in the United States has risen faster than any other major expenditure category in recent decades. Between 1970 and 1990, for example, the average tuition bill at private universities rose 474 percent while the consumer price index rose only 248 percent.[36] Other important factors behind tuition inflation have been the rapid growth of administrative staff (which has risen 123 percent in the last fifteen years[37]), and more expensive laboratories and libraries.[38]

Prestigious scientific laboratories have grown especially costly in recent years, as schools eager to move up in the academic pecking order have attempted to bid established labs away from rival institutions. Education analysts trace this latest development to an expensive campaign in which Florida State University lured a prominent magnet laboratory from MIT.[39] Florida State's successful effort was joined by the University of Florida and the Los Alamos National Laboratory, which were promised greater access to the lab than they had enjoyed at MIT, and by the state of Florida, which contributed $66 million for new lab installations. "It's a jungle out there," said David Merkowitz, a spokesman for an educational trade association. "A lot of the competition is for existing money, and these are ways for institutions to build prestige fairly quickly. It's kind of like competing for an automobile plant."[40] "It's not unlike professional sports," said Yale University spokesman Gary Fryer when informed that Yale had lost its prestigious Arbovirus Research Unit to the University of Texas, which offered new laboratories and a promise to integrate the unit with its own tropical disease center. "You have people who are very talented, and sometimes they move."[41]

The battle for elite educational credentials entails many consequences, some of them positive, others negative. But this much is sure: It will continue to put upward pressure on the cost of higher education. In chapter 11 we will suggest how at least some of the negative consequences of the educational arms race might be avoided.

9

Curbing Wasteful Competition

Centuries ago a European gentleman's response to a profound insult was to challenge the offending party to a duel. Accompanied by their seconds, the antagonists would typically assemble at dawn for their contest, which was governed by several formal rules. One specified the physical distance between the antagonists at the actual moment of the duel itself. It called for them to stand back to back, then march off a given number of paces before each turned to fire. A second rule governed the characteristics of the guns employed. Among other things, it specified that the barrels of the guns must be smooth, as opposed to having spiral grooves; and it called for weapons that fired only a single shot.

The transparent purpose of each of these rules was to reduce the odds of being killed. Establishing physical separation between the duelists made it more likely that their shots would miss than if they simply turned and fired at point-blank range. The purpose of requiring smooth gun barrels was to make the trajectories of the bullets less true. "Rifling"—the engraving of spiral grooves on the inner surface of a gun barrel—imparts a spin to the bullet as it leaves the weapon. This causes the bullet to follow a much straighter trajectory than it would if the barrel had been smooth, much as a football thrown with a tight spiral tends to be more accurate than one without. Projectiles that lack spin tend to wobble and flutter erratically, like the knuckleball in baseball. To appreciate the utility of the single-shot restriction, we need only imagine the fate of duelists who faced off with one-hundred-shot assault rifles.

These restrictions served their intended purpose. Thus one study of some two hundred British duels concluded that only one in six duelists was even hit by his opponent's bullet, and only one in fourteen was killed.[1] These figures probably overstate the true casualty rates, since "very many duels which left no business for the coroner must have gone unregistered."[2] Yet even these odds were a high price to pay for defending one's honor. And indeed, virtually all industrial societies have now made dueling illegal.

Unregulated dueling has many of the characteristics of a winner-take-all contest. In chapter 7 we described how such contests almost invariably result in mutually offsetting, and hence socially wasteful, patterns of investment. Here we will examine how the resulting inefficiencies, in turn, appear to have spawned a variety of formal and informal institutional arrangements aimed at restricting socially wasteful investment. Because these arrangements function like treaties that limit military weapons, we call them "positional arms control agreements." Not all of these arrangements play out in markets that bestow large prizes. Indeed, many affect ordinary citizens in their daily lives. As we have repeatedly seen, however, small early advantages often become decisive over time, and hence the attraction of controlling positional arms races even when the stakes seem small.

Positional Arms Control Agreements in Sports

The world of sports provides a rich source of examples not only of positional arms races, but also of the kinds of agreements, norms, and rules that have been developed to curtail them. The primary vehicle for the enforcement of these restrictions is the sports league, or governing body: in college sports, the NCAA and various regional conferences; in professional basketball, the NBA; in professional football, the NFL; and in professional baseball, the commissioner and league presidents. All these leagues enforce a variety of rules and regulations whose primary purpose is to curtail patterns of mutually offsetting investment.

Many of these regulations curtail expenditures. Most sports, for example, impose team roster limits for this purpose. Major-league baseball permits franchises to have only twenty-five players on their rosters during the regular season. The NFL sets roster limits at forty-nine, the NBA at twelve, and so on. In the absence of these limits, any team could increase its chances of winning by adding players. But other teams would inevitably follow suit, and teams taken as a whole would continue to win exactly 50 percent of all games played. On the plausible view that, beyond some point, larger rosters do not add appreciably to the entertainment value delivered to fans, roster limits are a sensible way to deliver this entertainment at a more reasonable cost.

Revenue sharing—the practice whereby team owners pool and share gate and television revenues with each other—is another common device for limiting expenditures. Because fans strongly prefer to watch winning teams, there is a strong link between a team's winning percentage and the amount of television and gate revenues the team generates. Without revenue sharing, owners thus face powerful incentives to bid for star players, coaches, scouts, and other inputs that make winning more likely. Revenue sharing weakens these incentives and thus helps to restrain player salaries and other key costs.

Some sports leagues, the NBA and NFL in particular, employ pay caps that limit each team's payroll to a given percentage of total league revenues. One purpose here is to preserve competitive balance by preventing large-city franchises from bidding top players away from small-city franchises.[3] But the more interesting feature of pay caps is that they prevent both large- and small-city franchise owners from getting into an all-out bidding war for one another's players. Even with pay caps in place, of course, salaries for the best players are very high. And since lots of highly talented athletes are still willing to play for these salaries, the effect of the pay caps is to reduce the total outlay required to field a competitive team.

Now, it might seem that this particular positional arms control mechanism is little better than a cartel that cuts payrolls while doing nothing to assure that owners pass the savings along to fans. Yet franchise owners have reason to worry that fans will complain to their elected representatives if the owners appear to be profiting excessively at fan expense. Given a sufficient desire to maintain the goodwill of fans, or a sufficient fear of regulation, pay caps are likely to constrain ticket prices.

Drug rules are another common positional arms control agreement in sports. Almost all athletic leagues and conferences now have regulations that prohibit the consumption of anabolic steroids, human growth hormones, and other performance-enhancing drugs. Most leagues also have programs of mandatory random testing to enforce these rules.

Some leagues have even attempted to limit the number of times teams can practice. Most NCAA Division I college football teams, for example, are limited to two practice seasons, one in the spring, the other in late summer. Both sessions are arduous and time-consuming, but the spring session imposes a particular burden on student athletes, coming as it does in the midst of the academic term. If all schools were to eliminate the spring practice session, the absolute quality of play would fall a bit, but the competitive balance within each conference would be largely unaffected. Indeed, the Ivy League once had a rule that no members could conduct football practice sessions during the spring term, a rule that it reluctantly abandoned in the wake of consistent losses to nonleague opponents that were not bound by it.

Eligibility requirements are another way of holding competitive pressures in check. Escalating pressures in college sports have resulted in a gradual erosion of the academic standards applied to student athletes. In some football programs, graduation rates of less than 10 percent are not uncommon, and some players cannot read at even the sixth-grade level. For any one school to tighten its academic standards unilaterally would weaken its competitive position, since it would then be recruiting from a smaller pool than its rivals. But if schools moved in unison to adopt higher academic standards for student athletes, competitive balance would be maintained. And since the presence of unqualified students undercuts a school's educational mission, there would be clear advantage in taking such a step. Armed with this view of the problem, the NCAA adopted a rule making freshman varsity eligibility contingent on the achievement of a threshold combined score on the SAT. Similarly, the Ivy League has long had a policy that student athletes are to be admitted according to the same criteria applied to other students. And Texas has a policy that high school athletes are ineligible for competition unless they pass all their courses.

Protective equipment requirements are another common positional arms control agreement. Economist Thomas Schelling has observed that when hockey players are left to decide for themselves, they generally play without helmets. And yet when given a chance to vote in a secret ballot, most favor a rule that mandates helmet wearing. The apparent contradiction is rooted in the logic of the positional arms race. Going without a helmet creates a marginal competitive advantage— perhaps by enabling players to see and hear a little better, or perhaps by making it easier to intimidate their opponents psychologically. But when all athletes play without helmets, the competitive advantage each seeks is neutralized. One team wins and another loses, whether no players wear helmets or all wear them. Helmets reduce risk of serious injury, and hence the attraction of helmet rules.

Runaway spending in yachting competitions—contestants spent $500 million on the last America's Cup[4]—has also spawned a series of new positional arms control agreements. America's Cup contestants, for example, will henceforth be limited to a maximum of two boats. In 1992, the last year before the imposition of this rule, the cup champion United States team, America, spent $65 million on four boats while Italian challenger II Moro di Venezia spent more than $120 million on five boats.[5] Other new rules specify deadlines for disclosing hull designs and impose limits on the number of sails each yacht may carry. There are even rules to limit the scope of "spying and reconnaissance activities."[6]

Finally, we note that many of the rules of athletic competition themselves may be interpreted as positional arms control agreements. Consider, for example, the rule against excessive roughness found in virtually every contact sport. One football team could enhance its chances of winning if it could somehow injure important players on opposing teams. Other teams would inevitably retaliate, however, and in the end each side would suffer injuries with no net gain in competitive advantage. Roughness penalties curb this tendency, to the benefit of players, owners, and spectators alike.

Social Norms as Positional Arms Control Agreements

The examples discussed above involve formal rules backed up by an organization with significant enforcement powers. Although officials of the National Hockey League may not have legal authority to mandate helmet wearing, they can prevent a player who insists on going without one from playing in their league. But many other positional arms control agreements survive because of widely accepted social norms, despite the absence of formal sanctioning bodies.

The Academy Award-winning film *Chariots of Fire* portrays British collegiate track-and-field competitors who have developed an implicit norm that limits their training and practice time. Their apparent understanding is that since the most talented runner will win whether all train arduously or none does, the sensible thing is for no one to train very hard. This arrangement is challenged by an outsider with a rigorous training regimen. In response the incumbents bring considerable social pressure to bear upon the maverick. In the face of such pressure, most normal challengers might have succumbed. But this particular runner is tough, and he goes on to win in the end.

This is not to say that the social norm he helped to destroy in the process was a desirable one. Deciding races on the basis of talent alone may be efficient, but it is not necessarily fair. The underlying distribution of running talent, after all, is essentially a matter of luck. Even so, many of us who believe that effort should also matter are troubled by the types of efforts that emerge when competition is *completely* unregulated.

Social norms for curtailing effort are also common on the shop floor. In many manufacturing and sales jobs, it is possible to measure with reasonable precision what each worker produces. According to traditional economic theory, such conditions strongly favor the use of piece-rate pay schemes, which reward workers in direct proportion to the amounts they produce. One of the enduring puzzles in labor economics is the relative scarcity of these pay schemes. Even in sales, perhaps the easiest activity in which to monitor productivity, a National Industrial Conference Board study found that more than half of all compensation plans imposed caps on total sales commissions.[7] Similar pay ceilings are described in a large literature that examines the widespread practice whereby workers on piece rates establish their own informal production quotas and impose strong sanctions on those who violate them.[8] Cases have even been reported in which firms themselves impose limits on production.

Worker-imposed production quotas have been described as devices whereby workers fool management about the difficulty of their production tasks, out of fear that if they earn too much under existing piece rates, management will simply lower the rates.[9] But this explanation ignores the fact that management has ample means for discovering how much time production tasks require. One author, for example, describes an electrical assembly plant strike during which supervisors were easily able to double existing production quotas.[10] So if these quotas substantially understate what workers are capable of producing, and management knows it, why doesn't management elicit higher production by simply reducing current piece rates?

Management's implicit tolerance of production quotas makes much more sense if we interpret such agreements as devices whereby workers attempt to curb positional arms races with one another. The difficulty is that if promotion depends in part on relative productivity, the conditions are ripe for a mutually offsetting effort pattern. Each worker attempts to produce more in the hope of gaining ground relative to the others, yet when all workers double their efforts, relative position remains largely the same. From a collective vantage point, the extra output summoned by unregulated piece rates is not sufficient to compensate for the extra effort required to produce it. When workers care about relative income, social enforcement of informal production quotas may bring private incentives more in line with collective interests.

We also see social norms against excess effort in the world of education. Consider, for example, the positional arms race that arises when students are graded on the curve—that is, on the basis of their performance relative to other students. On the assumption that students care more about their grades than about how much they learn, grading on the curve has the undesirable effect (from students' perspective) of making extra effort more attractive to each individual student than it is to students as a whole. For if all students increase their efforts in an attempt to improve their grades, the aggregate grade distribution will remain much the same as before.

Whether a positional arms race is inefficient depends, of course, on the perspective from which it is viewed. Students think grading on the curve leads to excessive effort. Parents and teachers, by contrast, are more likely to view the competitive struggle for higher grades as benign. Recalling their own youth, many are inclined to believe that students would tend to spend far too little time on their studies in the absence of competitive pressures. In their view a positional arms race is just what the doctor ordered.

It is not surprising, then, that different social norms about academic effort have evolved among students on the one hand and concerned adults on the other. Students are quick to brand as "nerds" or social misfits those among them who "study too hard," or in other ways attempt to curry favor with teachers. Parents and teachers, for their part, try to counter this norm with norms of their own that extol the virtues of academic achievement.

The net effect of these opposing forces is by no means clear. But because social norms are at best imperfect instruments for achieving collective aims, we should not be surprised that at least some inefficiencies of both types persist. That is, despite nerd norms, relative performance evaluation probably continues to lead some students to work too hard; and despite rewards for relative performance and norms encouraging academic achievement, many other students probably continue to work too little.

Many social norms regarding dress and fashion may also be interpreted plausibly as positional arms control agreements. This claim springs from the well-documented finding in experimental psychology that perception and evaluation are strongly dependent on the observer's frame of reference.[11] Consider, for instance, the person who wishes to make a fashion statement that he or she is among the avant garde. In some American social circles during the 1950s, that could be accomplished by wearing pierced earrings. But as more and more people adopted this practice, it ceased to communicate avant-garde status. At the same time, those who wanted to make a conservative fashion statement gradually became freer to wear pierced earrings.

For a period during the 1960s and 1970s, one could be on fashion's cutting edge by wearing two pierced earrings in one earlobe. But by the 1990s multiple ear piercings had lost much of their social significance, with some people wearing upward of a dozen pierced earrings, or a smaller number of piercings of the nose, eyebrows, or other parts of the body. Consider, for example, this description of Boone, Ohio, body piercer Bert DuChene, who as of 1994 still qualified for membership in fashion's avant-garde:

> Sunlight shines through the two ear rivets designed to stretch the skin of his ear lobes. A tiny barbell pierces his tongue, and just above that, a ring hangs from his septum—the cartilage that separates the nostrils.
>
> A bit further down, both nipples are pierced—the left one twice. The tiny silver loops quiver slightly with each heartbeat.
>
> And don't forget the Prince Albert.
>
> The what?
>
> "The needle goes through the tip of the penis, through the urethra, and comes out underneath," DuChene, 21, says. "There's a surgical steel ring."[12]

A similar escalation has taken place in the number, size, and placement of tattoos that define avant-garde status.

There is unlikely, however, to have been any corresponding increase in the value of avant-garde fashion status to those who desire it. Being on the outer edge of the fashion distribution means pretty much the same now as it once did. So, to the extent that there are costs associated with body piercings, tattoos, and other steps required to achieve avant-garde status, the current situation is basically wasteful compared to the earlier one, which required fewer steps. In this sense, the erosion of social norms against tattoos and body piercings has given rise to a social loss. Of course, the costs associated with this loss are small in most cases. Yet, since each body piercing carries with it a small risk of infection, the costs will continue to rise with the number of piercings. And once these costs reach a certain threshold, support may again mobilize on behalf of social norms that discourage body mutilation.

Similar cycles occur with respect to behaviors considered to be in bad taste. In the 1950s, for example, prevailing norms prevented major national magazines from accepting ads that used nude photographs to draw readers' attention. Advertisers naturally have powerful incentives to chip away at these norms, for as we have seen, sellers must compete vigorously for the buyer's limited attention. And indeed, norms regarding good taste have evolved in a way similar to those regarding body mutilation.

Consider, for instance, the evolution of perfume ads. First came the nude silhouette; then increasingly well-lighted and detailed nude photographs; and more recently, photographs of what appear to be group sex acts. Each innovation achieved just the desired effect—drawing the reader's instant attention. Inevitably, however, competing advertisers have followed suit, and the effect has been merely to shift our sense of what is considered attention grabbing. Photographs that once would have shocked readers now often draw little more than a bored glance.

Whether this is a good thing or a bad thing naturally depends on one's view about public nudity. Many believe that the earlier, stricter norms were ill-advised in the first place, the legacy of a more prudish and repressive era. And yet even those who take this view also are likely to believe that *some* kinds of photographic material ought not to be used in advertisements in national magazines. Where this limit lies will obviously differ a great deal from person to person. And each person's threshold of discomfort will depend in part on the currently observed standards. But we should not be surprised that as advertisers continue to break new ground in their struggle to capture our attention, the point may come when social forces again mobilize in favor of stricter standards of "public decency." Such forces, we suggest, are yet another example of a positional arms control agreement.

A similar claim can be made on behalf of social norms that discourage cosmetic surgery. Plastic surgery has produced dramatic benefits for many people. It has enabled badly disfigured accident victims to recover a more normal appearance and so to continue with their lives. It has also eliminated the extreme self-consciousness felt by people born with strikingly unusual or unattractive features. Such surgery, however, is by no means confined to the conspicuously disfigured. "Normal" people are increasingly seeking surgical improvements in their appearance. Some two million cosmetic "procedures" were done in 1991, six times the number just a decade earlier. Although having undergone any kind of cosmetic surgery was once a carefully guarded secret, such procedures are now offered as prizes in charity raffles in Southern California.[13]

In individual cases cosmetic surgery may be just as beneficial as reconstructive surgery is for accident victims. Buoyed by the confidence of having a straight nose or a wrinkle-free complexion, patients sometimes go on to achieve much more than they ever thought possible.

But the growing use of cosmetic surgery also has an unintended side effect—it has altered our standards for normal appearance. A nose that would once have seemed only slightly larger than average may now seem jarringly big; the same person who once would have looked like an average fifty-five-year-old may now look nearly seventy; and someone who once would have been described as having slightly thinning hair or an average amount of cellulite, may now feel compelled to undergo hair transplantation or liposuction. Because such procedures shift our frame of reference, their payoffs to individuals are misleadingly large, and from a social perspective, reliance on them is therefore likely to be excessive.

It is difficult to imagine legal sanctions against cosmetic surgery as a remedy for this problem. But at least some communities embrace powerful social norms against cosmetic surgery, heaping scorn on the consumers of facelifts and tummy tucks. In individual cases these norms may seem cruel. And yet, without them, many more people might feel compelled to bear the risk and expense of cosmetic surgery.

Contracts as Positional Arms Control Agreements

Given the potential for the wasteful escalation of positional arms races, we should expect contestants in the business world to seek contractual means of curtailing them. Of course, businesses also have an incentive to make anticompetitive agreements with their rivals even when the behaviors in question are not socially wasteful. It has long been the function of cartels, for example, to prevent their members from using price cuts to lure away one another's customers. Indeed, much of modem antitrust law is designed to frustrate collusive agreements. But the drafters of antitrust legislation implicitly recognized that many other forms of business competition do not serve the public interest.

And so the law permits a variety of contracts whose effect is to limit competition.

Some of these take the form of agreements to avoid litigation. With the explosion of litigation in recent decades, corporate contracts are increasingly likely to call for arbitration procedures in the event of disputes. Parties to these contracts recognize the potential for honest mistakes, or even for malfeasance, leading to disputes regarding the proper discharge of specific contract terms, But they also recognize the potential for an escalating legal battle if they try to resolve their disagreements in the courts. By committing themselves to binding arbitration, they sacrifice the ability to pursue a claim as fully as they might later wish; in return, they expect a reduction in their long-run costs.

Employers and workers likewise recognize the possibilities for disagreement over wages, working conditions, and other provisions in their labor contracts. But they also recognize the cost to both sides when such disputes escalate into strikes or lockouts. By committing dispute resolution to arbitrators chosen in advance, both sides limit their latitude to pursue legitimate grievances; but in return they expect higher long-run payoffs.

Positional Arms Control Agreements in Education

In college athletics there is a common practice called "redshirting," which means to withhold a player from competition for one year, usually the freshman year, thus making him eligible to play during his fifth year. (Most athletes don't graduate in four years.) The advantage, for a team that follows this practice, is that most athletes are larger, stronger, and more experienced in their fifth year than in their first. For the intercollegiate athletic system as a whole, however, redshirting yields no comparable advantage. For when all teams routinely redshirt their freshmen, the competitive balance among teams is much the same as if none did.

A similar calculus applies to the decision about when to start a child in school. A child who is a year older than most of his kindergarten classmates is likely to perform better, in relative terms, than if he had entered with children the same age. And since most parents are aware that admission to prestigious universities and eligibility for top jobs on graduation depend largely on *relative* academic performance, many will be tempted to keep their children out of kindergarten a year longer—to redshirt them, as it were. But, as in the case of athletic redshirts, there is no social advantage from holding all children back an extra year, since relative performance would then be essentially unaffected.

In most jurisdictions parents are not free to decide for themselves when to start their children in school. Laws typically require children who reach their fifth birthday before December 1 of a given year to start kindergarten that year. Although such laws deprive parents of flexibility that might be used to great advantage in special cases, they also eliminate a collectively futile attempt to enhance relative performance.

Another common positional arms race in the schools is the tendency for clothing expenditures to escalate as students attempt to match or exceed the fashion statements of influential peers. (At some inner-city schools, there have been reports of students' being killed for their Nike Air Jordans.) At least some schools have curbed escalating clothing expenditures by requiring that all students wear uniforms. Such requirements obviously rob students of one outlet of creative expression, but in the eyes of the parents and educators who ultimately decide these matters, the price is apparently worth paying.

Recent attempts to make SATs cram-proof constitute another positional arms control agreement in education. Most students who aspire to attend a prestigious college or university are well aware that their chances depend in part on how well they do on the SAT. Administered several times each year by the Educational Testing Service, a nonprofit corporation in Princeton, New Jersey, the SATs are intended to measure not academic achievement (there are separate tests for that purpose), but rather aptitude for doing successful college work.

Because strong SAT performance is viewed as crucial to success at the top of the educational hierarchy, there has developed a booming industry of educational service specialists who promise to boost performance on the tests. Launched by Stanley H. Kaplan more than fifty years ago, this industry offers an array of products, including printed manuals, computer software, individual tutoring, and group classroom instruction. Although some high school guidance counselors continue to tell students that these services have little effect on SAT scores, available evidence suggests the contrary. One study found, for example, that students who used a leading SAT software package improved their scores by almost 17 percent relative to a control group.[14]

To the extent that the SATs are supposed to measure aptitude, not achievement, and to the extent that what is learned in SAT prep courses alters neither aptitude nor achievement, these courses constitute a social waste. It appears clearly impractical to outlaw them, however, because of the ease with which students could turn to less formal and less easily monitored forms of coaching.

The one avenue available to control this particular positional arms race is to revise the tests themselves, making them less sensitive to the effects of coaching. This was indeed one of the primary goals of the redesign of the SAT in 1990. Of course, no conceivable format for the SAT would be completely invulnerable to student investments in performance enhancement. But designing the test so that performance is only minimally affected by these investments is a positional arms control agreement that students and parents have every reason to favor.

Law and Public Policy as Positional Arms Control Agreements

As we saw in chapter 7, competition among workers leads to a variety of positional arms races. A host of laws, regulations, and public policies are plausibly interpreted as collective agreements to curtail these positional arms races.

Consider, for example, the regulation of safety in the workplace. As Adam Smith emphasized more than two centuries ago, decisions involving workplace safety and other desirable working conditions confront people with a trade-off. Safer conditions can be had, but only at a price. A machine tool with a safety shield, after all, costs more to buy and maintain than one without. Smith argued that competition among firms for workers would lead to an optimal resolution of this trade-off: Firms would install those—and only those—safety devices whose costs were less than or equal to their benefits as perceived by workers. Firms that failed to install safety equipment that passed this cost-benefit test would risk losing their workers to a competitor that did.

A pivotal, if often unstated, assumption in Smith's argument is that when workers weigh the trade-off between risk and income, they care about absolute, but not relative, income. Yet when, as all evidence suggests, workers care about relative income as well, the choice between a safe job and a risky one becomes precisely analogous to the hockey player's choice about whether to wear a helmet. Just as hockey players are tempted to go without helmets as a means of gaining a competitive edge, workers are tempted to accept risky jobs to move higher on the economic totem pole. And just as it is impossible for opponents in a hockey game to simultaneously increase their odds of winning, so it is impossible for all workers to move higher in relative terms. If all workers accept riskier jobs, everyone's ranking in the income distribution will remain the same as before.

Critics of the market system have charged that safety regulations are needed to prevent firms with market power from exploiting their employees. Yet safety regulations bind with greatest force in those labor markets that are, by every measure, most competitive. Safety regulations are much more plausibly viewed as devices for softening the consequences of competition for relative economic position.

In chapter 7 we also noted that workers confront positional arms races in their decision of how many hours to work. They may be tempted to work longer hours in order to move forward in relative terms, yet when all work longer hours, relative position remains unchanged. Workers might thus find it attractive to limit their working hours, which in effect is what the Fair Labor Standards Act does: It requires firms to pay premium wage rates whenever employees work more than a given number of hours in a day or week—a strong incentive to limit hours.

Local statutes often tackle the same problem by limiting the hours stores can remain open for business. For example, the list of commercial activities prohibited on Sunday in at least one state includes barbering, general retail sales, sales of alcoholic beverages, motor vehicle sales, fresh meat sales, and tobacco warehouse sales.[15] Such statutes are often called "blue laws," and in at least some jurisdictions their apparent purpose is to scale back the workweek.[16]

The Social Security Act is another law that functions as a positional arms control agreement. Under this legislation wages are taxed during people's working lives, and the proceeds are used to finance an income stream for retired persons. Critics of the marketplace often contend that the Social Security program is needed because consumers would otherwise succumb to manipulative advertising and spend their retirement savings. Maybe so, yet we suggest that many consumers would find the program attractive even in a society in which no one was exploited by advertising.

Once again the reason is that the rewards of consumption are often relative. Parents have the choice of saving some of their current income for retirement or spending that income now on, say, a house in a better school district or on some other form of current consumption. As with decisions involving safety or the length of the workweek, positional pressures often make the second option compelling. The aggregate effects of such choices, however, often turn out to be disappointing.

Government pension programs mitigate this dilemma by keeping a portion of each person's income unavailable for spending. Programs of this type would be attractive even in a society in which consumers had perfect foresight and were impervious to the manipulations of advertisers.

Campaign finance rules are another clear example of legislation as positional arms control agreement. One candidate can increase her odds of winning by spending an additional million dollars on advertising, but when her opponent matches that expenditure, the original odds of winning are approximately restored. A similar outcome would be achieved in most cases if both candidates were to spend less money. Following an extended period of steep escalation in campaign expenditures, Congress recognized this simple logic and enacted legislation that limits spending by presidential candidates.

Spending limits are further justified by the belief that the imperatives of fund-raising may lead candidates to become political prostitutes, distorting their positions on policy issues or forcing them to make commitments that do not square with their sense of the public interest. In contrast to most of the cases discussed earlier, in which investments by competitors enhance the value of the final product, here the social payoff to winning is *negatively* affected by the winning candidate's investment.

Income, consumption, and luxury taxes are further examples of positional arms control agreements in the legislative arena. This interpretation is clearest in the case of luxury taxes, whose explicit purpose is to discourage wasteful expenditures on status seeking. The primary purpose of income and consumption (or sales) taxes, by contrast, is to raise revenue for government activities. But, like all others, these taxes have additional effects as well. For example, income taxes are often said to discourage investment and work by reducing the net gains from these activities. Sales taxes similarly discourage consumption and encourage savings. All three kinds of tax—income, consumption, and luxury—reduce the return on investments in performance enhancement by contestants in winner-take-all markets, and hence their utility as positional arms control agreements.

Monogamy: The Ultimate Positional Arms Control Agreement

Perhaps the most bitterly fought winner-take-all contest in the entire animal kingdom is the struggle between individuals for access to mates. For humans and other animals, the most intense of these struggles are typically those among males. The reason lies in an asymmetry in the reproductive strategies of the two sexes. Females, who in most species invest heavily in the gestation and care of offspring, have limited reproductive capacity relative to males, whose only contribution in many instances consists of cheaply manufactured sperm cells.

This asymmetry means that any single male is capable, in principle, of siring an almost unlimited number of offspring. And since, in the Darwinian scheme of evolution by natural selection, each individual's goal is to transmit as many copies of its genes as possible to the next generation, the result for males is a genetic tournament with enormously high stakes. In one species of seals, for example, 4 percent of the breeding-age males sire almost 90 percent of all surviving offspring.[17]

In a winner-take-all contest with so much at stake, we expect rivals to leave no stone unturned in their efforts to gain competitive advantage. In the species of seals just mentioned, for example, the battles for access to females are almost indescribably intense and bloody.

The variability of male reproductive success in humans, although smaller than in many other animal species, is nonetheless substantial. More than 85 percent of past and present human societies for which data are available were polygynous. In these societies high-ranking males often take numerous wives, and the biggest winners enjoy prodigious reproductive success. For example, Moulay Ismail, the last Sharifian emperor of Morocco, fathered more than a thousand children in the late seventeenth and early eighteenth centuries.[18]

Human societies have employed two basic strategies for keeping the contest for mates from getting out of control. One is to curtail the contest for high social rank itself, allocating top positions—and the entitlements to multiple wives that go with them—by caste membership or other ascriptive characteristics. This has been the strategy of choice in traditional human societies. But by far the more common strategy in modern societies is to enact legislation that prohibits people from taking more than one spouse at a time.

Needless to say even monogamy laws don't completely eliminate the competition for mates. To the extent that there is consensus on what constitutes a "high quality" mate, for example, monogamy laws do nothing to stem the competition for the most desirable partners. And in societies that permit divorce, serial monogamy often becomes, in effect, a form of polygyny in which wealthy males like Johnny Carson monopolize the reproductive capacity of a series of highly attractive females.[19] Imperfect though monogamy laws may be, however, there can be little doubt that the level of social competition would be dramatically higher in any modern society that lacked them.

On the Horizon

We mention a final positional arms race, one that emerging technology will almost surely launch in the near future. We refer to the ability to control the characteristics of one's children by genetic screening and manipulation. Limited capacities of this sort already exist, as with the use of amniocentesis to test for fetal genetic defects. This test permits parents to abort fetuses discovered to have serious deformities. And there are other mechanisms that actually enable parents to choose the sex of their offspring.

By themselves, neither the ability to eliminate deformities nor the ability to choose sex portends a significant positional arms race. Moral questions about abortion aside, screening out serious fetal deformities serves both the parents' interests and those of society as a whole. Some have voiced concern that the ability to choose sex might lead to a preponderance of one sex in some societies. This seems in fact to have happened in China, where the government's one-child policy, in combination with ultrasound imaging and ready access to abortion, has produced a generation in which there are now three single males over the age of fifteen for every two single females. These numbers suggest that "tens of millions of men alive at the turn of the century will be lifelong bachelors because there will not be enough women available as wives."[20]

There are already signs, however, that the demographic imbalance has begun to enhance the economic and social power of women in China. In time we might reasonably expect parents to respond by altering subsequent choices in favor of greater demographic balance. Most parents, after all, want to become grandparents, and this goal is best served by a sex selection that bucks any prevailing trend.

As the Human Genome Project continues, many other genetic screening and manipulation capabilities will inevitably emerge. And at least some of these raise far more ominous possibilities than the abilities to select a child's sex or eliminate serious deformities. Consider, for example, the ability to select for size, through either genetic screening or genetic manipulation. In athletic competition, there is generally an advantage to being larger than one's peers. This advantage is small in some cases, as in tennis; it is much larger in others, as in basketball. There is also a slight economic and social advantage to being larger than one's rivals. In all but a handful of cases, for example, the winning presidential candidate was taller than his opponent.[21] And a University of Pittsburgh study reported that men over six feet two earn 12.4 percent higher salaries than men under six feet.[22]

Unlike the sex and deformities cases, individual and collective interests clearly conflict with respect to the size of offspring. The collective effect of each parent's choosing slightly larger offspring is simply an upward shift in the aggregate size distribution of the population. And whereas it is generally to an individual's advantage to be somewhat larger than his peers, there is no comparable social gain from having a generally larger population. On the contrary, additional size actually becomes a handicap beyond some point because larger people require more food and are more susceptible to orthopedic ailments.

One response to positional arms races of this form is simply to ignore them. Similar arms races have gone essentially unregulated, after all, for as long as organisms have evolved under the pressures of Darwinian natural selection. These selection pressures have molded a human population whose average size is almost surely larger than optimal already. But the consequences of purposeful, unregulated genetic manipulation may in some cases be sufficiently troubling for us to at least consider the possibility of collective intervention.

To consider an extreme, but perhaps not overly fanciful, example, suppose there were a cheap, readily available, genetic manipulation whose sole effect in 99 percent of cases is to produce offspring who, although no more intelligent than before, are able to score 15 percent better on standardized tests like the SAT. In the remaining 1 percent of all cases, however, this manipulation has no effect on test-taking ability but produces severe emotional disability. This is a grim gamble indeed, yet one can imagine some parents' being willing to take it. The assumption is that 99 percent of their offspring would turn out to be winners who, because of their superior test-taking skills, would displace others' offspring from the best schools, and later from the best jobs. Many abstainers, seeing their genetically "natural" offspring fall further and further behind, would feel increasing pressure to roll the genetic dice. And as more and more did so, the pressures on the remaining holdouts would increase still further.

In this hypothetical example, there is a gain to the individual from the genetic manipulation (higher scores on standardized tests) but no gain to society as a whole (no one is made any smarter by the manipulation, and when everyone's test scores go up by 15 percent, the same students are admitted to the same schools as before). The cost of the manipulation, both to adversely affected people and to society as a whole, is extreme, although concentrated on only 1 percent of participants. We can imagine societies in which many parents would avail themselves of this genetic manipulation, yet at the same wish fervently that it had never been discovered. In these cases it seems likely that there would be interest in some form of positional arms control mechanism.

Yet, depending on the nature of the technologies available, regulation might not be simple. Just as we currently have generally insufficient testing mechanisms to prevent athletes from consuming anabolic steroids, so too it might be difficult to monitor and control opportunities for genetic manipulation. We are fortunate that not many such troubling opportunities are currently available to us. But this happy state will not last much longer, and it is by no means premature to consider policies for dealing with these issues.

10

Media and Culture in the Winner-Take-All Society

Writing on the *New York Times* daily book page, reviewer Michiko Kakutani recently offered this commentary on the work of a young best-selling author:

> After three earlier novels (*Less Than Zero*, *The Rules of Attraction*, and *American Psycho*), readers pretty much know what to expect from Bret Easton Ellis's fiction: shallow, cynical young people with empty, meaningless lives; lots of drugs; perfunctory, sometimes violent sex, and some sort of sensationalistic crime (gang rape, torture, and mutilation).
>
> His latest novel, *The Informers,* is no exception. It's got another cast of young, dissolute nihilists and their equally dissolute parents, and it takes place in familiar Ellis territory: a Los Angeles in which drugs, aerobics, sex and narcissistic navel-gazing seem to be the only activities in town. There are the usual desultory affairs between Mr. Ellis's various characters—less affairs, really, than weary, passionless couplings. There is a lot of pill-popping, spacing out and complaining. And finally, there are a couple of horrifying murders and mutilations, described in gruesome, stomach-turning detail.[1]

Shortly after this review appeared, the *Times* previewed Oliver Stone's film, *Natural Born Killers,* a chronicle of two psychopathic killers who become celebrities through a series of appearances on a national tabloid television show. "I began this film as a satire," Stone said. But that was before "the Menendez brothers, before the Bobbins, before Amy Fisher and Joey Buttafuoco, before the O. J. Simpson case. Well, it's not so much satirical now, but reality-based."[2]

Television programming, much of it targeted at children, has also taken a nasty turn. There have consistently been more violent acts shown during morning and after-school hours than in prime time, but with the spread of cable, children now have access to more vividly portrayed violence than in the past. Even MTV, a cable channel devoted primarily to music videos, now televises at least one incident of violence in more than half of its videos.[3]

Similar trends are evident in electronic video games. Early versions of games by Nintendo, Sega-Genesis, and others featured ample violence, but not nearly as much or as graphic as the versions on sale today. Midway's popular Mortal Kombat, for instance, now portrays "grisly scenes showing beating human hearts being torn out of bodies."[4]

Social critics cite examples like these in defense of their charge that popular culture has grown more formulaic, vulgar, sensational, and violent in recent years. Skeptics dismiss these charges as elitist and insist that there is little sense in arguing about inherently subjective cultural evaluations. As if to drive home their point, a second *New York Times* reviewer, Columbia University professor George Stade, offered this contrarian assessment of Ellis's *The Informers:* "In fact, a case could be made for Mr. Ellis as a covert moralist and closet sentimentalist, the best kind, the kind who leaves you space in which to respond as your predispositions nudge you, whether as a commissar or hand-wringer or, like me, as an admirer of his intelligence and craft."[5] Skeptics might well ask, if even the *Times*' own distinguished reviewers can't agree whether a book is art or trash, what standards do the elitist critics propose to employ, other than their own pious opinions, for passing judgment on popular culture?

Skeptics go on to point out that notwithstanding the offerings that social critics find so distasteful, our menu of cultural choices is in fact more diverse now than at any time in the past. Critics respond that the apparent diversity is an illusion; with the spread of cable and video, we may have more choices than ever, yet there is precious little worth watching. And there, typically, the debate over popular culture ends in stalemate, an apparently unresolvable quarrel over tastes.

There is indeed little to be gained by arguing whether Rachmaninoff is better than the Rolling Stones, Yet careful analysis of the forces that drive markets for popular culture affords insights that help push the tired debate in fruitful new directions. Our goal here is to explain why the recent intensification of winner-take-all markets might have molded popular culture in ways that even free marketeers might not favor. Our claim is not that people choose unwisely as individuals, but that the collective consequences of their choices often turn out to be very different from what they desire or anticipate.

Cultural Markets Are Winner-Take-All Markets

That many markets in the cultural arena are winner-take-all markets becomes evident once we look at the forces that give rise to them. On the supply side, most culture is currently produced in forms that allow the services of the most popular performers to be reproduced at very low cost. Through the magic of film, video, television, radio, recorded music, books, and newspapers, we thus have ready access to the world's most talented actors, comedians, singers, authors, columnists and newscasters.

On the demand side, the market for culture is also driven by many of the forces that give rise to winner-take-all markets. Books, movies, sporting events, and television programs are often entertaining in their own right, but most people also enjoy discussing them with friends. Just as a fax machine becomes more valuable when more of one's friends also have one, so entries in these categories become more valuable the more popular they are. Television audiences worldwide, for example, enjoyed speculating about "who shot J.R." during the summer of 1981. By the same token, the popularity of certain cultural offerings may impose costs on those who do not consume them. For instance, in the 1970s male office workers could not participate in conversations around the water cooler on autumn Tuesday mornings if they had not watched *Monday Night Football* the night before.

Quite apart from this networking value of popularity, a rational consumer will often use popularity as an index of quality in deciding which books to read, or which television programs to watch. When it was reported that Donald Trump had purchased thousands of copies of his own book, *The Art of the Deal*, thereby prolonging its stay on the best-seller lists, his critics saw this as further evidence of his egomania. They may be right, but Trump is also a shrewd businessman. Since a book's appearance on the best-seller lists assures that thousands of additional readers will buy it, Trump's move may have made sense even in cold financial terms.

Of course, as anyone who has read *The Art of the Deal*, or sat through an episode of *Beavis and Butthead* can attest, popularity in itself is no guarantee of quality. Yet a typical consumer with no other information to go on would be correct to assume that popular books and programs are, on average, more likely than unpopular ones to appeal to his tastes.

Our preference for popular entries has important consequences for the marketing of culture. As we have repeatedly seen, a failure to achieve early success in such markets often means having no chance to succeed at all. Increasingly, books that fail to sell briskly during their first month of publication are shipped back to their publishers in order to make room for other titles still in the running. Similarly, movies that fail to open big are whisked ever more quickly from first-run theaters to make room for the next wave of new releases.

How the Race to Achieve Quick Success Affects Quality

At first glance it might seem that this need to succeed early would tend to increase rather than reduce the quality of cultural offerings. After all, if quality is what buyers really want, why wouldn't producers try to achieve early success by simply offering higher quality products?

Quality does indeed appear to matter to many buyers. And although social critics have always denigrated popular culture, each generation has in fact produced an abundance of high quality offerings. During the depths of the Great Depression, for example, moviegoers flocked to see Chaplin's *Modern Times,* a film that has won enduring praise no less for its trenchant social commentary than for its finely crafted comic sequences. Reruns of Jackie Gleason's hit television series of the 1950s, *The Honeymooners,* continue to charm audiences even while instructing them about the vicissitudes of married life. Joseph Heller's *Catch-22* continues to draw belly laughs even as it conveys deep truths about the nature of bureaucracy. John Le Carré's espionage novels are perennial best-sellers, partly because of their bracingly fresh prose ("The day had been sullen and damp, an evening that began at breakfast"), but also because of their penetrating insights into human nature. Steven Spielberg's film *Schindler's List* proved that mass audiences could sit through a three-hour portrayal of a small segment of one of the grimmest episodes in history and yet emerge feeling enriched by the experience.

Yet quality by itself does not ensure commercial success. The world's libraries, after all, are filled with high-quality books that never succeeded commercially. The book buyer is faced with literally thousands of new books from which to choose each year, and, no matter how high their average quality, only a small number of these books can hope to make their way onto his mental agenda.

Imagine yourself a publisher faced with the choice of publishing one of two books, each of high quality (however measured), but the first of marginally higher quality than the second. If the first book is written by an unknown author and the second by a celebrity, or it has a slightly simpler, more easily summarized message, which should you publish?

Faced with these choices, any publisher under pressure to deliver on the bottom line (which is to say, virtually every publisher) will not hesitate to choose the second book. It is almost as good as the first, after all, and it stands a much greater chance of attracting the early attention that is so critical if it is to break out of the pack. Let the quality difference between the two books grow sufficiently large, of course, and the publisher will begin to agonize. Within broad limits, however, the financial incentives to publish sensational, simplistic, or formulaic offerings by well-known authors are often all but irresistible.

Such publishing decisions have implications for subsequent

decisions made by other publishers. If all publishers begin to publish slightly lower quality books with properties that make it easier to attract attention in the early going, the standards that define acceptable quality will begin to decline. By the same token, as more books come to be written by celebrity authors, or to have sensational or easy-to-summarize messages, the standards for attracting readers' attention also shift. And this, in turn, sets in motion a second dynamic process that causes quality to decline. Viewed in isolation, Bret Easton Ellis's books might seem like curious aberrations, works that could never have been published in the 1940s. Seen in the context of these dynamic processes, however, their publication seems hardly surprising.

Similar dynamics are at work in the film industry. With their attention focused on achieving a fast launch, producers are under heavy pressure to bid for the handful of actors, directors, and scripts that assure widespread media attention. Increasingly, studios have focused on the sequel—or more precisely, on strings of sequels—as a means for attracting large early audiences. As Verna Fields, a former film editor and production executive at MCA-Universal put it: "Producers are investing the money, and I don't think they feel very courageous about being daring and experimental. I don't blame them. They want to be safe. They know that *Jaws* made money, so *Jaws II* is sure to make it . . . They want . . . something proven. I can't blame them for being nervous about trying anything new."[6]

Jaws was the film that launched the modern blockbuster era, according to *New York Times* movie critic Janet Maslin. It proved dramatically that a single film could appeal strongly to people in all demographic categories. Maslin notes that moviegoers in the pre-*Jaws* 1970s could choose from a host of innovative, often quirky films targeted at narrow audiences, citing titles like *Mean Streets*, *The Conversation*, *Chinatown*, *McCabe and Mrs. Miller*, *Nashville*, *Klute*, *Three Days of the Condor*, *Don't Look Now*, and the early Woody Allen films.[7] Moviegoers of the 1990s, by contrast, are increasingly forced to choose among titles like *Beverly Hills Cop 3*, *Home Alone 2*, *Lethal Weapon 3*, *Terminator 2*, *Aliens 3*, and *Batman Returns*. (The Nicholas Hytner film *The Madness of King George*—which was based on the British play *The Madness of George III*—was retitled for fear that American audiences would be reluctant to see a film whose first two installments they had missed!) As Maslin goes on to observe:

> [In the earlier era], risk taking was deemed more artistically valuable than commercially foolhardy, which is one good way of distinguishing between the creative climate of the early 1970s and that of today. Peter Bogdanovich, who made his reputation with the small, perfect film *The Last Picture Show* in 1971, and whose latest film (*The Thing Called Love*, starring River Phoenix) went straight to video after it performed disappointingly in regional markets, recently speculated about whether he could ever have begun his career in a cutthroat, bottom-line oriented atmosphere like today's. The answer, he thought, was probably no.[8]

As in the publishing industry, the standards that define quality in the film industry depend on the quality of the offerings in previous seasons. Here, too, when studios move in tandem to accept small sacrifices in quality to gain greater early visibility, they inadvertently redefine the standards of acceptable quality. In the process they set in motion a cycle of similar trade-offs in future seasons.

On the buyer's side of the market, similarly, the standards that make a film attention-getting depend on context. Scenes and subject matter that startle viewers in one season are likely to lose some of their punch the next. The growth in sensationalism during any one year will often be too small to attract comment. Yet, over the past several decades, the cumulative effect of these changes has been dramatic.

Growing sensationalism is by no means confined to books and movies. Indeed, it is perhaps nowhere more evident than in evening television. Tabloid journalism, once confined to weekly newspapers sold in supermarket checkout lines, gained its first toehold in television in the "dead hour" between 7:00 and 8:00 P.M.[9] The early tabloid shows were produced independently for syndication to local stations and featured little-known hosts with no reputations to defend. Increasingly, however, tabloid television has invaded prime time, with programming now under network supervision and with genuine national celebrities as hosts.

Even the nightly network news broadcasts have assumed an increasingly tabloid quality. To get a feel for how much things have changed, try to imagine that Peggy Fleming, who won the Olympic gold medal in figure skating in 1968, had assaulted her principal rival before the competition began; and then try to imagine Walter Cronkite scurrying about the Olympic Village in Grenoble, vying with the tabloid journalists for a chance to interview Fleming about the details of her crime. Hard to picture? Of course, and yet, a scant twenty-six years later, no one seemed particularly surprised at the nightly spectacle of CBS coanchor Connie Chung in hot pursuit of Tonya Harding throughout the Lillehammer Winter Olympics of 1994.

Not even political coverage is immune from market forces. In a recent book, political scientist Thomas Patterson points to a fundamental change in the way the media cover politics.[10] Prior to the Vietnam and Watergate years, he argues, most journalists limited their criticisms of political leaders to demonstrable claims. In the years since, however, journalists have increasingly followed a different strategy. Rather than try to analyze a politician's position on some issue in detail, they simply ask his opponents to comment on it. And as opponents quickly discovered, the nastier their criticism was, the more likely it was to be quoted in print or to appear as a sound bite on the evening news.

Over time investigative journalism thus gave way to "attack journalism." Patterson notes that every president from Kennedy onward has received increasingly harsh treatment from the press, irrespective of how well he was performing on objective criteria. Bill Clinton, for instance, has received the most consistently negative press coverage of any president in modern history, despite his largely successful efforts in shepherding an ambitious legislative agenda through Congress. (Among postwar presidents, only Lyndon Johnson had a higher success rate in passing contested bills.) The point is not that Clinton is a president without flaws. But his predecessors were flawed as well, and, even after controlling for objectively measurable differences in job performance, each one received rougher press treatment than the one before.

Political commentary has also been transformed in recent decades by the appearance of what journalist James Fallows has called the "celebrity journalist." Since the dawn of the television era, but increasingly so since the 1970s, successful columnists and reporters have been invited to join teams of television news commentators, on such programs as *The McLaughlin Group* or *The Capitol Gang,* In the process they have become household names, which puts them in line to command five-figure appearance fees on the trade association lecture circuit.

ABC's Jeff Greenfield offered this description of one prominent news-talk-show panelist's standard routine on the circuit:

> He gets up, drops the fact that he was in the Oval Office last month, and says, "This is what the President told me." He makes five or six plati-tudinous observations and then takes questions, and it's worth, what, eight or ten grand. The journalist is delivering to that audience the same thing a lobbyist delivers. He's delivering the delicious sense of insider-ness, in a way there was no market for fifteen or twenty years ago.[11]

Our concern here is not that trade associations are failing to get their money's worth. These are worldly groups for the most part, and well able to fend for themselves. The real problem, as Fallows argues, is that the lure of celebrity journalists' seven-figure incomes shapes the behavior of aspiring young journalists in a variety of harmful ways. For one thing the demands of talk-show journalism encourage reporters to cultivate one of the stereotyped personas needed to fill the casting requirements of talk-show producers. Invariably, Fallows explains, these include "a Liberal, a Conservative, a Colorful Young Critic, a Respected But Twinkly-Eyed Authority, etc."[12]

One result is that subtlety and nuance all but disappear from talk-show discussions of important public issues. Those commentators who do try to look at both sides of an issue are often hammered for it by fellow panelists. Another problem, Fallows argues, is that the demands of celebrity journalism have introduced a nasty, bullying tone into our political discourse. The talk-show format, after all, thrives on the excitement generated by name-calling and *ad hominem* argument. *The McLaughlin Group*'s Robert Novak epitomizes this new style. "Novak knows he's the star of the show, and that his fame and lecture fees go up each time he acts the *terrible.*"[13]

Nasty, one-sided discourse may be an inevitable response to the winner-take-all forces of the modern media marketplace. But it is by no means clear that it helps us make more intelligent policy decisions.

What's New?

Winner-take-all markets in media and culture are of course nothing new. Nor, for that matter, is our fascination with matters lurid and sensational. So why have the offerings of popular culture been catering so much more overtly to this fascination in recent years? Why have President Clinton's personal adventures become the object of obsessive media scrutiny whereas President Kennedy's were considered strictly off limits? The dynamic processes just described are only part of the story. More fundamental has been growth—both in the top prizes at stake in cultural markets and in the openness of the competition for these prizes. These changes not only make it more tempting for any given player to break with tradition, they also simultaneously weaken the social forces that hold industry norms together.

As we discussed briefly in chapter 4, there are numerous factors that account for growth in the top prizes in media and culture markets. For example, whereas books published by American authors once earned most of their revenues in the United States, an increasing number now earn most of their revenues in foreign markets. A growing number of books, moreover, earn the lion's share of their revenues from the sale of various subsidiary rights. For instance, the film rights to John Grisham's first novel, *A Time to Kill,* recently fetched $6 million, far more than he and his publisher earned from direct sales of the book itself.[14]

The top prizes in the film industry have also benefited from the globalization of markets, from growing television revenues, and, more recently, from burgeoning revenues from the video aftermarket, and even more dramatically from product licensing. For films like *ET*, *Batman, Jurassic Park*, and *The Lion King*, such revenues can run several times higher than from ticket sales.

Growth in the top prizes in television has been less dramatic, the result mostly of increasing exports of programming and increasing sophistication in the marketing of syndication rights. Yet here, too, there have been some enormous product-spinoff bonanzas from shows like *Star Trek*, *Teenage Mutant Ninja Turtles*, and *Power Rangers*.

In both television and the print media, by far the more important change in recent years has been the movement toward more open competition for audiences. In television this has resulted from the proliferation of cable and the addition of a fourth major broadcast network. The print media, for their part, have faced growing competition from television, from magazines targeted at specialty audiences, and from the addition of one new national newspaper (*USA Today*) and the increased availability of two others (the *New York Times* and the *Wall Street Journal*).

Both the larger prizes and the more competitive environment have worked in tandem to fuel the growing trend toward sensationalism. In the past a relatively small number of competitors interacted repeatedly with one another. With only three TV networks, a small number of movie studios, and a handful of major publishers, it was possible for the news and entertainment industries to implement implicit social norms about the kind of material that could be shown or written about. The fact that the prizes were relatively small, moreover, kept the temptation to violate these norms within reasonable limits.

Thus, for example, each television network and each major newspaper knew that it could attract larger audiences momentarily if it covered President Kennedy's extramarital affairs while its rivals did not. Similarly each publisher knew it could make extra profits in the short run by publishing books like Bret Easton Ellis's. But each also knew that the advantage would be short-lived because its defection would spell the breakdown of their implicit agreements. And in the smaller markets of yesteryear, the potential gains from breaking ranks were not all that large anyway.

In today's competitive climate, such restraints have proved virtually impossible to sustain. There is simply too much at stake and too many loose cannons on the periphery. Thus it should have come as no surprise that all four major television networks plus numerous cable stations carried extended live coverage of O. J. Simpson's flight from police on the Southern California freeways, even though NBC had to interrupt its telecast of game six of the NBA finals in order to do so.

Television executives are well aware that many viewers sit with their remote controls in hand, rolling through the channels in search of the action. If one channel has stimulating images on the screen and others do not, it is sure to land a good percentage of these channel surfers. Yet programming designed to attract channel surfers inevitably entails compromise on quality dimensions that many viewers care about.

One of the last attempts at restraint in the publishing industry may have come in 1990 when Simon & Schuster forfeited its three-hundred-thousand-dollar advance to Bret Easton Ellis by abandoning its contract to publish *American Psycho* after seeing the final manuscript. In the event, the publisher's restraint was of little avail, as the manuscript was snapped up within forty-eight hours by Sonny Mehta, head of rival publisher Alfred Knopf.

Restraint was nowhere in evidence in the case of Joe McGinniss's *The Last Brother*, an unauthorized biography of Ted Kennedy that made extensive use of invented dialogue between the major characters. Such dialogue obviously makes for a much more engaging narrative, and thus increases the prospects for a best-seller. The problem is that invented dialogue also conveys information and emotional tone whose authenticity the author has no way to vouch for. But McGinniss is the ranking superstar of the true-crime genre, and in the current climate, he is apparently free to write his own ticket.

It may be tempting to think that the network anchormen of earlier decades—men like Chet Huntley, David Brinkley, Walter Cronkite, and John Chancellor—simply had too much dignity to have spent several prime-time hours narrating live coverage of the flight of a former football star suspected of murdering his ex-wife. But to assume that would be to ignore the fact that those men labored under different market conditions. Perhaps any or all of them would have refused to do what is expected of today's news anchors. But if so, they would have been quickly replaced. Tom Brokaw, Peter Jennings, and Dan Rather receive multimillion-dollar annual salaries and in return are expected to deliver the ratings points.

Does the Quality of Culture Matter?

The skeptic's most powerful response to the critic of popular culture has nothing to do with its quality or lack thereof. It is to ask simply: Why shouldn't people consume whatever kind of culture they want?

After all, the philosophical foundation of a free-market economy is that although people may not always spend their money wisely, they remain the final arbiters of their own tastes. The market's job is to provide a rich menu from which people can choose the options that promise the greatest satisfaction.

This response strikes a resonant chord, yet elements of it begin to look shaky on closer scrutiny. For example, although Adam Smith's invisible hand assures that markets do a speedy and efficient job of delivering the goods and services people desire, it tells us nothing about where people's desires come from in the first place. If tastes were fixed at birth, this would pose no problem. But if culture shapes tastes, and if market forces shape culture, then the invisible hand is untethered. Free marketeers have little to cheer about if all they can claim is that the market is efficient at fulfilling desires that the market itself creates.

So where do tastes come from? Some, like the drives for food and sex, are clearly rooted in biology, but even these basic appetites are powerfully mediated by cultural forces. With others, like tastes in music and literature, the influence of culture is even more transparent and powerful.

Just as culture affects preferences, so also do markets influence culture. Markets in the cultural domain are like markets for ordinary goods and services: They serve up only those offerings that people are most willing to pay for. For example, because many people are willing to pay to watch violent films, the market provides a rich menu of them, and the prevalence of such films, in turn, affects cultural attitudes toward violence. Of course, most people give little thought to how the films they watch might affect their attitudes or preferences. But even people who recognize that watching violent films might breed a taste for violence toward others have insufficient reason to avoid such films, because any resulting costs will be borne largely by others.

Activities that affect our preferences affect the well-being of others, just as activities that generate pollution affect the well-being of others. And just as there is no presumption that market forces will lead to a socially optimal amount of pollution, there can be no presumption that market forces will cause preferences to develop, as if led by an invisible hand, in socially beneficial ways.

Culture shapes not only tastes but also abilities. Neuroscientists now know that the brain's neural circuitry is extremely malleable under the influence of environmental stimuli. Our DNA provides the basic framework, but the rich details of synaptic development are powerfully dependent on experience. If the proper stimuli do not occur at critical stages of development, certain capabilities often cannot emerge at all. People who take up foreign languages as adults, for example, seldom learn to speak them without a heavy accent.

Experiments with young cats illustrate this point even more vividly. In ordinary natural environments, cats are exposed to a rich variety of visual stimuli and almost always develop the constellation of visual and motor skills they need to navigate successfully. These same skills do not develop reliably, however, in environments that lack certain kinds of stimuli. For example, kittens reared in a laboratory that lacks vertical lines will never develop the capacity to perceive vertically oriented objects. These cats, which appear normal in most other respects, routinely walk right into the legs of tables and chairs as if they weren't there.[15] No amount of subsequent training or conditioning seems able to repair this deficit.

To function successfully as an adult, a person must acquire not only the capacity to perceive vertical objects, but also a host of other problem-solving abilities and social skills. In the natural environments in which humans evolved, children acquired these skills through practice at solving problems and by grappling with the social situations that arise in family and peer groups. Modern environments are different in countless ways from the environment of evolutionary adaptation, but for developmental purposes, there is one difference of special concern: The typical child in the United States now spends several hours a day passively watching television. And television simply does not provide many of the stimuli that are required for normal cognitive and emotional development.

Of course, the primary goal of producers of television programs is to attract large audiences, not to foster development. Their offerings are seductive by design. Given a choice many children prefer to watch rather than to go out and play, where, after all, various problems and disputes invariably arise. Yet it is precisely the experience of grappling with these problems that fosters development. The brain of a child who watches cartoons four hours a day develops very differently from the brains of children who spend those same hours reading and playing with friends. And, as in the case of the experimental cats, deficits with which children emerge from childhood often cannot be overcome by training later in life.

In addition to social and problem-solving skills, one of the most important capacities for a child to develop on the way to adulthood is patience—the ability to defer gratification. This is important because the alternatives that look most attractive in the short run are often distinctly inferior in the long run. A job flipping hamburgers after school, for example, holds the immediate attraction of providing money to buy a car, but it also entails having less time to qualify for admission to a good university, and hence a lifetime of diminished opportunity.

The inability to set one's sights on larger, more distant rewards is associated with, among other difficulties, criminal behavior,[16] alcohol and other substance abuse,[17] marriage dissolution,[18] and pathologically low savings rates.[19] Our cultural offerings—which increasingly celebrate the simple over the complex, the formulaic over the inno-vative, sensationalism over nuance, the present over the future—could hardly be less well chosen to help foster patience in young people.

Increasingly impoverished political debate is yet another cost of our current cultural trajectory. Complex modern societies generate complex economic and social problems, and the task of choosing the best course is difficult under the best of circumstances. And yet, as in-depth analysis and commentary give way to sound bites in which rival journalists and politicians mercilessly ravage one another, we become an increasingly ill-informed and ill-tempered electorate. We become ever less inclined to compromise, ever more likely to choose leaders on the basis of single issues.

The cultural imperatives that spring from winner-take-all markets have also altered the nature of discourse more generally. Never before, for example, have people seemed so preoccupied as they are today with the lives of celebrities. This obsession has spawned a prime-time television show (*Lifestyles of the Rich and Famous*), a popular weekly magazine (*People*), and a host of imitators. Virtually every major newspaper now has a daily space that reports tidbits from the lives of movie stars, athletes, singers, politicians, and other public figures. Some have several: the *New York Daily News,* for instance, has five gossip columns, and the *New York Post* has three. Monthly magazines, such as *Esquire* and *Vanity Fair,* now have gossip columns.

New York Times culture reporter Trip Gabriel published a recent piece on the rising star of Donovan Leitch, son of the 1960s pop singer of the same name, who was known as Donovan. The message of the article was that even though the younger Leitch has become a celebrity of sorts—a regular fixture in the gossip columns, on everyone's guest list for high-profile gatherings, and so on—he doesn't seem ever to have *done* anything. How does this happen? Gabriel quotes Nancy Kand of Jason Weinberg & Associates, the public relations firm whose task it is "to get Mr. Leitch mentioned in columns and invited to the right movie openings and parties." According to Kand: "In January I'd be like, 'We're handling Donovan Leitch—you know, the son of the 60's crooner.' That was my spiel: Remember the 60s? 'They Call Me Mellow Yellow'? This is his son Donovan Leitch. Now it's just 'Donovan.' Or 'Dono.' Now people beg him to come to parties."[20] Ostensibly Donovan Leitch is a singer in a band called Nancy Boy. But this band, Gabriel notes, is, like Leitch, famous primarily for the company it keeps.

Neil Gabler, author of a recent biography of the late gossip columnist Walter Winchell, notes that although there have always been people whose main achievement it was to be seen with the right people in the right places, the phenomenon has grown sharply in recent years. "So much of what drives this culture is the desire by general Americans, particularly in places like New York and Los Angeles, to *know*," says Gabler. "To know who Donovan Leitch is, even though it doesn't make a damn bit of difference. That makes you feel good. Think about how peculiar this is. There is this validation in *knowing* about people who do nothing and get written about for doing nothing."[21]

Peculiar though it may be, the motive is strong enough to sustain a booming segment of the publishing industry. In the apparently well-founded expectation that its readers would want to know, *People* magazine reported that Donovan Leitch had pierced his navel in order to prod himself to lose weight. "It didn't work," he reports in the caption next to a photo portraying his already wraithlike torso.[22]

Is the fact that it makes some people feel good to know who Donovan Leitch is a matter of social concern? Who is harmed, after all, if some people read the *National Enquirer* and *People* while others read the *New York Times* and the *Atlantic*? Why can't the person whose friends find him dull for not knowing who Donovan Leitch is simply choose a different set of friends?

He can, of course, and, indeed, people everywhere have always tended to stratify according to their interests. Yet we often face compelling incentives to join social networks whose members may not be entirely to our liking. For example, someone may choose to work for the company that offers the best prospects for advancement, even though she may have much more in common socially with the employees of some other company. Once a part of the former group, she will face strong incentives to adopt its norms and values.

Still less under any individual's control are the contents of books, movies, and television programs. We are free to choose, of course, from the existing menu of these items. But as individuals we have virtually no control over the contents of that menu.

No one is truly independent of the culture at large, and we thus have a shared interest in the direction that culture takes. What we read and watch affects the kinds of people we become. And the kind of people we become, in turn, affects what the purveyors of popular culture offer us, and so on in an endless cycle. As more people become preoccupied by the details of celebrities' lives, knowing these details becomes increasingly necessary just to participate in ordinary social exchange.

Not even the ostensibly elite cultural outlets are immune to these environmental pressures. The *New York Times,* for example, has always claimed to have a no-gossip policy, "yet some of its regular columns are amazing simulacra of gossip, and gossipy news increasingly makes it as far as the front page."[23] Even the venerable *New Yorker,* once the epitome of journalistic dignity and good taste, has also adapted to the changing environment. In the summer of 1994, it ran a detailed series on the O. J. Simpson case, and in one 1993 issue published three separate cartoons on the theme of the Bobbitt episode.[24]

Imagine yourself a parent faced with a choice between two societies in which to raise your children: In the first, news media dwell obsessively on the intimate and sensational details of celebrities' lives. In the second, much of this material is replaced by news, feature, and editorial coverage of the events of the day. A choice like this is never offered, of course; but if it were, we suspect that few parents would regard it as a matter of indifference. The financial imperatives of winner-take-all markets are pushing us increasingly toward the first society, and yet it is by no means obvious that this is what most of us favor.

We do not mean to deny the obvious allure of sensationalism. But the things we are most strongly drawn to in the short run are not always in our long-term interest, either as individuals or as a society. Indeed, even those who have become most absorbed by the cult of celebrity often have misgivings about their own behavior. Outside O. J. Simpson's home one day during the week following the murders of Nicole Brown Simpson and Ron Goldman, for example, a female jogger appeared carrying a small camera. When a reporter asked if she always ran with a camera, she responded, "I hate myself for being here. But I can't stay away."[25]

More troubling than any of the other effects of winner-take-all forces on media and culture, however, is the fact that these forces have almost certainly raised the level of violence in society. Here, too, the difficulty is that in markets for media and culture, the need to achieve quick success places a premium on being able to attract attention. Violence has played diverse roles in different human cultures at different points in history, but one constant across time and place is its unerring capacity to compel our attention. As a means of attracting television viewers, moviegoers, and readers, it is rivaled only by sex. Confronted with a murder scene in progress, the channel surfer reflexively lifts his finger from the channel-advance button.

To the producers of television programming, the proof is in the numbers. These executives know that violent programming draws viewers. Newspapers and magazines likewise sell many more copies when their headlines and cover stories deal with violence. And movie goers have always flocked to films in which the protagonist is provoked mercilessly by evil forces before finally erupting in paroxysms of retributive violence.[26]

There would be cause enough for concern if the only consequence of attending to so much violence were that we had less time to devote to other activities. But it appears that exposure to violence has the more profoundly troubling effect of causing violent behavior in viewers themselves. The relationship between violent behavior and exposure to media violence has been studied in many cultures over many decades. And although the precise nature and magnitude of this relationship continues to be debated, the balance of scholarly opinion strongly supports the existence of a positive causal relationship.

In her 1988 congressional testimony, for example, University of Kansas Professor Aletha C. Huston, chair of the American Psychological Association's Task Force on Television and Society, reported: "There is more published research on this topic than on almost any other social issue of our time. . . . Virtually all independent scholars agree that there is evidence that television can cause aggressive behavior."[27] Robert E. McAfee, president of the American Medical Association (AMA), voiced a similar judgment in his 1994 congressional testimony:

A growing body of scientific research has documented the relationship between the mass media and violent behavior. Reports by the Surgeon General, the National Institutes of Mental Health, the National Academy of Sciences, the Centers for Disease Control and Prevention, and the Society of Adolescent Medicine, among others, have arrived at a similar conclusion—namely, that programming shown by the mass media contributes to the aggressive behavior and, in particular, to aggression-related attitudes of many children, adolescents, and adults.[28]

A recent analysis of 188 studies covering almost a quarter of a million viewers in all found a correlation of .31 between exposure to violence and violent behavior.[29] Although statistical correlation by itself does not establish the existence of a causal relationship, more than 130 of the 188 studies were experiments in which the researchers attempted to ensure that the level of exposure to violent programming was the only relevant difference between treatment groups and control groups. The studies found that exposure to violence had a much more pronounced effect on the behavior of children than of adults.

In one of the pioneering studies from the 1950s, twelve four-year-olds were shown a Woody Woodpecker cartoon full of violent images (violent by 1950s standards, at any rate), while another twelve four-year-olds were shown "The Little Red Hen," a peaceful cartoon. Afterward, the children who watched Woody Woodpecker were found to be more likely to hit other children, break toys, and engage in a variety of other disruptive behaviors during free play.[30]

Several other studies attempt to measure actual changes in violence when television is introduced into communities that never had it. One study found, for example, that verbal and physical aggression increased among elementary school children when television was introduced into a community, this in contrast to no change in playground behavior in two control communities that had already had television service for many years.[31] In a similar study, a University of British Columbia researcher observed the behavior of first- and second-grade children in a town in a mountainous part of western Canada where there had been no television before the introduction of a cable system in 1973. By 1975, he found, the incidence of "hitting, biting, and shoving" had increased by 160 percent for students in his sample.[32]

A similar natural experiment took place in South Africa, where the Afrikaner regime banned television until 1975. One study found that in the eight years after television was introduced, South Africa's murder rate shot up dramatically, with the steepest and earliest increases observed in the white community, where television saturation was highest. These findings mirror a similar racial pattern in the sharp increase in murder rates observed in the wake of television's proliferation in the United States in the 1950s.[33]

There have also been studies of how violence in films affects attitudes. One experiment, for example, divided a group of male college students into four groups: The first, a control group, was shown no movies; the second group was shown "teenage sexual-innuendo" movies; the third group saw nonviolent X-rated movies; and the fourth watched the slasher films *Texas Chainsaw Massacre*, *Friday the 13th Part 2*, *Maniac*, and *Toolbox Murders*. The subjects were then empaneled as members of a mock jury and asked a series of questions to measure their empathy for a female rape victim. Subjects who had seen the slasher films scored lowest in empathy not only for the specific victim in the experiment but also for rape victims generally.[34]

Interactive video games, according to one veteran researcher, are even more harmful than television or film violence. As psychologist Leonard Eron explains: "It's because the child is actively involved. He's not just watching and listening; he's doing something. He's connecting kinesthetically. He's making the violence happen. Not only that, but also if he doesn't make the right choice—which is usually the most violent one—he loses the game."[35]

Yet despite the preponderance of evidence that violence in the media begets violence in real life, violence in the media continues. The AMA now estimates that by the time a typical American child has left grade school, he or she will have viewed some eight thousand televised killings and more than one hundred thousand other acts of violence.[36]

Reading interviews with media executives, one gets the sense that they often sincerely wish they could offer programming with less emphasis on violence. But these executives also understand the commercial imperatives of their current situation. As Sen. Paul Simon of Illinois put it, the competitive pressures on broadcasters have "spawned an 'arms race' from which none will retreat for fear of losing ratings points. As in all arms races, the public is the loser."[37]

It is common to hear that popular culture has been corrupted because media executives are evil or greedy people. Perhaps some of them are, but this is almost surely beside the point. We have argued that recent trends are the result not of executive personality traits, but of growing winner-take-all forces that often leave little room for discretionary action. And as we will see in the coming chapter, reform proposals that fail to take these forces into account often have little prospect of making any real difference.

11

Old Wine in New Bottles

In his short story "Harrison Bergeron," Kurt Vonnegut imagines a future world in which the inequality problem has been solved by "the unceasing vigilance of agents of the United States Handicapper General." Vonnegut's main character, George, has above-average intelligence, and is thus required to wear a "little mental handicap radio" in his ear that disrupts his thoughts every few seconds. As the story begins, George is watching a televised dance, with ballerinas that "weren't really very good—no better than anybody else would have been, anyway. They were burdened with sashweights and bags of birdshot, and their faces were masked, so that no one, seeing a free and graceful gesture or a pretty face, would feel like something the cat drug in."[1]

As Vonnegut's tale forcefully makes clear, equality achieved in this manner comes at far too high a price. A society in which the principle of a level playing field is replaced by a forcible insistence on equal outcomes is not for us. Yet reducing inequality is important nonetheless. What is to be done?

The conventional economic wisdom is not encouraging. As Nobel economist James Tobin put it: "The most difficult issues of political economy are those where goals of efficiency, freedom of choice, and equality conflict. It is hard enough to propose an intellectually defensible compromise among them, even harder to find a politically viable compromise."[2]

Yet despite the apparent bleakness of this forecast, our diagnosis of the problem suggests grounds for hope. The conventional wisdom is that income inequality is an inescapable byproduct of any system that provides adequate incentives for good performance. But as we have seen, the relevant incentives in winner-take-all contests are often *too* large, motivating both excessive entry and effort on the part of contestants. Public policies aimed at these problems can simultaneously reduce both wasteful activity *and* inequality. The famous trade-off between equity and efficiency simply need not apply

We illustrate this hopeful conclusion with a series of policy proposals. Many of them are not new, and in fact have been debated extensively in the "tournament of reason." Our aim is not to provide a comprehensive analysis of them, but rather to show how the arguments developed in this book strengthen the case for declaring them winners. The goal in each instance is to help forge a more equitable and productive society, with no loss in individual liberty.

Tax Policy

Fundamental changes in technology and institutions have allowed the most able performers to serve broader markets, and to capture a larger share of the economic pie. The resulting growth in inequality has occurred in a context of slow economic growth—far slower in the last two decades than in the earlier post-war period. Those in the bottom half have been losing ground not only relative to those in the top, but also relative to their parents' generation and their own reasonable aspirations. As the top performers sequester themselves in ever more opulent walled suburbs, inner-city residents lead increasingly desperate and chaotic lives.

We cannot expect an invisible hand to mitigate the economic and social ills that spring from winner-take-all markets. On the contrary, since the forces that create these markets are getting stronger, the most plausible projection is that, left untended, our problems will get even worse.

Many commentators have suggested education and technical

training as remedies for inequality and slow growth. These measures might make it easier for the least skilled persons to find useful jobs, and for that reason alone might be well worth undertaking. But education and training, important as they are, cannot be expected to do much to relieve inequality in the upper reaches of the income distribution. As we saw in chapter 5, for example, earnings inequality in the 1980s grew sharply even *within* the professional class—among people who are already near the top of the educational distribution. The top prizes in many winner-take-all markets are limited in number and will remain so. They will continue to be captured by those who perform best in relative terms, regardless of how well educated the field is.

One possible remedy is a more steeply progressive income tax. In chapters 6 and 7, we argued that higher taxes on the top prizes would curb overcrowding in winner-take-all markets and also reduce incentives to engage in positional arms races. The effect, on both counts, would be to promote equity and efficiency simultaneously.

Of course, higher income taxes would have negative effects as well. For one thing, by taxing the portion of income that people save, they would discourage savings and investment, the most important engines of long-term economic growth.

The prospect of curtailed savings is especially worrisome since the United States already has the lowest saving and investment rates in the industrialized world.[3] Whereas Germans save roughly 15 percent of their personal incomes, and Japanese almost 20 percent, the United States savings rate has fallen below 4 percent. Given the power of compound interest, these differences have important implications for future incomes. Within less than two generations, for example, a society with per capita income growth of 1.5 percent will become 30 percent poorer than another society with the same initial income and a 2 percent growth rate.[4]

If we taxed consumption instead of income, savings would be exempt from tax, which would sharply increase incentives to save. A consumption tax would stimulate savings in a second way—namely, by leaving more disposable income in the hands of people with high savings rates. The resulting higher saving, in turn, would mean more investment, higher economic growth, and reduced borrowing from abroad to finance government deficits.

A consumption tax also promises two other gains. Because the ultimate purpose of earning income is to consume it, a progressive tax on consumption makes entry into winner-take-all tournaments less attractive for the same reasons that a progressive tax on income does. And by effectively reducing the prizes received by winners, a progressive consumption tax also reduces the incentives to engage in positional arms races.

No tax is popular, of course, and yet consumption taxes enjoy support from a surprisingly broad spectrum of political opinion. As economist Laurence Seidman has pointed out, for example, both Lester Thurow and Milton Friedman have written articles advocating consumption taxes.[5] We have to tax *something,* after all, and both liberal and conservative economists seem to recognize that consumption taxes produce fewer negative side effects than income taxes do. Moreover, consumption taxes attack the problems caused by the spread of winner-take-all markets—thus demonstrating that taxes can have positive side effects as well as negative ones.

Proposals to tax consumption raise the specter of forbidding complexity—of citizens having to save receipts for each purchase, of politicians and producers bickering over which products are to be exempt, and so on. Yet a system of consumption taxation need entail no greater complexity than the usual systems of income taxation. The need to keep receipts can be easily avoided by calculating overall consumption as the difference between current income and current savings. There is simply no need to add up the value of each item purchased. The need to debate which, if any, consumption categories ought to be exempt can be avoided by having a large standard deduction—by making the first, say, $20,000 of annual consumption expenditures for each family exempt from taxation. This feature would serve two purposes: It would shield necessities like food, health care, basic clothing, shelter, and transportation from taxation; and it would make the tax progressive.

Consumption taxation is hardly a radical idea. It is already an important component of tax policy in most other developed nations, if not in precisely the form we advocate. For example, value added taxes, which are a form of consumption tax, provide large shares of government revenues in every European country. There are already provisions in the U.S. tax code that exempt specific categories of savings from taxation. But the amounts of income that can be sheltered under these provisions—which include IRAs, Keogh accounts, 401k pension accounts and others—are small. Simply removing the caps and other limitations on these provisions would be a step in the right direction.

It is safe to assume that once a family's consumption exceeds several hundred thousand dollars per year, the family will have long since purchased the things most people regard as necessities. Beyond some threshold, spending tends to be concentrated on second homes, premium automobiles, jewelry, and other luxury items. Since the satisfaction afforded by these items is largely social, or positional, in nature, little would be sacrificed if there were an across-the-board reduction in luxury consumption. If, for example, overall spending on luxury automobiles were to decline, the satisfaction from driving a *relatively* high-quality automobile would remain largely the same.

These observations suggest yet another attraction of a progressive tax on consumption, for such a tax would function, in effect, as a luxury tax. To the extent that certain goods are purchased in part *because* their prices are so high, taxing them leads to more efficient patterns of consumption. Ironically, they do this without imposing significant harm even on those who buy luxury items.

To illustrate, consider a young man's decision about how big an engagement diamond to give his fiancée. Because the function of this gift is to serve as a token of commitment, the ring he buys must necessarily cost enough to hurt. His jeweler will tell him that the custom is to pay two months' salary for a stone and setting. Thus if his annual salary is $42,000, he will have to come up with $7,000 or else be considered a cheapskate.

From the perspective of the economy as a whole, the outcome would be better if there were, say, a 25 percent consumption tax in place. The after-tax price of what is now only a $5,600 diamond would then rise to $7,000. In buying this smaller diamond, the young man would incur the same economic hardship as before, and since this is the essence of the gift's function, his goal would not really be compromised by the tax. Nor would his fiancée suffer any real loss. Because *everyone* would now be buying smaller diamonds, the smaller stone would provide much the same satisfaction as the larger one would have. On the plus side, the government gets an additional $1,400 to finance its expenditures. The only loser is the De Beers diamond cartel of South Africa, which would suffer a decline in the value of its stock of diamonds.

The standards that define acceptable schools, houses, wardrobes, cars, vacations, and a host of other important budget items depend on the amounts other people spend on them. When one job seeker buys a more expensive suit, the effect—even if unintended—is to make her rival's suit seem less attractive. Individual consumers have no reason to take account of how their own spending decisions affect community consumption standards. The result is that consumption goods generally appear much more attractive to individuals than to society as a whole. Taxing these goods makes them less attractive.

How would a progressive consumption tax affect labor supply? The supply-side economists of the Reagan era made confident claims that lower tax rates would stimulate people to work harder. In the major tax reforms of 1981 and 1986, the marginal rates for top earners were reduced from 43 to 28 percent.[6] But because tax reform also broadened the tax base, the average federal rate for this group declined only slightly. Thus the high-wage workers were not given any tax windfall, but were given a strong incentive to work longer hours. And sure enough, a group that economists expected to be most responsive to this change, married women in high-income households, did increase their hours of work substantially during the 1980s. We cannot confidently attribute this increase to the tax reform, however, since low-income, older women also increased their hours substantially during the 1980s, and they suffered an actual increase in marginal tax rates.

Supply-side economists also argue that the multimillion-dollar compensation packages of Fortune 500 CEOs are needed to provide "incentives" without which these CEOs would fail to manage aggressively on behalf of shareholders. Executives surely do perform in a more focused, energetic way when their pay depends in part on

"If those soak-the-rich birds get their way, I can tell you here's one coolie who'll stop putting his shoulder to the goddam wheel."
Drawing by Donald Reilly; © 1972 The New Yorker Magazine, Inc..

how well their companies perform. But there is reasonably clear evidence that CEO performance does not strongly depend on the *extent* to which pay varies with profitability.[7]

Vigorous executive performance is often the norm even under much weaker financial incentives than we find in the United States. In Japan and Germany, for example, CEOs earn much lower salaries and face much higher tax rates than do their American counterparts.[8] On the supply siders' view, it might seem puzzling that Japanese and German executives even bother to show up for work. And yet the companies they manage have provided much of America's stiffest competition in recent years.

In sum, neither the available empirical evidence nor our most carefully considered economic theories support the claim that higher tax rates would sharply reduce national income. On the contrary, we have argued that a progressive tax on consumption would be more likely to expand national income than to contract it. This point is important because the many compelling ethical and practical budgetary arguments for more progressive taxes have so often been trumped by the presumption that such a move would make us poorer.

An Ill-Advised Reform

Federal tax reform legislation enacted in 1993 eliminated tax deductions on any portion of an executive's salary in excess of one million dollars, a move that appears to have been motivated by public concern over runaway salaries in the executive suite. Although the political forces that led to this provision are easily understood, its consequences are likely to be far different from what its proponents had intended. For executives already on the job, the cap is like an increase in the tax rate on executive incomes. But because the policy is limited to executive salaries, its effect is to make top positions in business less attractive compared to top positions in some other arenas. For example, since most lawyers earn their incomes as partners in firms, or as independent contractors, such a policy would make law more attractive relative to management.

We see no persuasive reason to alter the existing incentive structure in this way. If the goal is to limit the highest incomes, this should be done so as to affect the incomes of employees and independent contractors alike. On both efficiency and equity grounds, multimillion-dollar annual salaries are no more problematic in executive suites than in sports, entertainment, law, consulting, or other areas. Taxing all such incomes—or, better, the corresponding consumption expenditures—at a higher rate makes more sense than capping the deductibility of executive incomes alone.

Another reason for questioning the wisdom of the deductibility caps is that similar caps in the past may actually have served to increase the average amounts paid rather than lower them. For example, in reaction to public outrage over proliferating "golden parachutes"—multimillion-dollar severance payments received by CEOs—Congress passed a law in the early 1980s that prohibited companies from taking tax deductions on severance payments larger than 2.99 times the average pay of the affected executive over the previous five years. Although the obvious intent was to curb golden parachutes, its effect was apparently just the opposite. By calling severance payments *larger than* the 2.99 multiple unacceptable, the law was implicitly suggesting that payments *up to* that amount were okay. And this, apparently, led many companies with smaller golden parachutes quickly to boost them to the limit.[9]

Tort Reform

Of all the winner-take-all markets we have discussed, the evidence of overcrowding is clearest in the legal profession. Unlike participants in many other winner-take-all markets, whose activities create new wealth, litigators usually battle over existing wealth. The private rewards of the top plaintiffs' attorneys are almost certainly much larger than the social value of their services.

Of course, we are not saying that the tort system accomplishes no good at all. Society clearly gains if the fear of being sued prompts cost-effective action to prevent injury to others. What we are arguing is that these gains can be realized at a fraction of the cost we incur under our current system. For it is the private interest of the litigants, not the broader social interest, that channels so many of our best and brightest students into the legal profession.

The tendency of law to attract top talent is not new. Before World War II, Stanford psychologist Lewis Terman recorded the occupations and other characteristics of a sample of 150 exceptionally gifted men, whose average age in 1940 was 30.5 years, and whose average IQ was 155. Sixteen percent of them were lawyers, by far the largest single occupation represented in the sample.[10]

With the litigation explosion of recent decades, the number of people choosing law has grown sharply. Legal services, which accounted for only 0.6 percent of gross domestic product in 1960, accounted for 1.39 percent in 1987. By 1987 there were almost 750,000 full- and part-time practicing attorneys, a more than threefold increase in twenty years.[11] Many of these are extremely able and energetic persons who could have made valuable contributions in other sectors of the economy.

A variety of simple reforms might help steer some of these people away from legal careers. Thus we could hold losing plaintiffs responsible for court costs and defendants' legal fees. Under the current American system, a plaintiff risks almost nothing by filing a lawsuit. The primary resource needed to file a suit is an attorney's time. A lawyer will handle a plaintiff's case for a contingency fee, so that the plaintiff incurs no legal expenses if he or she loses. There is the possibility of a countersuit to consider, but the standards for finding a lawsuit frivolous are so strict that this risk is negligible in most cases. Given the apparent randomness with which juries award large judgments, it is little wonder that many people regard an opportunity to sue as a free lottery ticket. People would be less inclined to file baseless lawsuits if they knew they would have to pay court costs and their opponent's legal fees if they lost. This is the system employed in many European countries, and the United States would do well to adopt it. True, this reform would make it harder for low-income persons to seek compensation for their injuries, but there are a host of better mechanisms for assuring equitable access to the legal system.

A second promising reform would be to impose caps on liability awards. Many tort judgments strike neutral observers as far in excess of any reasonable assessment of the damages actually suffered. In 1986, for example, a New York court awarded $65 million—$58 million of it for "pain and suffering"—to a woman who lost part of her small intestine when a hospital failed to diagnose an obstruction in her digestive tract.[12] But even if these vast sums accurately measured the amount of injury suffered, few of us would consider buying private insurance with as much as one-tenth as much coverage.[13] By allowing these awards, we force people to buy "insurance" in the form of higher prices of all goods and services. One author has estimated that this "liability tax" accounts for 30 percent of the price of ordinary stepladders and 95 percent of the price of childhood vaccines.[14] Large, highly publicized tort judgments are one of the factors that have lured excessive resources into the legal profession. A cap on these judgments would not only be equitable, it would also enhance efficiency.

Health Care Finance

Real health care expenditures per capita in the United States have grown more rapidly than real GNP per capita for as long as the relevant data have allowed us to measure.[15] As a share of GNP, health care costs have risen from only 4 percent in 1940 to roughly 14 percent today.

The reasons for this escalation are many. But it is clear that physicians' fees, especially those of highly trained specialists, are implicated. We saw in chapter 5, for example, that the incomes of the highest-paid physicians grew extremely rapidly even in the context of the 1980s, a decade of unusually strong growth in the nation's highest incomes.

This growth in the incomes of top physicians has been brought about largely by third-party payment schemes, which reimburse specialists at high rates for performing procedures that could have been performed by generalists at much lower rates. The resulting high incomes of specialists exacerbate the problem by confronting entering medical students with compelling financial incentives to become specialists rather than general practitioners. In ordinary markets, where consumers pay directly for the services they consume, this would spell an eventual decline in the fees charged by specialists. But this discipline is often conspicuously absent in markets driven by third-party payers.

The simple fix for this problem is to tailor reimbursements to the nature of the procedure being performed rather than to the physician's qualifications. Most government health care reform proposals, as well as the move to managed care in the private sector, have stressed the need to employ more primary care physicians in the delivery of health services. Such reforms will help smooth the distribution of income and, at the same time, help free up talented people to perform useful tasks in other sectors—once again, an improvement in both equity and efficiency.

Educational Finance

In chapter 8 we saw evidence that the demand for elite educational credentials has grown sharply in recent decades. As the forces that give rise to winner-take-all markets intensify, this trend is likely to continue or even accelerate. Universities will continue to respond by bidding for those things that contribute to elite status—leading research faculty talented administrators, successful fund-raisers, and so on. In the bidding war for top faculty, the principal inducements are higher salaries, bigger research budgets, and lighter teaching loads. Higher compensation at the top of the academic pyramid will inevitably filter downward, and the number of fund-raisers will continue to grow, as universities respond to the growing demand for elite educational credentials.

At present governmental expenditure policies help fuel these elements of the educational arms race. Thus, in addition to funding a large system of junior colleges and four-year state colleges, California taxpayers support an elite system in which nine separate University of California campuses vie for preeminence in the international intellectual arena. This competition is driven largely by the imperatives of the research agendas in the various disciplines. And there is no reason to suppose that the criteria by which, say, literary critics or economists score points in this competition are even loosely correlated with the interests of taxpayers.

It is one thing for a state to recognize a public interest in ensuring that all citizens receive a solid primary and secondary education. A case can also be made for public support for higher education in the increasingly sophisticated skills required in the modern workplace. And, from the perspective of state governments at least, there is even a case for subsidizing elite education at the university level, lest the state's best students migrate to other states and thereby vanish from local tax rolls. But it is far from clear that taxpayers should subsidize the competition for elite status across a broad range of disciplines in each of several separate state universities.

Both efficiency and fairness favor a narrower and more focused pursuit of excellence. Those states that wish to maintain elite public institutions of higher learning would be well advised to consider charging tuitions comparable to those charged by elite private institutions. Equity requires that a talented student not be denied access to the top institutions merely because of his or her family's inability to pay. But this goal can be served with need-based financial aid, rather than with across-the-board tuition subsidies, which largely benefit rich and upper-middle-income families.

The case for tuition reform is clearest perhaps in the case of law schools. Although the country already has far more lawyers than could possibly be justified on efficiency grounds, most states continue to subsidize the production of still more lawyers. For example, the law schools at the state-supported University of California campuses matriculate thousands of new law students each year, even though the state has run budget deficits of almost ten billion dollars in some recent years. UC law students pay tuition that covers only a fraction of the annual cost of their education. Similar situations exist in other state-supported law schools.

Why should the nation's taxpayers subsidize the production of additional lawyers? On both equity and efficiency grounds, the case for eliminating these tuition subsidies is compelling. There is a similar case for eliminating the tax-deductible status of private gifts to law schools.

A case can also be made that tuition policy constitutes a more effective lever than either income or consumption taxes for discouraging overcrowding in a variety of other winner-take-all markets. The financial success of lawyers like F. Lee Bailey, Alan Dershowitz, and any number of Wall Street deal makers surely contributes to the law profession's allure, yet we doubt that many would abandon their pursuit of a law degree on learning that the tax rate on high incomes had risen somewhat.

Tax rates on winners' incomes take effect in most cases only years after people commit themselves to compete in specific arenas. It is a widely documented principle of psychology that individuals are much more responsive to current rewards and penalties than to rewards and penalties that occur only after considerable delay.[16] Criminals, for example, are known to respond more to an increase in the likelihood of being caught than to an increase in the sentence they will ultimately receive if caught. And many fewer people would drink to excess if the ensuing hangover came immediately and not the next morning.

These observations suggest that, relative to the effect of taxes on winners, subsidies and penalties issued at a much earlier stage may be more likely to influence the career choices of young persons. Several philanthropists have demonstrated, for example, that the promise of financial support for college attendance sharply increases the graduation rates in inner-city high schools. In 1981, for example, businessman Eugene Lang promised sixth graders in East Harlem's

P.S. 121 that he would pay full college tuition for any of them who graduated from high school and wanted to go on. The school's principal at the time had told Lang that only one out of four students would ordinarily make it. In this particular class, however, 54 percent of the sixty-one students received a high school diploma or the equivalent.[17] More than half—thirty-two students—went on to "Bard, Swarthmore, and other universities."[18] Such experiences suggest that scholarships, fellowships, and the terms of student loans might be extremely effective mechanisms for leading students to favor certain career choices over others.

It is easy to imagine pitfalls in bureaucratic attempts to fine-tune the allocation of students to different fields of study. Yet failure to take *any* action along these lines is itself risky. In the increasingly competitive global marketplace, our economic prosperity will depend more and more on our ability to allocate our most talented people to our most important jobs. It is by no means clear that our current policy toward educational aid, which implies that law students and engineers are equally deserving of financial encouragement, is justifiable.

Tuition subsidies also provide a more effective means than tax policy for encouraging activities that markets would otherwise pursue insufficiently. In chapter 6, for example, we saw that the imperfections of patent protection often make it impossible for the creators of new technologies to reap more than a small fraction of the social benefit of their discoveries. The traditional approach of tax policy has been to offer tax exemptions or subsidies for research and development and other investments that society wants to encourage. The difficulty with this approach, however, is that it tacitly invites people to redefine whatever they do as technology production.

This problem is avoided if we use tuition subsidies to encourage the production of more graduates who are trained to do research and development. Of course, educating someone as an engineer does not guarantee that he or she will remain an engineer forever. But it is reasonable to expect that people with technical and scientific training will, on the average, find their most attractive opportunities in fields that make use of those skills. More important, the production of more scientists and engineers gives firms no incentive to tell the tax authorities that their accountants are doing R&D.

Information Remedies

In chapter 6 we argued that overcrowding in winner-take-all tournaments is a problem even when people are perfectly informed about their odds of winning. People tend to be unrealistically optimistic about their chances, thus exacerbating the problem. If only people could be made more vividly aware of their true odds of doing well in different fields.

Information remedies, however, are a less promising tack than might appear. For one thing, there are so many fields that wide dissemination of the odds of a winning outcome in each would be too cumbersome to do much good. Perhaps counselors in specific fields could do more to warn aspirants of the long odds against landing top positions. For example, before someone commits himself to spend eight hours a day for more than a decade, hoping to become a concert pianist, his teacher might counsel him that only a handful of the thousands who try each year ever perform before a paying audience. Aspiring lawyers might likewise be told that very few will ever become partners in Wall Street law firms.

Yet hope springs eternal, and one cannot feel very confident that these efforts would produce major changes in the career choices of young people. On the other hand, some of the relevant information could be disseminated through existing institutions at low cost, and might divert at least some people to other pursuits. Carefully chosen information remedies might thus be another mechanism that promotes both equity and efficiency.

Antitrust Policy

In chapter 9, we described a variety of positional arms control agreements implemented by .private citizens and organizations. These ranged from informal social norms, such as those that discourage cosmetic surgery, to formal contractual arrangements, such as the salary cap in the NBA.

Any positional arms control agreement, private or public, restricts the freedom of individuals to take certain actions.[19] Because we celebrate individual freedom as a value, there is a preference in the

West for private over public means of restricting individual behavior. It is thus incumbent on policy makers to permit private positional arms control agreements whenever they do not clearly conflict with some larger public interest. Particularly in the field of antitrust, however, such deference has often been missing.

Consider, for example, the court's decision in a suit filed by the M&H Tire Company against the New England Auto Racing Association (NEARA).[20] All auto racing associations take a variety of steps to limit the amounts individual contestants may spend on their cars and equipment. These include limits on engine displacement, fuel delivery systems, suspension components, and so on. The rules evolve as technology changes. In the late 1970s individual NEARA members discovered that they could gain an edge by spending more than their rivals on new designs of racing tires. To curb this arms race, NEARA amended its rules to specify that all racers must compete with identical brands and models of tires. To this end it posted technical specifications for the tires it wanted and invited tire manufacturers to submit bids. The winning bidder was announced, and this particular dimension of the positional arms race was solved. Or so NEARA thought.

Shortly after the tire contract was signed, the M&H Tire Company, one of the losing bidders, filed and won an antitrust suit against NEARA for price-fixing. Although the decision was later reversed on appeal, the fact that NEARA had to pay high legal fees to contest the issue was bound to have a chilling effect on others contemplating similar positional arms control agreements.

The winner-take-all perspective calls attention to another ill-advised antitrust suit, one filed by the Justice Department against the Ivy League universities and MIT. The schools were charged with price-fixing through collusion on their financial aid policies. Literally speaking, the accused were guilty as charged. They had an implicit policy of not using financial aid as a means of competing with one another for the brightest students, and enforced this policy by sharing information on how much financial aid each was offering to specific students. The suit was dropped when defendants signed a consent decree in 1991 in which they promised to abandon their existing financial aid policy.[21]

The unfortunate result has been the destruction of a valuable positional arms control agreement. As we saw in chapter 8, a university's reputation for excellence depends in large measure on its ability to attract the best possible students. In an unconstrained environment, schools must use all means at their disposal, including financial aid, to attract these students. In such an environment, financial aid will be captured disproportionately not by the students whose families most need it, but by the students with the highest grades and test scores.

The Justice Department charged, correctly, that the existing tuition policy worked to the disadvantage of the most talented students. But that was the whole *point* of the policy. We are all happy with the idea that people who work hard and do well should be rewarded. But the financial aid policy's purpose was to protect an even more deeply cherished social value—that financial limitations not stand in the way of students' receiving the best education for which they qualify. In the absence of cooperative financial aid policies, the increasingly limited stocks of financial aid will be ever less likely to help those who really need it.

We do not mean to suggest that our antitrust laws serve no useful purpose. Many of the agreements to restrict competition that businesses have made over the years have been harmful to the public interest, and the antitrust laws have almost surely inhibited at least some such agreements. Yet as the locus of competition has shifted from the local to the global marketplace, the threat from price-fixing, mergers, and other business practices proscribed by the antitrust laws has declined. Simultaneously, the escalating stakes of competition have created increasingly intense positional arms races. It is time to consider antitrust legislation and policies that are more sensitive to this shifting balance.

Leisure Policy

As we saw in chapter 7, Americans today are working longer hours than in the recent past. People at the top work harder because the top prizes have gotten bigger, whereas those near the bottom work harder to just keep from falling further behind. The continuing proliferation of winner-take-all markets all but ensures the continuation of these trends. Is this a good thing, and if not, is there any practical alternative?

The winner-take-all perspective suggests that when reward depends on relative performance, no individual can work less without compromising his or her chances of getting ahead. If *everyone* were to work a little less, however, no one's promotion prospects would be harmed. This insight suggests the attraction of policies that encourage people to work fewer hours. Instead of being triggered at thirty-nine hours per week, for example, overtime premiums could take effect after only thirty-five. Or the number of official national holidays could be increased.

Such steps have been taken without obvious ill effects in other places. Whereas in the United States many entry-level workers receive less than two weeks of paid vacation, the corresponding figure in many European countries is close to six weeks (counting national holidays in both cases). Of course, if people worked a little less, they would have to be paid a little less as well. But if *everyone* were paid less, then people would also need less to meet their obligations.

Media and Culture

In chapter 10 we argued that the intensification of winner-take-all forces has helped mold popular culture in a variety of troubling ways. These changes have come about partly because today's larger financial stakes create stronger incentives to employ attention-getting devices. The implicit positional arms control agreements by which suppliers refrained from employing such devices in the past have broken down both because of the higher stakes and because of the increase in the number of actual or potential competitors who are in a position to violate them.

Since both competition and the financial stakes will continue to grow, it would be naive to hope for a return to voluntary restraint on excessive sexual and violent content. Some of the same technological changes that have given rise to the problems, however, may also make possible a new class of solutions. Television circuitry now exists, for example, that enables parents to black out any programs they do not wish their children to see.[22] If this feature were more widely available, services would quickly develop to prescreen and rate programs and offer viewing guidelines to parents. The result would be a system far more flexible than the alternative of direct government regulation of program content.

A deeper understanding of how winner-take-all effects mold popular culture also lends additional weight to the case for government support for cultural offerings that might otherwise vanish from the private marketplace. Conservatives condemn the Public Broadcasting System and National Public Radio as entitlements for the rich, and perhaps they are right that more could be done to make offerings of these programs available to a broader spectrum of consumers. Yet, as we have seen, the basic premise behind the conservatives' complaint—that free markets lead to socially optimal outcomes in popular culture-—is flawed. We are not advocating the equally naive view that cultural offerings prescribed entirely by government bureaucrats would be an improvement. But between these extremes lies a prudent middle ground—one that preserves the vibrancy of market forces and at the same time acknowledges that, in matters of culture, our collective interests often differ profoundly from our individual interests.

Looking Ahead

The forces that give rise to winner-take-all markets have been growing stronger and will continue to do so. In all likelihood they will accelerate. Looking ahead, then, it would be unrealistic to expect even the most determined government programs to reverse the trend toward greater income inequality. After all, if one country's tax rates get too high, its top performers can simply emigrate.

If inequality cannot be contained by anything short of a world government, we must somehow find ways to soften its impact on our social fabric. As journalist Mickey Kaus described the problem in his recent book:

> We've always had rich and poor. But money is increasingly something that enables the rich, and even the merely prosperous, to live a life apart from the poor. And the rich and semi-rich increasingly seem to *want* to live a life apart, in part because they are increasingly terrified of the poor, in part because they increasingly seem to feel that they deserve such a life, that they are in some sense superior to those with less. An especially

precious type of equality—equality not of money but in the way we treat, each other and live our lives—seems to be disappearing.[23]

Perhaps the most promising accommodation to these stresses is to limit the domains of life in which income matters. James Tobin wonders "why we cannot arrange things so that certain crucial commodities are distributed less unequally than is general income—or, more precisely, less unequally than the market would distribute them given an unequal income distribution."[24]

Thinking along these lines, philosopher Michael Walzer argues that inequality creates greater psychological burdens in some spheres of life than in others.[25] It is easier to tolerate the fact that income controls access to luxury automobiles than to tolerate its controlling access to good schooling or essential medical care; and easier to tolerate its controlling access to overseas vacations than to tolerate its being a prerequisite for fair treatment by the criminal justice system. Walzer envisions an ideal world in which life is partitioned into different spheres. In some—his sphere of goods, for example—the amount of income you have matters; but in other important spheres, all citizens stand on equal footing, irrespective of their incomes. Unlike the current political sphere in the United States, for example, Walzer envisions political rules under which people's voices are heard with equal strength irrespective of their incomes. In the sphere of justice in this ideal world, similarly, the rules would assure that the quality of legal representation is independent of personal wealth.

In practical terms attempts to limit the domain of inequality begin with government support for those things for which equal access seems most essential. This impulse is embodied in proposals for universal health coverage and universal access to good public schools. Tobin also includes access to basic housing and nutrition.

The catch, in the conventional wisdom, is that even these essentials are beyond our means. Thus, the argument goes, the poor can't be taxed because they have no money, and the rest of us can't be taxed lest we stop working hard and stop making productive investments.

The conventional wisdom is wrong. Our prevailing beliefs about economic and social policy were forged in an environment in which winner-take-all markets were both less pervasive and much less clearly understood. The inaccuracy of these beliefs, however, does not ensure that they will be easily abandoned. All beliefs die hard, but none more so than those that support existing positions in the economic and social order. Yet the fact remains that the policies that once worked are increasingly ill suited to our current problems.

Change is never easy. Yet once we see clearly the role of winner-take-all markets in our current situation, the necessary adjustments become less daunting. The conventional wisdom portrays a world of agonizing trade-offs. We reject this pessimistic conclusion, for, as we have seen, a greater tax burden on the economy's biggest winners would not only help set our financial house in order but would also help steer our most talented citizens to more productive tasks. If this burden took the form of a progressive tax on consumption, it would also stimulate much needed savings and investment. Thus the redeeming feature of the modern winner-take-all society is that many of the same policies that promote equality also promote economic growth. If this is not quite a free lunch, it is surely an inexpensive one.

Notes

Chapter 1. *Winner-Take-All Markets*

1. Vonnegut, 1987, pp. 74, 75.
2. Ibid., p. 75.
3. Goode, 1978, p. 72.
4. For a detailed discussion, see Krugman, Fall 1992.
5. *The Economist,* November 5, 1994, p. 19.
6. Ibid.
7. *Fortune,* April 19, 1993, p. 162.
8. Marshall, 1947 (1890), p. 685.
9. Evidence for these and other similar tendencies is discussed in Gilovich, 1990, chap. 5.
10. Quoted by Whiteside, 1980, pp. 158, 159.
11. Sykes, 1988, pp. 5, 6.
12. See Ashenfelter and Bloom, 1990.
13. Boulding, 1966, p. 110.
14. Gleick, 1992, p. 128.
15. Lane, 1994, p. 90.
16. Ibid., p. 90.

Chapter 2. *How Winner-Take-All-Markets Arise*

1. *United States Tennis Association Yearbook,* 1993, 1994.
2. There is, however, an emerging literature that describes why some firms might deliberately structure employee compensation schemes as rank-order tournaments in situations where monitoring costs

would have otherwise led to insufficient effort (Lazear and Rosen, 1981; O'Keeffe, Viscusi, and Zeckhauser, 1984; Rosen, 1986). By contrast, our interest is in cases where the winner-take-all payoff structure is a natural feature of the competitive environment.

3. Rosen, 1981, p. 845.

4. Bell et al, 1994, p.2c.

5. Wriston, 1992, p. 36.

6. National Science Foundation, 1989.

7. Zuckerman, 1977, p. 171.

8. See Mnookin and Wilson, 1988. Texaco ultimately settled for three billion dollars in cash.

9. See, for example, Farrell and Saloner, 1985; and Katz and Shapiro, 1985.

10. Diamond, 1994, p. 30.

11. Arthur, 1988, 1989.

12. Arthur, 1989, p. 126.

13. Arthur, 1988, p. 16.

14. See, for example, Merton, 1968, 1988; Cole and Cole, 1973.

15. Merton, 1988, p. 445.

16. Kingston and Lewis, 1990, p. xx.

17. In a study based on college choices of high school seniors, for example, Fuller, Manski, and Wise, 1982, report that applicants tend to prefer colleges that matriculate students whose SAT scores exceed their own.

18. Quoted by Walton, 1986, p. 24.

19. Katz and Shapiro, 1994, p. 107.

20. For a discussion, see Adler, 1985.

21. See, for example, Miller, 1956.

22. Goode, 1978, p. 75.

23. Quoted by Berkowitz, 1986, p. 33.

24. See Laband, 1990, p. 133.

25. Berlyne, 1971, p. 193.

26. Adler, 1987, uses this observation to explain the success of chain restaurants.

27. Note that habit formation and acquired tastes give rise to winner-take-all effects only when they operate in conjunction with an economy of scale somewhere in the relevant production process. If

there were no extra costs, for example, in producing a customized news broadcast for each household, then each consumer could watch a different set of commentators, and the winner-take-all effect we now see in this area would be muted. The production technology of broadcast television, however, makes it much cheaper to produce a few newscasts than many, and this fact, together with a preference for the familiar, contributes to the observed concentrations of demand.

28. Berlyne, 1971, p. 193.
29. Hirsch, 1976.
30. For an extensive summary of the evidence for concerns about relative position, see Frank, 1985, chap. 2.
31. Quoted by Rial, 1990, p. 54.
32. Faulkner, 1983, p. 173.
33. Krugman, Fall 1992, p. 24.
34. Marshall, 1947, quoted in Rosen, 1981, p. 857.
35. See Buchanan, Tollison, and Tullock, 1980; Krueger, 1974.

Chapter 3. The Growth of Winner-Take-All Markets

1. Reported in Rosen, 1981, p. 857.
2. Kirkland, 1988, p. 42.
3. Reich, 1991, p. 83.
4. Greenspan, 1988, p. 12.
5. Pine, 1993, p. 44.
6. Wriston, 1992, p. 43.
7. Ibid.
8. Quoted by Tenner, 1991, p. 31.
9. Ibid.
10. See Griffin Miller, 1992.
11. *International Business*, March 1993, p. 104
12. MacKie-Mason and Varian, 1994, p. 76
13. *Time*, June 13, 1994, p. 62.
14. *Computergram International*, 1994.
15. McBee, 1985, p. 49.
16. Ibid., pp. 49, 50.
17. Adam Smith, 1910 (1776), book 1, p. 5.
18. Adam Smith, quoted by Heilbroner, 1986, p. 171.

19. Zuboff, 1988, p. 9.
20. Reich, 1991, pp. 177, 178.
21. This pattern has been alternatively rationalized on grounds of fairness or on the basis of high-ranked workers' willingness to buy high local status from their lesser-ranked colleagues. See Frank, 1985, chap, 2.
22. Krugman, Fall 1992, p. 21.

Chapter 4. Runaway Incomes at the Top

1. For a detailed discussion, see Whiteside, 1981, chap. 2.
2. PR Association, 1994.
3. Quoted by Whiteside, 1981, p. 105.
4. These and other contract figures come from Whiteside, 1981.
5. Quoted by ibid., p. 174.
6. *Business Week,* April 19, 1993, p. 92.
7. The results that follow were produced in collaboration with Chadwick Meyer as part of his Cornell Economics Honors Thesis in 1989.
8. For details, see Meyer, 1989.
9. Crystal, 1991, p. 164.
10. Ibid., p. 166.
11. Blair, 1994, p. 24.
12. Crystal, 1991, p. 27.
13. Burroughs and Helyar, 1990, p. 95.
14. Bok, 1993, chap. 1.
15. Crystal, 1991, pp. 207, 209. The implied comparison between foreign and American executive salaries may be overstated by the fact that nonmonetary fringe benefits tend to be more valuable in Japan and Germany. But this effect will be at least partially offset by the substantially higher tax rates on top earnings in Japan and Germany.
16. See Frank and Cook, 1995. Our analysis was based on *Forbes* survey data generously shared with us by Kevin M. Murphy.
17. McCarroll, 1993, p. 63.
18. Byrne, July 25, 1994, p. 61.
19. Huey, 1993, p. 56.
20. Byrne, July 25, 1994, p. 65.

21. Huey, 1993, p. 57.
22. *Television and Video Almanac,* 1988, p. 323.
23. Wecker, 1992, p. 18.
24. Ibid., p. 34.
25. Vogel, 1986, p. 92.
26. Leedy, 1980, p. 3, quoted in ibid., p. 105.
27. Wecker, 1992, p. 51.
28. Kilday and Thompson, 1994, p. 18.
29. Wecker, 1992, p. 49.
30. Kasindorf, 1992, p. 37.
31. Ibid.
32. Stevenson, 1991, p. 3–1.
33. Fabrikant, 1992.
34. Caen, 1993.
35. Reibstein, 1994, p. 58.
36. Ibid.
37. Auletta, 1994, p. 63.
38. Ibid.
39. The account that follows is based on Conover, 1978.
40. Heinfeld, 1993.
41. Behbehani, 1993,
42. Sperber, 1990, p. 42.
43. Schmuckler, 1994.
44. *Sports Illustrated,* December 28, 1988, p. 24. The same pressure to win that led to Sherrill's high salary apparently also led to numerous infractions of NCAA rules. In 1988, the year Sherrill left A&M, the school's football program was given two years' probation for recruiting and other violations.
45. Sperber, 1990, p. 149.
46. Wolff, 1992, p. 96.
47. Korr, 1990, p. 37.
48. Fainaru, 1991.
49. Chass, 1993.
50. Sandomir, 1994, p. B13.
51. Ladewski, 1991, p. 33.
52. Blum, 1991, p. 9A.
53. Sandomir, 1994, p. A1.

54. *Jet,* December 16, J.991, p. 52.
55. Sandomir, 1994, p. A1.
56. Watson, 1992.
57. Ibid., p. 103.

Chapter 5. Minor-League Superstars

1. Krugman, March 23, 1992.
2. Phillips, 1994, app. A.
3. Lawrence Katz, 1992/93, p. 11.
4. Kuttner, 1983.
5. Bound and Johnson, 1992; Katz, 1992/93.
6. Young people quickly got the message, and enrolled in colleges and universities in record numbers during the 1980s. Otherwise the "baby bust" generation would have been too small to fill the existing spaces.
7. Levy and Murnane, 1992, p. 1372.
8. There were 118 million people with earnings in 1989 (1990 census data supplied by Claritas Inc., Ithaca, N.Y.).
9. The most detailed data on earnings come from the decennial U.S. Census. The 1980 and 1990 censuses included questions about employment and earnings for the preceding year, asked of a huge random sample—5 percent of the population. These data enable us to compare earnings distributions for 1979 and 1989. By "earnings" we mean wage and salary income and self-employment income before taxes. We limit our analysis to those who work full-time: at least forty weeks, at thirty-five hours per week or more.
10. To be more precise, according to the Consumer Price Index the figure that is comparable to $70,000 in 1979 is $119,600 in 1989. Our statistical analysis uses this latter figure. But in the discussion, we round it off to $120,000 for simplicity of exposition,
11. The number of Centurions in 1989, P_{89}, is equal to the following expression:

$$(1+g)(1+m)(1+x)P_{79},$$

where

g = number of additional full-time workers in the occupation divided by the number in 1979

m = the difference between the fraction of workers who would have been Centurions in 1979 (if the median income in 1979 had been the same as it actually was in 1989) and the fraction of workers who actually were Centurions in 1979

x = residual growth after taking account of g and m, due to increase in inequality of earnings

12. Rosen, 1982.
13. Lewis, 1989, p. 163.
14. Ibid., p. 179.
15. Ibid., p. 36.
16. Eaton, 1994.
17. Jackson et al., 1988.
18. Novick, 1988.
19. See Furino and Douglass, 1990; and Douglass and Furino, 1990.
20. Rosen, 1992, pp. 242–43.
21. See, for example, Olson, 1991, and Huber, 1988. The figures that follow come from Huber.
22. Brimelow and Spencer, 1989, p. 197.
23. Ibid.

Chapter 6. Too Many Contestants?

1. Wright and Dwyer, 1990, p. 126.
2. Smith, 1937 (1776), pp. 107, 109.
3. Ibid., p. 109.
4. Wylie, 1979.
5. Svenson, 1981.
6. Parker et al, 1959.
7. College Board, 1976–77.
8. Cross, 1977.
9. Weinstein, 1980; Weinstein, 1982; Weinstein and Lachendro, 1982.
10. *Psychology Today,* October 1989, p. 16, quoted in Gilovich, 1991.
11. Gilovich, 1991, p. 77.
12. The anthropologist Lionel Tiger, for example, takes this approach in his 1979 book. See also Gilovich, 1991, chap. 5.
13. Alloy and Abramson, 1979.
14. Tversky and Kahneman, 1974.

15. Randall, 1994.
16. Consider the following illustrative example: Suppose that with one hundred contestants, the expected income of the winning singer is $1,000,000. If all potential contestants considered themselves equally likely to win at the moment they decided to enter the contest, each has an expected income of $10,000 (in effect, a lottery ticket worth this amount), the same as the potter's wage. There will thus be one hundred contestants for the recording contract if everyone chooses the occupation that maximizes her expected income. Let M denote the amount by which the winner's expected income rose when the number of contestants grew from ninety-nine to one hundred. We know that each contestant's expected income when there were only ninety-nine contestants—namely $(\$1,000,000 - M)/99$—must have been greater than ten thousand dollars (or else the one hundredth contestant wouldn't have entered). Thus we have $(\$1,000,000 - M)/99 > \$10,000$, which implies $M < \$10,000$. So if contestants enter up to the point where their expected income equals the potter's wage, entry will proceed past the income-maximizing point. For a more general demonstration of this result, see Frank and Cook, 1993.
17. The paper in which the phrase was coined is by Garrett Hardin, 1968.
18. In ordinary markets as well, the entry of a new supplier may cause harm to existing suppliers by driving the price of the product down. But every dollar suppliers lose because of a price reduction is a dollar gained by those who buy the product. There is no similar compensation, however, for the loss suffered by contestants in a winner-take-all market when a new person enters.
19. Just as Japanese baseball teams sometimes pay large sums to players no longer good enough to play in the major leagues.
20. If the nonmonetary aspects of being a loser are sufficiently unpleasant, we might see cases where the monetary wage for losers exceeds the wage in alternative occupations.
21. See, for instance, Frank, 1984; Konrad and Pfeffer, 1990; and Podolny, 1993.
22. See Frank and Cook, 1993.
23. DeMare, 1994, p. 57.

24. See Kunreuther, 1979.
25. Dasgupta, 1988, p. 74.
26. Mansfield et al, 1981.
27. For an extended discussion, see Okun, 1975.

Chapter 7. The Problem of Wasteful Investment

1. Personal communication.
2. See, for example, Congleton, 1980; Frank and Cook, 1993.
3. See Chung, 1994.
4. An important potential exception to this claim involves cases in which the prize being sought substantially understates the social value of the winner's performance. In such cases investment in performance enhancement may be insufficient despite the winner-take-all payoff structure.
5. Our description of Phillips's experience is based on an interview with her by Joan Ryan, 1992.
6. Ibid.
7. Ibid.
8. Quoted in ibid.
9. Pace, July 28, 1994.
10. Quoted by Hoberman, 1992, p. 251.
11. Janofsky, August 6, 2, and 1, respectively, 1992.
12. Hoberman, 1992, p. 266. In addition to Johnson, there were four East Germans and one Swiss.
13. Ibid., p. 100.
14. Windsor and Dumitru, 1988.
15. McCormick and Tinsley, 1990, quoting *USA Today,* April 3, 1985.
16. Ibid., quoting *Newsweek,* April 8, 1985.
17. Ibid.
18. Sperber, 1990, p. 2.
19. Ibid., p. 93.
20. Jenkins, 1992, pp. 71, 72.
21. Sperber, 1990, p. 247.
22. *Chronicle of Higher Education,* May 21, 1986.
23. Sperber, 1990, p. 85.
24. Ibid., p. 86.
25. Ibid., p. 87.

26. Moran, August 13, 1989.

27. *Sports Illustrated*, October 2, 1989.

28. *South Bend Tribune,* August 14, 1987, quoted by Sperber, 1990, p. 15.

29. *Chronicle of Higher Education,* May 11, 1988.

30. Purdy, February 4, 1993.

31. The following account of promotional activity in the publishing industry is drawn from Whiteside, 1981.

32. Ibid., p. 25.

33. Ibid., pp. 25, 26.

34. *Standard Directory of Advertisers,* various volumes.

35. For an extensive survey of this evidence, see Frank, 1985, chap. 2.

36. Quoted by Wallich, 1994, p. 77.

37. Ibid.

38. For a more detailed development of this argument see Frank, 1985, chap. 7.

39. Schor, 1991, p. 29.

40. The paper that launched this literature is by Lazear and Rosen, 1981. See also O'Keeffe, Viscusi, and Zeckhauser, 1984; Rosen, 1986.

Chapter 8. The Battle for Educational Prestige

1. Gannett News Service, 1991.

2. See Ehrenberg et al, 1993, p. 184. The decline in the ratio of doctorates actually understates the true shift because the proportion of foreign nationals among doctoral students in American universities has increased sharply during recent decades, especially in engineering and the sciences, and many of these students do not remain in the United States.

3. Lewis, 1989, p. 24.

4. Huey, 1993, p. 56.

5. Kingston and Lewis, 1990.

6. Coleman, 1973.

7. See Kingston and Lewis, 1990.

8. For a discussion, see McPherson and Winston, 1988.

9. See Krukowski, 1985, for evidence that students' definition of quality shifted during the early 1980s to focus more on the post-graduate success of the student body.

10. Fuller, Manski, and Wise, 1982.
11. McMillen, June 5, 1991.
12. Ibid.
13. National Science Foundation, 1983, pp. 79–80.
14. Blank, 1991.
15. Merton, 1988, p. 615.
16. Caminiti, June 18, 1990.
17. Ibid.
18. We used the list from the 1980 edition of *Barron's*. Colleges were rated by several factors to determine the competition for admission, including entrance exam scores and high school grades of the freshman class, as well as the proportion of applicants to whom the college offered acceptance.
19. The same list of schools matriculated 61 percent of the Presidential Scholars for the period 1987–1989, and 60 percent of the Westinghouse Talent Search Winners for the period 1960–89.
20. The list of schools was the same for 1979 and 1989, and was taken from the 1980 *Barron's*.
21. See Schenet, 1988, and Clotfelter, 1991.
22. Clotfelter, 1991.
23. Schapiro, O'Malley, and Litten, 1990.
24. Spies, 1990.
25. In 1987, about 56 percent of those who applied to an elite private school matriculated at such a school. See table 4 of Schapiro, O'Malley, and Litten, 1990.
26. Astinetal., 1988, p. 8.
27. For details of the survey, see Cook and Frank, 1992.
28. Shea, 1994.
29. McPherson and Schapiro, 1990.
30. Quoted by Merton, 1973, p. 428.
31. Ibid., pp. 428, 429.
32. See Hearn, 1990, and Spies, 1990.
33. Sykes, 1988, p. 72.
34. Ibid.
35. U.S. Department of Education, 1993, table 225.
36. Ibid., table 305.
37. Associated Press, September 28, 1994.

38. Clotfelter, 1994.
39. Celis, 1994, p. 38.
40. Ibid., 1994, p. 1.
41. Ibid.

Chapter 9. Curbing Wasteful Competition

1. Wilkinson, 1979, pp. 45, 46.
2. Kiernan, 1988, p. 144.
3. Oddly enough, however, there has been greater competitive balance in baseball, which despite not having pay caps has seen small-city franchises win seven of the last fourteen World Series. By contrast, no small-city franchise has won the NBA title during the same period, and only one (Portland) has made it to the finals.
4. Hine, March 12, 1993.
5. Bell and White, May 25, 1993.
6. Ibid.
7. National Industrial Conference Board, 1970, p. 79.
8. For a survey of this literature, see Frank, 1985, chap. 5.
9. Scc, for example, Whyte, 1955, p. 201.
10. Mangum, 1964, p. 48.
11. See, for instance, Helson, 1964.
12. Reed, August 10, 1994.
13. *The Economist,* January 11, 1992, p. 25.
14. Fine et al, 1991, p. 402.
15. Laband and Hienbuch, 1987, p. 3.
16. Ibid., pp. 144, 145.
17. Dawkins, 1976, p. 154.
18. Wright, 1994.
19. See ibid.
20. Shenon, August 18, 1994.
21. See, for example, Dowd, June 28, 1992.
22. Reported by Doup, September 28, 1992.

Chapter 10. Media and Culture in the Winner-Take-All Society

1. Kakutani, August 2, 1994.
2. Quoted by Weinraub, August 16, 1994.
3. McAfee, 1994.

4. *South China Morning Post,* February 20, 1994.

5. Stade, 1994, p. 14.

6. Quoted by Faulkner, 1983, p. 172.

7. Maslin, May 1, 1994.

8. Ibid.

9. This period was created by an FCC ban on network programming between 7 and 8 P.M., which was supposed to encourage the development of more local programming. Instead local stations turned largely to independent syndicators to fill this time slot.

10. Patterson, 1994.

11. Quoted by Fallows, 1986, p. 44.

12. Ibid, p. 45.

13. Ibid.

14. Associated Press, August 12, 1994.

15. Held and Hein, 1963.

16. Wilson and Herrnstein, 1985.

17. Ainslie, 1992.

18. Frank, 1988.

19. Thaler and Shefrin, 1981.

20. Quoted by Gabriel, 1994, p. 31.

21. Ibid., p. 34.

22. *People,* September 19, 1994.

23. Szabo, 1994, p. 24.

24. These cartoons appeared in the November 29, 1993 issue.

25. Janofsky, 1994, p. 14.

26. This is a one-sentence plot summary of the enormously successful Bruce Lee films and a series of hit films starring Charles Bronson. For an insightful discussion, see Romer, 1996.

27. Quoted by Cannon, 1993.

28. McAfee, 1994.

29. Comstock and Paik, 1991.

30. Quoted by Cannon, 1993. See also Bandura, Ross, and Ross, 1963; and Steuer, Applefield, and Smith, 1971.

31. Joy, Kimball, and Zabrack, 1986.

32. Quoted by Cannon, 1993.

33. Ibid.

34. Ibid.

35. Quoted by Meltz, 1994, p. 2.
36. McAfee, 1994.
37. Quoted by Hickey, 1994, p. 11.

Chapter 11. Old Wine in New Bottles

1. Vonnegut, 1970, p. 8.
2. Tobin, 1970, p. 263.
3. Boskin, 1988, p. 71.
4. Ibid., p. 72.
5. Seidman, 1994, p. 66.
6. Bosworth and Burtless, 1992.
7. Jensen and Murphy, 1990.
8. See Crystal, 1991. Crystal's non-U.S. figures may understate executive compensation to the extent that a greater share of compensation in other countries comes in the form of fringe benefits. On the other hand, the tax rate comparison is probably biased in the other direction because of the prevalence of high value-added taxes outside the United States.
9. Byrne, April 24, 1994, p. 57.
10. Shurkin, 1992.
11. Rosen, 1993, table 1.
12. Huber, 1988, p. 122.
13. On this point see Cook and Graham, 1977.
14. Huber, 1988, p. 3.
15. See Newhouse, 1992, p. 4.
16. The definitive treatment of this issue is found in Ainslie, 1992.
17. Freifeld, 1991, p. 4.
18. Neff, March 25, 1990.
19. Actually, this language is misleading, since if an individual favors having his actions restricted in some way, it hardly makes sense to call this a reduction in his freedom. But inevitably there will be some who do not favor a particular positional arms control agreement, and for these people at least, the restrictions represent a genuine loss of freedom. The idea is not that private restrictions on individual freedom are never onerous. On the contrary, social norms are sometimes far more oppressive than formal laws. But in general it will be easier for strongly affected individuals to escape

the consequences of private restrictions. Someone who doesn't approve of a poker game's conservative betting limits can move to a game with higher stakes. It is much more difficult for someone who doesn't approve of a law against bigamy to form a new society in which bigamy is permitted.

20. Soocher, 1984.
21. Wortman, 1993, p. 67. MIT refused to sign the consent decree and eventually prevailed in court.
22. For a discussion, see Hamilton, 1994.
23. Kaus, 1992, pp. 5, 6.
24. Tobin, 1970, p. 265.
25. Walzer, 1983.

Bibliography

Ackoff, R. L., and M. H. Halbert. *An Operations Research Study of the Scientific Activity of Chemists.* Cleveland: Case Institute of Technology Operations Research Group, 1958.

Adler, Moshe. "Stardom and Talent." *American Economic Review* 75 (March 1985): 208–12.

———. "Economies of Scale in Imitative Consumption and the Size of the Firm: Theory and an Application to Chain Restaurants." Davis: University of California Department of Economics Working Paper No. 287, 1987.

Allison, Paul D., and John A. Stewart. "Productivity Differences Among Scientists: Evidence for Accumulative Advantage." *American Sociological Review* 39 (August 1974): 596–606.

Alloy, L. B., and L. Y. Abramson. "Judgment of Contingency in Depressed and Nondepressed Students: Sadder But Wiser?" *Journal of Experimental Psychology: General IQS* (1979): 441–85.

Arthur, W. Brian. "Self-Reinforcing Mechanisms in Economics." In Philip W. Anderson and Kenneth J. Arrow, eds., *The Economy as an Evolving Complex System.* Reading, Mass.: Addison-Wesley, 1988, pp. 9–31.

———. "Competing Technologies, Increasing Returns, and Lock-In by Historical Events." *Economic Journal* 99 (March 1989): 116–31.

Ashenfelter, Orly, and David Bloom. "Lawyers as Agents of the Devil in a Prisoner's Dilemma Game." Working Paper #270, Industrial Relations Section, Princeton University, 1990.

Associated Press. "Study: College Tuition Up 6 Percent." *Ithaca Journal,* September 28, 1994, p. 5A.

———. "Grisham's Next Film Nets Him $6 Million." *Ithaca Journal,* August 12, 1994, p. 2A.

Astin, Alexander W, K. C. Green, W. S. Korn Schalit, and E. R. Berz. *The American Freshman: National Norms for Fall 1988.* Los Angeles: University of California Higher Education Research Institute, 1988, 9–31.

Auletta, Ken. "Promise Her the Moon." *The New Yorker,* February 14, 1994, pp. 61–63.

Bandura, A., D. Ross, and S. A. Ross. "Imitation of Film-mediated Aggressive Models." *Journal of Abnormal and Social Psychology* 66, 1 (1963): 3–11.

Becker, Gary S., and Kevin M. Murphy. "A Theory of Rational Addiction." *Journal of Political Economy* 96, 4 (1988): 675–700.

Behbehani, Mandy. "The Making of a '90s Mega-model." *San Francisco Examiner,* January 31, 1993, pp. D1, D2.

Bell, Jarrett, Bob Abramson, and Eric Brady. "Deion Who?" *USA Today,* August 17, 1994, p. 2C.

Bell, Jarrett, and Carolyn White. "Several Rules Changes to Buoy America's Cup." *USA Today,* May 25, 1993, p. 9C.

Berkowitz, Peggy. "Bomb at Home, Best-Seller in Canada." *Wall Street Journal,* June 24, 1986, p. 33.

Berlyne, D. E. *Aesthetics and Psychobiology.* New York: Appleton-Century-Crofts, 1971.

Blair, Margaret M. "CEO Pay: Why Such a Contentious Issue?" *Brookings Review,* Winter 1994, pp. 23–31.

Blank, Rebecca, "The Effects of Double-Blind versus Single-Blind Reviewing: Experimental Evidence from the *American Economic Review.*" *American Economic Review* 81 (December 1991): 1041–67.

Blum, Ronald. "Big Stars Play for Big Bucks." *Ithaca Journal,* September 3, 1991, pp. 1A, 9A.

Bok, Derek Curtis. *The Cost of Talent: How Executives and Professionals Are Paid and How It Affects America.* Newark: Free Press, 1993.

Boskin, Michael. "Tax Policy and Economic Growth: Lessons from the 1980s." *Journal of Economic Perspectives* (Fall 1988): 71–97.

Bosworth, Barry, and Gary Burtless. "Effects of Tax Reform on Labor Supply, Investment, and Saving." *Journal of Economic Perspectives* 6 (Winter 1992): 3–26.

Boulding, Kenneth. *The Impact of the Social Sciences,* Rutgers, N.J.: Rutgers University Press, 1966.

Bound, John, and George Johnson. "Changes in the Structure of Wages in the 1980s: An Evaluation of Alternative Explanations." *American Economic Review* 82 (June 1992): 371–92.

Brimelow, Peter, and Leslie Spencer. "The Plaintiff's Attorney's Great Honey Rush." *Forbes,* October 16, 1989, pp. 197 ff.

Buchanan, James, Robert Tollison, and Gordon Tullock, eds. *Toward a Theory of the Rent-Seeking Society,* College Station: Texas A&M Press, 1980.

Burrough, Bryan, and John Hellyar. *Barbarians at the Gate.* New York: Harper & Row, 1990.

Byrne, John A. "The Craze for Consultants." *Business Week,* July 25, 1994, pp. 60–66.

———. "That's Some Pay Cap, Bill." *Business Week,* April 25, 1994, p. 57.

Caen, Herb. "One Thing After Another." *San Francisco Chronicle,* January 26, 1993, p. B1.

Carniniti, Susan. "Where the CEOs Went to College." *Fortune,* June 18, 1990, pp. 120–22.

Cannon, Carl. M. "Honey I Warped the Kids: Television, Violence, and Children." *Mother Jones*, July 1993, pp. 16ff.

Celis, William. "The Big Stars on Campus Are Now Research Labs." *New York Times,* December 4, 1994, pp. 1, 38.

Chass, Murray. "Motivation Upon Arrival for Henderson." *New York Times,* March 3, 1993, p. B10.

Chi, Victor. "Football Abolished at Santa Clara." *San Jose Mercury News.* February 4, 1993, pp. 1G, 9G.

Chung, Tai-Yeong. "Rent-Seeking Contest When the Prize Increases with Aggregate Efforts." University of Western Ontario Department of Economics Research Report 9407, 1994.

Clotfelter, Charles T. "Demand for Undergraduate Education." In Charles T. Clotfelter, Ronald G. Ehrenberg, Malcolm Getz, and John J. Siegfried, *Economic Challenges in Higher Education.* Chicago: University of Chicago Press, 1991, pp. 19–139.

———. *Buying the Best: Cost Escalation in the Arts and Sciences.* Unpublished Monograph, Duke University, September 1994.

Cole, Jonathan R., and Stephen Cole. *Social Stratification in Science.* Chicago: University of Chicago Press, 1973.

Coleman, James S. *Power and the Structure of Society.* New York: Norton, 1973.

College Board. *Student Descriptive Questionnaire.* Princeton, N.J.: Educational Testing Service, 1976–77.

Comstock, G., and H. Paik. *Television and the American Child.* San Diego, CA: Academic Press, 1991.

Congleton, Roger. "Competitive Process, Competitive Waste, and Institutions." In J. Buchanan, R. Tollison, and G. Tullock, eds. *Toward a Theory of the Rent-Seeking Society.* College Station: Texas A&M Press, 1980, pp. 153–79.

Conover, Carole. *Conover Cover Girls.* Englewood Cliffs, NJ: Prentice-Hall, 1978.

Cook, Philip J., and Robert H. Frank. "The Growing Concentration of Top Students at Elite Schools." In Charles Clotfelter and Michael Rothschild, eds. *Studies in Supply and Demand in Higher Education.* Chicago: University of Chicago Press, 1993, pp. 121–40.

Cook, Philip J., and Daniel A. Graham. "The Demand for Insurance and Protection: The Case of Irreplaceable Commodities." *Quarterly Journal of Economics* 91 (1977): 143–56.

Cowan, R. *Backing the Wrong Horse: Sequential Technology Change under Increasing Returns.* Ph.D. dissertation, Stanford University, 1987.

Cross, R. "Not *Can* But *Will* College Teaching Be Improved?" *New Directions for Higher Education* (Spring 1977): 1–15.

Crystal, Graef. *In Search of Excess; The Overcompensation of American Executives.* New York: W. W. Norton, 1991.

Dasgupta, Partha. "Patents, Priority and Imitation or, the Economics of Races and Waiting Games." *Economic Journal* 98 (March 1988): 66–80.

Dawkins, Richard. *The Selfish Gene.* New York: Oxford University Press, 1976.

DeMere, Mac. "BMW M3 versus Toyota Supra: Hormone-Enhanced 3-Series Tackles Turbo-less Super Car." *Motor Trend*, September 1995, pp. 56–64.

Diamond, Edwin. "The Last Word." *New York,* January 10, 1994, pp. 8–35.

Doup, Liz. "Tall or Short, Life Is a Game of Inches." *Chicago Tribune,* September 7, 1992, Tempo section, p. 1, zone C.

Dowd, Maureen. "Presidential Timber Seems to Be Tall." *New York Times,* June 28, 1992, p. E1.

Eaton, Leslie. "Brokers' Paychecks Kept Swelling in 1993." *New York Times,* August 9, 1994, p. D1.

Ehrenberg, Ronald G., Daniel Rees, and Dominic Brewer. "How Would Universities Respond to Increased Federal Support for Graduate Students?" In Charles T. Clotfelter and Michael Rothschild, eds., *Studies of Supply and Demand in Higher Education.* Chicago: University of Chicago Press, 1993, pp. 183–206.

Fabrikant, Geraldine. "Blitz Hits Small Studio Pix." *New York Times,* July 12, 1992, p. F7.

Fairanu, Steve. "The Real Green Monster." *Boston Globe Magazine,* August 25, 1991, pp. 13 ff.

Fallows, James. "The New Celebrities of Washington." *New York Review of Books,* June 12, 1986, pp. 45–49.

Farrell, Joseph, and Garth Saloner. "Standardization, Compatibility, and Innovation." *Rand Journal of Economics* 16 (1985): 70–83.

Faulkner, Robert R. *Music on Demand: Composers and Careers in the Hollywood Film Industry.* New Brunswick, N.J.: Transaction Books, 1983.

Fine, Larry F, R. C. Bialozor, and T. F. McLaughlin. "An Analysis of Computer-Assisted Instruction on Scholastic Aptitude Test Performance of Rural High School Students." *Education* 111 (Spring 1991): 400–403.

Frank, Robert H. "The Economics of Buying the Best." Cornell University Department of Economics Working Paper, 1978.

———. *Choosing the Right Pond: Human Behavior and the Quest for Status.* New York: Oxford University Press, 1985.

Frank, Robert H., and Philip W. Cook. "Winner-Take-All Markets." Cornell University, 1993. Mimeo.

———. "Winner-Take-All Markets and Executive Pay." Paper presented at the annual meetings of the American Economic Association, Washington, D.C. January, 1995.

Freifeld, Karen. "College Promise Pays Off." *Newsday,* June 24, 1991, p. 4.

Fuller, Winship C., Charles F. Manski, and David A. Wise. "New Evidence on the Economic Determinants of Postsecondary Schooling Choices." *Journal of Human Resources* 27, 4 (1982): 477–98.

Fullerton, Don, and Diane Lim Rogers. *Who Bears the Lifetime Tax Burden?* Washington, D.C.: The Brookings Institution, 1993.

Gabler, Neil. *Winchell; Gossip, Power and the Culture of Celebrity.* New York: Alfred A. Knopf, 1994.

Gabriel, Trip. "Donovan Leitch: He's It! He's Hot! He's . . . Who?" *New York Times,* July 31, 1994, pp. 31ff.

Gale, David, and Lloyd S. Shapley. "College Admissions and the Stability of Marriage." *American Mathematical Monthly* 69 (January 1962): 9–15.

Gannett News Service. "Lawyer Numbers Grow." *Ithaca Journal,* May 1, 1991, p. A8.

Gilder, George. *Microcosm.* New York: Simon & Schuster, 1989.

Gilovich, Thomas. *How We Know What Isn't So.* New York: Free Press, 1991.

Gleick, James. *Genius.* New York: Pantheon, 1992.

Goldin, Claudia. "Labor Markets in the Twentieth Century." Cambridge, Mass.: NBER Historical paper no. 58, 1994.

Goode, William J. *The Celebration of Heroes,* Berkeley: University of California Press. 1978.

Greenspan, Alan. "Goods Shrink and Trade Grows." *Wall Street Journal,* October 24, 1988, p. A12.

Griffin, Larry, and Karl Alexander. "Schooling and the Socioeconomic Attainments: High School and College Influences." *American Journal of Sociology* 84 (1978): 319–47.

Hamilton, James T. "Marketing Violence: The Impact of Labeling Violent Television Content." Duke Program in Violence and the Media Working Paper, January 1995.

Hardin, Garrett. "The Tragedy of the Commons." *Science* 162 (1968): 1243–48.

Hearn, James C. "Pathways to Attendance at the Elite Colleges." In Paul W. Kingston and Lionel S. Lewis, eds. *The High-Status Track: Studies of Elite Schools and Stratification.* Albany: State University of New York, 1990, pp. 121–47.

Heilbroner, Robert. *The Essential Adam Smith.* New York: W. W. Norton, 1986.

Held, Richard, and Alan Hein. "Movement-Produced Stimulation in the Development of Visually Guided Behavior." *Journal of Comparative and Physiological Psychology* 56 (5) (1963): 872–76.

Helson, Harry. *Adaptation Level Theory.* New York: Harper & Row, 1964.

Hickey, Neil. "How Much Violence Is There?" In *Violence On Television: TV Guide Symposium on Television Violence.* Newark: 1994.

Hine, Tommy. "The Glory Isn't Worth It; Koch Says Price Too High." *Hartford Courant,* March 12, 1993, p. E4.

Hirsch, Fred. *Social Limits to Growth.* Cambridge, Mass.: Harvard University Press, 1976.

Hoberman, John M. *Mortal Engines: The Science of Performance and the Dehumanization of Sport.* New York: Free Press, 1992.

Huber, Peter W. *Liability: The Legal Revolution and Its Consequences.* New York: Basic Books, 1988.

Huey, John. "How McKinsey Does It." *Fortune,* November 1, 1993, pp. 56–81.

Jackson, Donald W, William H. Cunningham, and Isabella C. M. Cunningham. *Selling: The Personal Force in Marketing.* New York: John Wiley and Sons, 1988.

James, Estelle, Nabeel Alsalam, Joseph C. Conaty, and Duc-Le To. "College Quality and Future Earnings: Where Should You Send Your Children to College?" State University of New York at Stony Brook, 1988. Photocopy.

Janofsky, Michael. "Americans Finish 1–2 in Shot Only to Field Heavy Questions." *New York Times,* August 1, 1992, Sec. 1, p. 31.

——. "Devers and Christie Get to Dazzle in the Dash." *New York Times*, August 2, 1992, Sec. 8, p. 1.

——. "Watts and Marsh Blaze to Glory on the Track." *New York Times*, August 6, 1992, p. B13,

——. "With Envelope, Simpson's Lawyer Keeps World Guessing for Weekend." *New York Times,* July 3, 1994, p. 14.

Jenkins, Sally. "Sorry State: Football in the Southwest Conference Isn't What It Used to Be and Texas and Texas A&M Are Looking to Bail Out." *Sports Illustrated,* November 16, 1992, pp. 70–76.

Jensen, Michael C, and Kevin J. Murphy. "CEO Incentives—It's Not How Much You Pay, But How." *Harvard Business Review* 68 (May–June 1990): 138–49.

Joy, J., M. Kimball, and M. Zabrack. "Television and Children's Aggressive Behavior." In T. M. Williams, ed., *The Impact of Television: A Natural Experiment in Three Communities.* Orlando, FL: Academic Press, 1986, pp. 303–60.

Kakutani, Michiko. "Some Familiar Terrain After *American Psycho*." *New York Times,* August 2, 1994, p. B2.

Kasindorf, Jeanie. "Payback Time." *New York,* January 27, 1992, pp. 34–40.

Katz, Lawrence F. "Understanding Recent Changes in the Wage Structure." *NBER Reporter* (Winter 1992/93): 10–15.

Katz, Lawrence, and Kevin M. Murphy. "Changes in Relative Wages, 1963–87: Supply and Demand Factors." Cambridge, Mass.: NBER Working Paper No. 3927, 1992.

Katz, M, L., and Carl Shapiro. "Network Externalities, Competition and Compatibility." *American Economic Review* 75 (1985): 424–40.

———. "Systems Competition and Network Effects." *Journal of Economic Perspectives* (Spring 1994): 93–115.

Kaus, Mickey. *The End of Equality.* New York: Basic Books, 1992.

Kiernan, Y. G. *The Duel in European History: Honour and the Reign of Aristocracy.* New York: Oxford University Press, 1988.

Kilday, Gregg, and Anne Thompson. "Offers They Can't Refuse." *Entertainment Weekly*, April 8, 1994, pp. 16–23.

Kingston, Paul William, and Lionel S. Lewis, eds. *The High-Status Track: Studies of Elite Schools and Stratification.* Albany: State University of New York, 1990.

Kingston, Paul W. and John C. Smart. "The Economic Pay-off of Prestigious Colleges." In Paul W. Kingston and Lionel S. Lewis, eds. *The High-Status Track: Studies of Elite Schools and Stratification.* Albany: State University of New York, 1990, pp. 147–74.

Kirkland, Richard. "Entering a New Age of Boundless Competition." *Fortune,* March 14, 1988, p. 41.

Kleinfeld, N. R. "No Superstar, Just a Working Model: A 'Great Smile' and a 6-Figure Income." *New York Times,* January 5, 1993, p. B1.

Kolbert, Elizabeth. "Study Reports TV is Considerably More Violent Despite Outcry." *New York Times*, August 5, 1994, p. A13.

Konrad, Alison, and Jeffrey Pfeffer. "Do You Get What You Deserve? Factors Affecting the Relationship between Productivity and Pay." *Administrative Science Quarterly* 35 (June 1990): 258–85.

Korr, Chuck. "Twenty Years Later: A Look at the Curt Flood Case." *Sporting News*, January 15, 1990, p. 37.

Krueger, Alan. "How Computers Have Changed the Wage Structure:

Evidence from Microdata, 1984–89." Cambridge, Mass.: NBER Working Paper No. 3858, 1992.

Krueger, Anne O. "The Political Economy of the Rent-Seeking Society." *American Economic Review* 64 (June 1974): 291–303.

Krugman, Paul R. "Disparity and Despair." *U.S. News & World Report,* March 23, 1992, p. 54.

———. "The Right, the Rich, and the Facts." *The American Prospect* 11 (Fall 1992): 19–31.

Krukowski, Jan. "What Do Students Want? Status." *Change,* May–June 1985, pp. 21–28.

Kunreuther, Howard. "The Changing Societal Consequences of Risks from Natural Hazards. *Annals, AAPSS* 443 (May 1979): 104–16.

Kuttner, Robert. "The Declining Middle." *The Atlantic,* July 1983, pp. 60–72.

Laband, David N. "How the Structure of Competition Influences Performance in Professional Sports: The Case of Tennis and Golf." In Brian L. Goff and Robert D. Tollison, eds., *Sportometrics.* College Station: Texas A&M Press, 1990, pp. 133–50.

Laband, David N., and Deborah H. Hienbuch. *Blue Laws: The History, Economics, and Politics of Sunday Closing Laws.* Lexington, Mass.: Lexington Books, 1987.

Ladewski, Paul. "Sports Salaries." *Inside Sports,* April 1991, pp. 30–33.

Lane, Anthony. "The Top Ten." *The New Yorker,* June 27 & July 4, 1994, pp. 79–92.

Lazear, Edward, and Sherwin Rosen. "Rank-Order Tournaments as Optimal Labor Contracts." *Journal of Political Economy* 89, 5 (1981): 841–64.

Leedy, D. J. *Motion Picture Distribution: An Accountant's Perspective.* Los Angeles: David Leedy, CPA, P O. Box 27845.

Levy, Frank. *Dollars and Dreams: The Changing American Income Distribution.* New York: Russell Sage Foundation: 1987.

———. "Incomes, Families, and Living Standards." In Robert E. Litan, Robert Z. Lawrence, and Charles Schultze, eds., *American Living Standards.* Washington, D.C.: Brookings Institution, 1988, pp. 108–53.

Levy, Frank, and Richard J. Murnane. "U.S. Earnings Levels and Earnings Inequality: A Review or Recent Trends and Proposed Explanations." *Journal of Economic Literature* 30, 3 (1992): 1333–81.

Lewis, Michael M. *Liar's Poker: Rising Through the Wreckage on Wall Street.* New York: W. W. Norton, 1989.

Lotka, Alfred J. "The Frequency Distribution of Scientific Productivity." *Journal of the Washington Academy of Sciences* 16 (June 19, 1926): 317.

Loury, Glenn. "Market Structure and Innovation." *Quarterly Journal of Economics.* 93 (1979): 395–410.

Mangum, Garth. *Wage Incentive Systems.* Berkeley: Institute of Industrial Relations, University of California, 1964.

Mansfield, E., M. Schwartz, and S. Wagner. "Imitation Costs and Patents: An Empirical Study." *Economic Journal* 91 (December 1981): 907–18.

Marantz, Steve. "Fehr and Ravitch on the Campaign Trail." *Sporting News,* August 8, 1994, pp. 10–15.

Marshall, Alfred. *Principles of Economics, Eighth Edition.* New York: Macmillan, 1947.

Maslin, Janet. "Just Before They Invented the Blockbuster." *New York Times,* May 1, 1994, Sec. 2, Arts & Leisure, p. 30.

McAfee, Robert E. "Statement of the American Medical Association to the Subcommittee of Telecommunications and Finance, House Committee on Energy and Commerce." FDCH Congressional Testimony, June 30, 1994.

McBee, Susanna. "English: Out to Conquer the World." *U.S. News & World Report*, February 18, 1985, pp. 49–52.

McCarroll, Thomas. "A Builder Not a Slasher." *Time*, November 8, 1993, p. 63.

McCormick, Robert E., and Maurice Tinsley. "Athletics versus Academics? Evidence from SAT Scores." In Brian L. Goff and Robert D. Tollison, eds., *Sportometrics.* College Station: Texas A&M Press, 1990, pp. 179–91.

———. "Athletics and Academics: A Model of University Contributions." In Brian L. Goff and Robert D. Tollison, eds., *Sportometrics.* College Station: Texas A&M Press, 1990, pp. 193–204.

McMillen, Liz. "Foundations and Corporations Concentrate Giving at Top Universities, Study Finds." *Chronicle of Higher Education,* June 5, 1991, pp. A1, A21, A23.

McPherson, Michael S., and Morton Owen Schapiro. *Selective Admission and the Public Interest.* New York: The College Board, 1990.

McPherson, Michael S., and Gordon C. Winston. "Reflections on Price and Quality in U.S. Higher Education." Williamstown, Mass.: Williams College, 1988, Draft.

Meltz, Barbara F. "Video Violence Can Translate Into Real Life." *Houston Chronicle,* January 30, 1994, p. 2.

Merton, Robert K. "Priorities in Scientific Discovery." *American Sociological Review*, 22, no. 6 (December 1957): 635–59. Reprinted in Robert K. Merton, *The Sociology of Science.* Chicago: University of Chicago Press, 1973, pp. 286–324.

———. "'Recognition' and 'Excellence': Instructive Ambiguities." In Adam Yarmolinsky, ed., *Recognition of Excellence: Working Papers.* New York: Free Press, 1960, pp. 297–328. Reprinted in Robert K. Merton, *The Sociology of Science,* Chicago: University of Chicago Press, 1973, pp. 419–38.

———. "The Matthew Effect in Science." *Science,* 159, no. 3810 (January 5, 1968): 56–63. Reprinted in Robert K. Merton, *The Sociology of Science,* Chicago: University of Chicago Press, 1973, pp. 439–59.

———. "The Matthew Effect in Science, II." *Isis* 79 (1988): 606–23.

Meyer, Chadwick. *So You Want to Turn Pro?* Department of Economics Honors Thesis, Cornell University, 1989.

Meyer, Herbert H. "The Pay for-Performance Dilemma." *Organizational Dynamics* 3 (Winter 1975): 39–50.

Miller, G. A. "The Magical Number Seven, Plus or Minus Two: Some Limits on Our Capacity for Processing Information." *Psychological Review* 63 (1956): 81–97.

Miller, Griffin. "For Any Tie that Binds, There Is a Club to Join." *New York Times*, October 3, 1992, p. 32 (national edition).

Mnookin, Robert H., and Robert B. Wilson. "Rational Bargaining and Market Efficiency: Understanding Pennzoil v. Texaco." Stanford Center on Conflict and Negotiation, Working Paper No. 1, December 1, 1988.

Moran, Malcolm. "Colleges Try to Buck a Troubling Trend." *Raleigh News & Observer*, August 13, 1989, pp. 1B, 8B.

Murphy, Kevin J. "Top Executives Are Worth Every Nickel They Get." *Harvard Business Review* 64 (March-April 1986): 125–32.

Murphy, Kevin M., Andrei Shleifer, and Robert W. Vishny. "The Allocation of Talent: Implications for Growth." *Quarterly Journal of Economics* 106 (May 1991): 503–30.

Murphy, Kevin M., and Finis Welch. "The Structure of Wages." *Quarterly Journal of Economics* 107 (February 1992): 285–326.

National Industrial Conference Board. "Incentive Plans for Salesmen." *Studies in Personnel Policy* 217 (1970): 75–86.

National Science Foundation. *Federal Support to Universities, Colleges, and Selected Nonprofit Institutions, Fiscal Year 1981.* Washington, D.C.: U.S. Government Printing Office, 1983, pp. 79–80.

——. *Grants and Awards for 1988.* Washington, D.C.: U.S. Government Printing Office, 1989.

Neff, Joseph. "Millionaire's Scholarship Offer Pays Off for Students in Harlem." *Los Angeles Times,* March 25, 1990, p. A34.

Newhouse, Joseph P. "Medical Care Costs: How Much Welfare Loss?" *Journal of Economic Perspectives* 6 (Summer 1992): 3–21.

Norris, Floyd. "Bought Wilt Chamberlains? Relax, You're Off the Hook." *New York Times*, February 17, 1993, p. C1.

Novick, Harold J. *Selling Through Independent Reps.* New York: AMACOM, 1988.

Nystrom, Paul H. *The Economics of Fashion.* New York: The Ronald Press Company, 1928.

O'Keeffe, Mary, W. Kip Viscusi, and Richard J. Zeckhauser. "Economic Contests: Comparative Reward Schemes." *Journal of Labor Economics* 2 (January 1984): 27–56.

Okun, Arthur M. *Equality and Efficiency: The Big Tradeoff.* Washington, D.C.: Brookings Institution, 1975.

Olson, Walter. *The Litigation Explosion: What Happened When America Unleashed the Lawsuit.* New York: Dutton, 1991.

Osder, Scott. "Andre Even Flies Like a Champ." *San Francisco Chronicle,* February 8, 1993, pp. C1, C8.

Pace, Eric. "Christie Henrich, 22, Gymnast Plagued by Eating Disorders." *New York Times* July, 28, 1994, p. D24.

Parker, J. W. E. K. Taylor, R. S. Barrett, and S. Martens. "Rating Scale Content: The Relationships Between Supervisory- and Self-Rating." *Personnel Psychology* 12 (Spring 1959): 49–63.

"Patrick Ewing's $33 Million Pact Highest Ever in Team Sports." *Jet*, December 16, 1991, pp. 52, 53.

Patterson, Thomas. *Out of Order.* New York: Vintage Books, 1994.

People Magazine, [untitled article on Donovan Leitch.] September 19, 1994, p. 146.

Phillips, Kevin. *Boiling Point: Democrats, Republicans, and the Decline of Middle-Class Prosperity.* New York: Harper Perennial, 1994.

Pine, Joseph. *Mass Customization: The New Frontier in Business Competition.* Boston, Mass.: Harvard Business School Press, 1993.

Podolny Joel. "A Status-based Model of Market Competition." *American Journal of Sociology* 98 (1993): 829–72.

PR Newswire Association. "K-Mart Corporation Announces Borders-Walden 1993 Results." *PR Newswire,* February 28, 1994.

Prial, Frank J. "What Price Glory? Too High." *New York Times*, March 25, 1990, sec. 6, p. 54.

———. "Wine Talk." *New York Times*, March 3, 1993, p. B4.

Purdy, Mark. "Financial Strain Caught Up with SCU Football." *San Jose Mercury News*, February 4, 1993, pp. 1G, 9G.

Randall, Eric D. "What Could You Do With $1.1 Billion?" *USA Today*, June 15, 1994, p. IB.

Reed, Raquel. "Piercing Into the Mainstream." *Ithaca Journal,* August 10, 1994, p. 9B.

Reibstein, Larry. "A Star Is Rehired, Fabulously." *Newsweek,* February 29, 1994, p. 58.

Reich, Robert B. *The Work of Nations: Preparing Ourselves for 21st-century Capitalism.* New York: Alfred A. Knopf, 1991.

Rogerson, William. "The Social Costs of Monopoly and Regulation: A Game Theoretic Analysis." *Bell Journal of Economics* 13 (1982): 391–401.

Romer, Paul. *Tastes, Preferences, and Values.* Cambridge: Cambridge University Press, 1996, forthcoming.

Rosen, Sherwin. "The Economics of Superstars." *American Economic Review* 71 (December 1981): 845–58.

———. "Authority, Control and the Distribution of Earnings." *Bell Journal of Economics* 13 (October 1982): 311–23.

———. "Prizes and Incentives in Elimination Tournaments." *American Economic Review* 76 (September 1986): 701–16.

———. "The Market for Lawyers." *Journal of Law and Economics* 35 (October 1992): 215–46.

Roth, Alvin E., and Marilda Sotomayor. *Two-Sided Matching: A Study in*

Game-Theoretic Modeling and Analysis. Econometric Society Monograph Series. Cambridge, England: Cambridge University Press, 1990.

Ryan, Joan. "Too Much, Too Young." *San Francisco Examiner*, July 12, 1992, pp. C1, C6, C7.

Sandomir, Richard. "Why Baseball Faces a Strike." *New York Times*, August 10, 1994, p. A1.

Schapiro, Morton O., Michael P. O'Malley, and Larry H. Litten. "Tracing the Economic Backgrounds of COFHE Students: Has There Been a Middle-Income Melt?" Williamstown, Mass.: Williams College, 1990. Draft.

Schelling, Thomas. "Hockey Helmets, Concealed Weapons, and Daylight Saving: A Study of Binary Choices with Externalities." *Journal of Conflict Resolution* 17, 3 (September 1973): 381–428.

Schenet, Margot A. "College Costs: Analysis of Trends of Costs and Sources of Support." CRS Report for Congress, Washington, D.C., 1988.

Schmuckler, Eric. "Nothin' But Net at CBS: CBS Pays Record Fee to Retain National Collegiate Athletic Association Broadcasting Rights." *Mediaweek* 4 (December 12, 1994): 3.

Schor, Juliet B. *The Overworked American.* New York: Basic Books, 1991.

Seidman, Laurence S. *Saving for America's Economic Future: Parables and Policies.* Armonk, N.Y.: M.E. Sharpe, 1990.

——. "A Better Way to Tax." *Public Interest*, Winter 1994, pp. 65–72.

Shea, Christopher. "A Flood of Applications: Many Colleges See Increases Despite Dip in the Number of High-School Seniors." *Chronicle of Higher Education* 40 (April 27, 1994): A31.

Shenon, Philip. "China's Mania for Baby Boys Creates Surplus of Bachelors." *New York Times*, August 16, 1994, pp. A1, A8.

Shurkin, Joel N. *Termans Kids: The Groundbreaking Study of How the Gifted Grow Up.* Boston: Little, Brown, 1992.

Smith, Adam. *An Inquiry Into the Nature and Causes of the Wealth of Nations.* London: J.M. Dent and Sons, 1910 (1776).

Soocher, Stan. "Equality and Price Justify Use of Single-Tire Rule." *The National Law Journal,* June 11, 1984, p. 44.

South China Morning Post. "Jojo Moyes Reports on Recent Allegations Linking Brutality and Pornography in Video Games and Real Life Violence." February 20, 1994, p. 4.

Sperber, Murray. *College Sports, Inc.: The Athletic Department vs. The University*. New York: Henry Holt, 1990.

Spies, Richard R. *The Effect of Rising College Costs on College Choice*. New York: College Entrance Examination Board, 1978.

——. "The Effect of Rising Costs on College Choice." Princeton University, July 1990. Mimeo.

Stade, George. "Hopping, Popping, and Copping." *New York Times Book Review*, September 18, 1994, p. 14.

Standard Directory of Advertisers. New Providence, N.J.: National Register Publishing, 1994.

Stevenson, Richard W. "Taming Hollywood's Spending Monster." *New York Times*, April 14, 1991, Sec. 3, pp. 1, 6.

Svenson, O. "Are We All Less Risky and More Skillful Than Our Fellow Drivers?" *Acta Psychologica* 47 (1981): 143–48.

Sykes, Charles J. *ProfScam: Professors and the Demise of Higher Education*. Washington, D.C.: Regnery Gateway, 1988.

Television and Video Almanac. Quigley Publishing Co. 33rd edition. 1988.

Tenner, Edward. "The Impending Information Implosion." *Harvard Magazine,* November–December 1991, pp. 31–34.

Thaler, Richard, and H. M. Shefrin. "An Economic Theory of Self-Control." *Journal of Political Economy* 89, 2 (1981): 392–406.

Tiger, Lionel. *Optimism*. Newark: Simon & Schuster, 1979.

Tobin, James, "On Limiting the Domain of Inequality." *Journal of Law and Economics* 20 (1970): 263–277.

Tversky, Amos, and Daniel Kahneman. "Judgment Under Uncertainty: Heuristics and Biases." *Science* 185 (1974): 1124–31.

United States Tennis Association Yearbook. Lynn, Mass.: H. O. Zimman, 1992, 1993, 1994.

U.S. Department of Education. *Digest of Education Statistics*. Washington, D.C.: U.S. Government Printing Office, 1993.

Vogel, Harold L. *Entertainment Industry Economics*. New York: Cambridge University Press, 1986.

Vonnegut, Kurt. "Harrison Bergeron." In *Welcome to the Monkey House*. New York: Dell, 1970.

——. *Bluebeard*. Newark: Delacorte Press, 1987.

Vesalis, Charles E., and R. Craig Kammerer. "The Strengths and Failures of Drug Tests." *New York Times*, February 4, 1990. Sec. 8, Sports Desk, p. 10.

Wald, Matthew. "Going Beyond Batteries to Power Electric Cars." *New York Times*, March 3, 1993, p. C2.

Wallich, Paul. "The Workaholic Economy." *Scientific American,* August 1994, p. 77.

Walton, Mary. "How Penn Became a Hot School." *Inquirer: The Philadelphia Inquirer Magazine,* April 13, 1986, pp. 22–34.

Walzer, Michael. *Spheres of Justice.* New York: Basic Books, 1983.

Watson, Peter. *From Manet to Manhattan: The Rise of the Modern Art Market.* New York: Random House, 1992.

Wecker, Jonathan. *So You Want to Stay Home.* Ithaca, N.Y: Cornell University Economics Honors Thesis, 1992.

Weinraub, Bernard. "How a Movie Satire Turned into Reality." *New York Times,* August 16, 1994, p. C15.

Weinstein, N. D. "Unrealistic Optimism About Future Life Events." *Journal of Personality and Social Psychology* 39 (1980): 806–20.

———. "Unrealistic Optimism About Susceptibility to Health Problems." *Journal of Behavioral Medicine* 5 (1982): 441–60.

Weinstein, N. D., and E. Lachendo. "Egocentrism and Unrealistic Optimism About the Future." *Personality and Social Psychology Bulletin* 8 (1982): 195–200.

Whiteside, Thomas. *The Blockbuster Complex.* Middletown, Conn.: Wesleyan University Press, 1981.

Whyte, William F. *Money and Motivation.* New York: Harper and Brothers, 1955.

Wilkinson, F. *The Illustrated Book of Pistols.* London: Hamlyn, 1979.

Windsor, Robert, and Daniel Dumitru. "Anabolic Steroid Use by Athletes: How Serious Are the Health Hazards?" *Postgraduate Medicine* 84 (1988): 37–49.

Wolff, Alexander. "Something for Nothing." *Sports Illustrated,* December 7, 1992, p. 96.

Wortman, Marc. "Can Need-Blind Survive?" *Yale,* October 1993, pp. 63–67.

Wright, John W., and Edward J. Dwyer. *The American Almanac of Jobs and Salaries.* New York: Avon, 1990.

Wright, Robert. *The Moral Animal: Evolutionary Psychology and Everyday Life.* New York: Pantheon, 1994.

Wriston, Walter B. *The Twilight of Sovereignty: How the Information Revolution Is Transforming Our World.* New York: Scribner, 1992.

Wylie, R. C. *The Self-Concept*, vol. 2. Lincoln: University of Nebraska Press, 1979.

Zuboff, Shoshana. *In the Age of the Smart Machine.* New York: Basic Books, 1988.

Index

Kand, Nancy, 204
Kaplan, Stanley H, 179
Karolyi, Bela, 132
Kaus, Mickey, 229–230
Keillor, Garrison, 105, 150
Kellogg Corporation, 141
Kellogg Graduate School of
    Management,
Northwestern University, 129–130
Kennedy, Edward M., 200
Kennedy, John E, 58, 198, 199
Kerrigan, Nancy, 145
Kids Say the Darndest Things
    (Linkletter), 140
King, Alexander, 139–140
King, Stephen, 65
Kingston, Paul, 36, 149
KKR, xi–xii
Knopf, Alfred A., Inc., 200
Koppel, Ted, 76
Krabbe, Katrin, 134
Krantz, Judith, 9–10, 18, 64
Krugman, Paul, 86
Kuttner, Robert, 87

Labor, division and specialization
    of, 53–54
Labor unions, decline of, 5, 87
Laffer curve, 123
Lake Woebegon effect, 105, 150
Landier, Augustin, xii
Lane, Anthony, 18
Lang, Eugene, 223–224
Languages, 28, 52–53
Last Brother, The (McGinniss), 200
Law School Admissions Test, 31
Law schools, 222–223

Layard, Richard, 42
Le Carre, John, 18, 193
Legal profession, 3, 11, 16–17, 26,
    88, 97–98, 111, 119–120, 147,
    219–220, 222–223
Leisure policy, 227–228
Leitch, Donovan, 204–205
Lendl, Ivan, 39
Letterman, David, 75
Leveraged buyouts, 70
Levy, Frank, 87, 94
Lewis, Lionel, 36, 149
Lewis, Michael, 92–94
Liar's Poker (Lewis), 92
Linkletter, Art, 140
Litigation, 97–98, 111, 119–120,
    178, 219–220
Lock-in through learning, 35, 36
Los Alamos National Laboratory,
    166
Lotteries, 30, 32
Lottery game, 130–131
Lovers (Krantz), 18
Ludlum, Robert, 65
Luxuries, prices of, 82–84
Luxury tax, 15, 183, 215

M&H Tire Company, 226
MacNeil/Lehrer Newshour, 40
Macpherson, Elle, 78
Madden, John, 76, 77
Madness of King George, The
    (film), 194–195
Madonna, 75
Magic Video Corporation, 73
Magowan, Pete, 6
Malpractice suits, 98

The Number 1 *Sunday Times* Bestseller

THE ECONOMIC NATURALIST

By Robert H. Frank

Why is there a light in your fridge but not in your freezer?
Why do 24-hour shops bother having locks on their doors?
Why did Kamikaze pilots wear helmets?
The answer is simple: economics

Discover the secrets behind these and hundreds of other everyday enigmas and why many of the most puzzling parts of everyday life actually make perfect economic sense.

'Fascinating . . . provides the answers to some of life's quirkiest conundrums' *Daily Mail*

'Don't miss this addictive book' Tim Harford, author of *The Undercover Economist* and *The Logic of Life*

ISBN 9780753513385

www.rbooks.co.uk

THE RETURN OF THE
ECONOMIC NATURALIST

By Robert H. Frank

**Discover how economics explains some of
life's most puzzling problems**

Should we just leave everything to the market?
Why do we all save so little?
Do nice guys always finish last?

The Economic Naturalist is back with a whole batch of intriguing new
questions and answers that reveal how we really behave when
confronted with economic choices.

'In *The Return of the Economic Naturalist* Robert Frank guides us
skilfully and elegantly through our complex, and sometimes strange,
economic environment – helping us to see more clearly the essence of
our world.' Dan Ariely, author of *Predictably Irrational*

ISBN 9780753519660

www.rbooks.co.uk